What is Islamic Philoso[

"This excellent book provides a user-friendly introduction to the emergence and subsequent developments of Islamic philosophy. Jackson's problem oriented approach also shows, in a skilful manner, the relevance of this philosophy to some of the most pressing issues of our time in important fields such as politics, ethics and religion."

Ali Paya, *University of Westminster (UK), Islamic College (UK), and National Research Institute for Science Policy (Iran)*

What is Islamic Philosophy? offers a broad introduction to Islamic thought, from its origins to the many challenging issues facing Muslims in the contemporary world. The chapters explore early Islamic philosophy and trace its development through key themes and figures up to the twenty-first century.

Topics covered include:
- ethical issues such as just war, abortion, women's rights, homosexuality and cloning
- questions in political philosophy regarding what kind of Islamic state could exist and how democratic can (or should) Islam really be
- the contribution of Islam to 'big questions' such as the existence of God, the concept of the soul, and what constitutes truth.

This fresh and original book includes a helpful glossary and suggestions for further reading. It is ideal for students coming to the subject for the first time as well as anyone wanting to learn about the philosophical tradition and dilemmas that are part of the Islamic worldview.

Roy Jackson is Reader in Philosophy of Religion at the University of Gloucestershire, UK. He has many years' experience of lecturing in Philosophy and Religion at a number of universities. His books include *Fifty Key Figures in Islam* (2006), *Nietzsche and Islam* (2007), *Mawlana Mawdudi and Political Islam* (2010), and *The God of Philosophy* (2011).

What is Islamic Philosophy?

Roy Jackson

Routledge
Taylor & Francis Group

LONDON AND NEW YORK

First published in 2014
by Routledge
2 Park Square, Milton Park, Abingdon, Oxon OX14 4RN

And published in the USA and Canada
by Routledge
711 Third Avenue, New York, NY 10017

Routledge is an imprint of the Taylor & Francis Group, an informa business

British Library Cataloguing in Publication Data
A catalogue record for this book is available from the British Library

Library of Congress Cataloging in Publication Data
Jackson, Roy, 1962-
What is Islamic philosophy? / Roy Jackson.
pages cm
Includes bibliographical references.
1. Islamic philosophy. I. Title.
B741.J29 2014
181'.07–dc23
2013034764

ISBN: 978-0-415-63202-7 (hbk)
ISBN: 978-0-415-63203-4 (hbk)
ISBN: 978-1-315-81755-2 (ebk)

Typeset in Bembo
by Taylor & Francis Books

Printed and bound by CPI Group (UK) Ltd, Croydon, CR0 4YY

To Annette … my 'LC'

Contents

Preface

The aim of this book is to present Islamic philosophy in an accessible way, making no assumptions in terms of the reader's background knowledge of either philosophy or Islam (or, for that matter, Muslim languages). There are now many excellent introductions to Islam, and also to philosophy, but there is still very little out there to satisfy what is a growing demand for some understanding of Islamic philosophy. I hope this little book goes some way to alleviating this demand.

The book is a result of my many years of studying and teaching, first within the field of Western philosophy, and then into Islamic Studies. My background caused me to make links between philosophy and Islam, and my studies have been helped tremendously over the years by my students, who have patiently been prepared to devote their own time and energies to my enthusiasms in this respect.

What isn't in this book

With the hope of anticipating criticisms that this little book leaves out so much, my response is to simply say that, yes, it does leave out plenty. The publisher provides a specified word limit and the author has a limited lifespan, which may or may not be specified. My intention has always been to introduce Islamic philosophy to those who know nothing or little about it and may not even be aware that Islam has a philosophical tradition at all. In this respect, this book is a taster, and I sincerely hope that readers will be sufficiently interested in some of the topics or philosophers covered here to then move on to read some more. Thankfully, more and more works are being translated into English every year, and at the end of each chapter I recommend just a few good books for further reading. I did not wish this book to end up as merely a series of bullet points in an attempt to cover such a massive subject, and so I have focused on certain specific philosophers and themes, while also being aware that I do not do them justice by any means.

Arabic names, terms and dates

My students, when confronted with variation in the spellings of Arabic or Persian or Urdu words and terms, have asked me which is the 'correct' one.

Ultimately, there is not always one 'correct' way of writing these down and, for this book, I have followed the Occam's (slight pun there, as 'Occam' can also be written as 'Ockham') Razor principle of parsimony. Simplicity is best. Inevitably, sometimes I will use Arabic words and names, though sometimes they will be in the more recognized Anglicized form. In this respect, I may be bowing to familiarity rather than accuracy. It is not my intention to overwhelm the reader with unfamiliar names and words, and I have also left out all diacritical marks in transliteration. In addition, when introducing a Muslim name for the first time, I will provide the name in bold that the reader may use to find his or her full (or fuller, some are quite long) name in Appendix I; but from then on, I will keep to a shortened name. For example, choosing randomly one name that will appear in this book on occasion:

Abū Ḥāmid Muḥammad ibn Muḥammad al-Ghazzālī

(Full name with diacritics)

Without diacritics, and shortened, you will often come across his name in introductory texts as 'al-Ghazali' (or al-Gazzali, etc). However, the 'al' in Arabic is the definite article, which is the equivalent of 'the' in English and is often used to refer to the birthplace of that person or his ancestors (again, Occam's name derives from William *of* Occam). Many Muslim names also have 'ibn' (Ibn Arabi, for example), which indicates a person's heritage and means 'son' ('bint' means daughter), so Ibn Arabi means 'son of Arabi', though this need not be the father, but a more distant ancestor. These are just a couple of examples, which I am leaving out of the names once used on first introduction: al-Ghazzali becomes Ghazzali, Ibn Arabi becomes Arabi, and so on.

However, again, on occasion familiarity must take precedence. For example, with some names the absence of 'al' may make a name seem rather alien if entirely omitted, and in these circumstances it will be added to produce a surname. For example, al-Kindi becomes Alkindi, and al-Farabi becomes Alfarabi. All the names appear in Appendix I where the reader can check the spellings used in the book with the Islamic name.

Latinized names

Another complication is that a number of Arabic names have become 'Latinized'. As Muslim thinkers were introduced to the Western world, their names were converted into a Latinized form to make them easier to pronounce. Now, here, I shall bow to familiarity: for example, Ghazzali's Latinized name is Algazel, but this name is so uncommon as to cause confusion if I were to use it, and so **Ghazzali** it is. The same cannot be said for Ibn Rushd, who is much better known by his Latinized name Averroes, and so I stick to the latter.

To italicize or not to italicize

When to italicize an Arabic word? These days, generally speaking, you will not find the word 'Quran' in italics, yet you may find 'sharia' in italics some of the time, and not others. Again, unless a word has become so Anglicized ('Quran' being an example here, although, again, I am going for simplicity and not writing it out as 'Qur'an') I will put Arabic words and phrases in italics and bold upon first usage only, and a list of words is contained in Appendix II.

Dates

The Muslim calendar is lunar and consists of twelve months in a year, but is shorter than the 'solar' calendar, being 354 or 355 days. Sometimes you will see 'AH' after the date, the Latin 'anno Hegirae' ('in the year of the Hijra') because the first year of the Islamic calendar begins when the nascent Muslim community migrated from Mecca to Medina, which was in 622 of the Gregorian calendar. Again, I will go for what is more familiar for most readers here, and will restrict myself to the Gregorian calendar.

Acknowledgements

I have mentioned already the trials my students have had to undergo over the years as a result of my particular hobbyhorses. There are, of course, far too many names to mention (or remember!) but, as a cohort, they have frequently brought me entertainment, enthusiasm, enlightenment, and a constant renewal in a faith that human beings are not all that bad really.

Always at the back of my mind when writing this book is the memory of my teacher and friend Dr John Bousfield, who is sorely missed, and is an example of someone who saw no distinction between religion and philosophy, for it was all about truth. I would also like to thank my colleague Dr David Webster for never ceasing to be enthusiastic about whatever crazy idea I have, but that is probably because he has so many crazy ideas himself.

A debt of gratitude is also owed to Annette, for being Annette, and to my children Raef and Nadiya, for being children (long may that last!).

Finally, much appreciation goes to all the staff at Routledge. This is not the first project I have worked on with them, and I have found them to be professional, dedicated, and eager for new ideas. A special mention to Katherine Ong, who has been at the 'front desk' in terms of dealings with this book, but also a big thanks to all those others who contributed by correcting my failings and bringing the book to fruition.

1 What is Islamic philosophy?

Bismillah

One of the greatest philosophers is the German **Immanuel Kant** (1724–1804) and, as this is a book on philosophy, his name and thought will inevitably crop up on occasions throughout this work. Kant is, of course, a 'Western' philosopher and not an Islamic philosopher, although I might add that it is quite possible to be 'Western' and 'Islamic' at the same time (more about that below), but I begin here with Kant and a curious fact, for there exists a copy of Kant's doctoral thesis, dated 1755, which has inscribed at the top of the title page the Arabic words *bismillah al-rahman al-rahim* (most common translation: 'in the name of God, most Gracious, most Compassionate'). This short and poetic phrase is regarded as containing the true essence of the **Quran** (the Islamic holy scripture) and it is frequently cited at daily prayers and other contexts by Muslims. Why this Arabic phrase should appear at the top of Kant's doctoral thesis is puzzling, and we will likely never know the answer. It is unlikely Kant placed it there himself, for he makes little mention of Islam in his writings, but I remark upon the existence of this thesis here because, in many ways, it symbolizes the key theme of this book, and that is the relationship between the firmly established Western philosophical tradition – with such giants as Kant – and the perhaps more fragile existence of Islamic philosophy. Is it really possible to propose that there is congruence between such philosophical system-builders as Kant and what Islamic philosophers have to say in their great volumes or, for that matter, what can be found in the Quran? Or does this bismillah merely poke fun at the very idea that Islam could offer anything of value to philosophical discourse when compared with the earth-shattering contributors to modern thought that Kant, amongst others, represents? This is why I declare that Islamic philosophy seems more 'fragile' in this respect, for the ground upon which it rests *seems* more slippery. But why is this the case, and does it really make any sense at all to even speak of an 'Islamic philosophy'?

What is Islam?

This writer does his very best to write an accessible introduction to Islamic philosophy, and no assumptions are made that the reader has any background knowledge or previous understanding of philosophy as such. However, when it comes to Islam, we are dealing with a very large subject here, and this work cannot provide an introduction to such a complex and diverse belief system. The reader is advised to familiarize him- or herself with some of the basic beliefs and practices in Islam, and some good introductions are recommended at the end of this chapter. Having said that, I like to think you can get by perfectly well without any supplementary reading: all Islamic terms are explained, however briefly, and there is a glossary at the end of the book. Something the reader will quickly become aware of is the diversity that exists within Islam, a feature it shares with all world religions. Therefore, one of the first problems we have when talking of Islamic philosophy is what constitutes 'Islamic'.

From a historical perspective, Islam begins with the **Prophet Muhammad** (*c.* 570–632) who, it is traditionally regarded, was born in Mecca in Arabia. In the year 610, Muhammad received revelations from God that were then written down in what is called the Quran ('recitation'). For all Muslims, belief in the one God and that Muhammad is the prophet (indeed, the final prophet) of God are essential articles of faith. As the Quran is seen as literally the word of God, Muslims look to this scripture for guidance on how to be a good Muslim, which is synonymous with how to be a good human being. God created Man with a purpose, and Man must, in turn, determine what this purpose is.

Today there are over one and a half billion people who call themselves Muslim, and they are spread across the world. Anyone who reads a newspaper will quickly appreciate just how many countries are 'Islamic' in one sense or another as a result of, for example, the events of the Arab Spring, civil war in Syria or unrest in Turkey. Alas, it is the nature of newspapers that bad news tends to sell better than good, and so an image of Islamic states tends to be associated with such things as 'unrest', 'war', 'terrorism', 'protest' and so on, but the fact is that the majority of Muslims live peaceful lives and, should you visit a Muslim country, you are likely to discover how welcoming, courteous and generous these pious people can be.

Islam, at its most essential level, is a belief in God. This, of course, is a very personal and inward matter, although it inevitably has consequences in terms of how the believer lives his or her life. Nonetheless, in terms of outward expression of this belief, this can vary quite a lot from one person to the next. Some may well be considered more 'devout' than others by praying five times a day (or more), fasting during the holy month of **Ramadan**, making one or more pilgrimages to Mecca and so on, but this raises the question of what constitutes a good Muslim, and this need not necessarily be because someone is diligent in engaging in the practices and rituals. For some, it is enough, and even more important, to simply believe with one's heart in God.

Islam, as we shall see, also refers to a culture and a civilization although, again, due to the diversity that is Islam, it is difficult to pinpoint what constitutes an Islamic culture or civilization: there are Arabic Muslims, Persian Muslims, Chinese Muslims, African Muslims, Southeast Asian Muslims and

'Western' (European and American) Muslims, amongst others. There are also 'nominal' or 'cultural' Muslims whereby identity is determined by being born to a Muslim father, much like a Jew born to a Jewish mother. Other than that, it is not required to subscribe to beliefs and practices of the faith; rather it is a matter of ethnicity or group allegiance. A modern example of this is Bosnia, where a person is described (or describes him/herself) as a Bosnian Muslim to be distinguished from Bosnian Serbs (Orthodox) and Bosnian Croats (Catholic). Other than that, the Bosnian Muslims are

> [d]rinkers of slivovitz, strong plum brandy, eaters of pork, for many Bosnian Muslims their only connections with Islam until the [Bosnian] war were that they had names like Amra and Emir and left their shoes outside their houses. Bosnian Muslims were largely secular and those that were religious emphasized that they were 'European Muslims', something quite different to the Ayatollahs of Iran and the Islamic clergy of Saudi Arabia.
>
> (LeBor 1997: 20)

It is, perhaps, not surprising that the Muslims from Saudi Arabia and Algeria that went to Bosnia to fight during the conflicts there were shocked by the Bosnians' lifestyle, and equally the Bosnians themselves were not enamoured of the orthodoxy of these **Mujahidin**.

However, the concern in this work is primarily with those who do wish to assert a belief in God and resist any accusations of atheism, but as we shall see there is considerable tension in being both 'Islamic' and a 'philosopher'.

What is philosophy?

The word 'philosophy' derives from the ancient Greek '*philosophia*' which means 'love of wisdom', and it makes great sense to state that philosophy as we understand it begins with the ancient Greeks. When the so-called pre-Socratics such as Thales, Anaxagoras, Parmenides and so on were investigating the nature of the world and, by doing so, were not relying upon mythic explanations, they were effectively 'doing philosophy', although what they were doing may remind us more of scientific enquiry today than what we regard as philosophy. The term 'philosophy' for most of them covered a broad and varied school of thought. What they generally all have in common is a concern with matters of 'cosmology' (from the Greek word *kosmos*, meaning something like 'good order'). The ancient Greek philosophers were intent on finding a unifying principle of the cosmos, an order for the apparent chaos of the world they occupied.

It was really **Plato** (427–347 BC) and **Aristotle** (384–322 BC) who laid the foundations for what we understand by philosophy to this day. Although also concerned with matters relating to cosmology, Plato and his teacher Socrates (*c.* 470–399 BC) are very different from the so-called pre-Socratic philosophers before them because of their more rigorous and rational method of enquiry.

What they did was to invent the method and terminology of philosophizing that is still used today. By introducing analysis, cogent argument and a rational approach to thought, Plato especially laid the foundations for all philosophers who came after him. This is why the British philosopher Alfred North Whitehead (1861–1947) famously said that the history of philosophy is but a series of footnotes to Plato. Plato's main concern, initially, was with moral philosophy, with how we ought to live our lives. However, although this was his main inspiration, as he matured his writings covered many of the branches of philosophy, including political philosophy, education, aesthetics (philosophy of art), metaphysics (the study of the features of reality) and epistemology (the study of knowledge and what can we know).

In a nutshell, philosophy concerns itself with all those kinds of knotty problems such as: What can we know for sure? What is the best form of political government? What does it mean to be good? Is there a mind and is it separate from the body? As a *method*, it attempts to address these 'big questions' systematically (usually!), critically and through rational argument. Now, it should be stressed that – like religion – philosophy is itself incredibly diverse; it is by no means always rational and systematic and, indeed, some philosophers would argue that reason gets in the way of 'proper philosophy'. Nonetheless, however rational or otherwise philosophy may be, the issue here is how philosophical methodology and enquiry relates to Islam. It is argued by many Muslims throughout history that God provides us with all the knowledge that we need. The Quran begins by retelling the story of an angel (who became Satan) who fell from grace by using his intellect to defy God. Such emphasis on using the mind to question what God decrees, then, is treated with suspicion, as well as being regarded as irrelevant so far as Islam is concerned.

The Islamic 'sciences'

Within Islam there are a number of disciplines or schools, what are referred to as the Islamic 'sciences'. The term 'science' in this respect needs to be understood in its broader context as the Latin derivation *scientia*, which simply means 'knowledge'. The pursuit of knowledge can take many different paths and two in particular, the 'science of theology' and the 'science of philosophy', have often been uncomfortable travelling companions along the Islamic paths.

Theology, or **kalam** (literally meaning 'spoken word') as it is known in Arabic, has on the whole confined itself to questions that are raised by revelation. For example, regarding such issues as the nature of God and His relationship with His creations: Does God's power mean that Man has no free will? Can God be described in human terms? (I.e. actually possess hands, eyes and so on.) In Arabic the word for philosophy is merely an Arabization of the Greek, hence **falsafa**. It is what in the Western world would be regarded as 'natural philosophy', and so encompasses the non-religious sciences such as logic, mathematics, physics, astronomy, psychology, ethics and politics to name just some.

Falsafa, then, is less restricted than kalam, the former being prepared to tackle any branch of philosophy. The distinction between kalam and falsafa is best summed up by the famous Islamic philosopher of history Ibn **Khaldun** (1332–1406) who, in his *Introduction to History*, noted that whereas philosophy explored both the realms of the physical and the metaphysical in all their aspects, theology's exploration of these realms was confined to how they could support arguments for the existence and nature of God. This confinement of the discipline of theology, for Khaldun, was not seen as a weakness. On the contrary, its strict boundaries were its strength and could be used as a powerful weapon, so that 'innovations may be repulsed and doubts and misgivings concerning the articles of faith removed'. What is particularly revealing about this quote is the concern for 'innovations', that is ideas that are not considered to be part of the Islamic worldview, and hence Khaldun's determination to have intellectual tools to defend the faith against such ideas. This gives some indication of the suspicious eye that many theologians cast over philosophy or any other 'imported' science.

On the one hand, then, we have what are regarded as the Islamic, or religious, sciences: kalam, **fiqh** (jurisprudence) and **sharia** (law). Whilst on the other hand, we have the foreign sciences such as philosophy, mathematics, medicine, physics, astrology and astronomy, although, as already intimated, these foreign sciences were often placed under the broad umbrella term of 'falsafa'. For most Muslims, the former curriculum is considered superior to the latter for the very reason that it is specifically considered 'Islamic', it is a direct offspring of the prophetic-revelatory event that occurred during the life of the Prophet Muhammad and resulted in the creation of the Quran. The foreign sciences, however, are products of non-Muslims, and this immediately creates a tension in terms of fitting non-Islamic schools of thought into the Islamic worldview. Philosophy, by originating with ancient Greeks such as Plato and Aristotle in the fourth century BC, was by definition written by non-Muslims and hence 'infidels'. Still, this tension between the Islamic and the non-Islamic was alleviated somewhat by the well-known, oft-quoted **hadith** (saying) of the Prophet, 'Pursue knowledge even to China, for its pursuance is the sacred duty of every Muslim.'

Having said that, whilst it is true that there is considerable suspicion levelled against philosophy, the discipline of theology is also not immune from such misgivings either. The term 'kalam' is the Muslim equivalent of systematic theology in Christianity, but it is not so highly regarded. The term '*ilm al-kalam*' is 'the science of discourse' on divine themes, and Muslims sometimes prefer to use the phrase '*ilm al-tawhid*', 'the science of (divine) unity', thus avoiding the term 'kalam' which, as this translates as 'talk' or 'discourse', can be used in a pejorative sense of 'idle chatter'. The suggestion here is that when considering the unity of God, to engage in discussion is to lower God's divinity to human discourse. Hence the suspicions levelled against philosophy – that it is humans talking about what cannot be talked about – can also be levelled against theology. In fact, the term for a theologian is **mutakallim**, and such individuals are often considered in the same way Plato regarded the sophists: clever talkers but lacking in real wisdom. Ultimately, the most important of the Islamic sciences is fiqh ('understanding'), which is the science of jurisprudence. It is the attempt, the struggle, to truly understand God's guidance, or sharia. As the primary science, it is the experts of fiqh, the **ulama**, who are considered by the majority as the wisest Muslims.

What, then, is Islamic philosophy?

I have said above that the concern of philosophy is with the 'big questions', and what you will see in this book is chapters devoted to such questions as where does our knowledge come from?, or what is the best state?, etc. And so, this is certainly a work of 'philosophy'. However, it is a work of Islamic philosophy because those 'big questions' have been raised by people who *relate it to the concerns of Islamic belief and practice.* There is that ultimate, really big question here: *What does it mean to be human?* Whether we look to Plato or the Quran, it is the same question being asked, and attempts are made to answer that question. The Quran is a guide for Muslims, but it admits its own ambiguity and encourages its followers to seek knowledge, and so we should 'do philosophy' and make use of the tools and the knowledge it possesses in helping us to try and understand that ultimate question. This book is also an acknowledgement that, despite resistance at times, Muslims have been philosophical in their enquiries and would not hesitate to still consider themselves pious believers. We should study and learn from these great people.

Further reading

Some introductions to Islam:

Esposito, J.L. (1998), *Islam: The Straight Path*, 3rd edition, Oxford: Oxford University Press.
Rippin, A. (2012), *Muslims: Their Religious Beliefs and Practices*, 4th edition, Abingdon: Routledge.
Ruthven, M. (2000), *Islam in the World*, 2nd edition, London: Penguin.
Shepard, William (2013), *Introducing Islam*, 2nd edition, Abingdon: Routledge.

The Quran

Many Muslims would say that the Quran could only be truly understood in its original Arabic. Therefore, any 'translations' are considered 'interpretations', and to some extent this is certainly correct, considering the ambiguity of many Arabic words. The reader is advised to consult more than one 'interpretation' to see just how they can differ but, for consistency, I have relied on just the one for this book:

The Qur'an (2008), Oxford World Classics, trans. by M.A.S. Abdel Haleem, Oxford: Oxford University Press.

The hadith

The hadith record the sayings and acts of the Prophet Muhammad and they consist of a vast body of material from a number of hadith 'collectors'. In most cases I have named the collector in brackets, although many hadith sayings can be found in more than one collection (the idea of hadith collection as a 'science' is that one collector should corroborate another). Ultimately, only one excellent source is used here: www.hadithcollection.com. Here you will find hadiths from those collectors considered the most reliable (Bukhari, Dawud etc.) and an efficient search engine. Not all hadiths come from these sources, and some have been passed down with weak veracity; for example, the hadith quote I give in this chapter ('Pursue knowledge even to China, for its pursuance is the sacred duty of every Muslim') will not be found amongst the stronger hadiths. However, it is so well used, and, if nothing else, the spirit of the hadith is recognized amongst many Muslims so as to make it more powerful in determining Islamic discourse than many of the more reliable hadiths. For this reason, they are worth quoting.

Websites

Some good sources for the study of Islam:

Academic Islamic Studies and Middle East, Central Asian, and other Area Studies Sites: www.uga.edu/islam/MESCenters.html.

Islamic Studies Digital Library: www.academicinfo.net/Islammeta.html.

Academic Islamic Studies Resources: www.theamericanmuslim.org/tam.php/tam/linkcategory/C122.

Andrew Rippin's own website with many useful links: www.rippin.org.

The BBC provides basic knowledge, but you can also listen to radio programmes from the BBC World Service: www.bbc.co.uk/worldservice/people/features/world_religions/islam.shtml.

Also, there is lots of material here on Islam and the West: news.bbc.co.uk/2/hi/talking_point/special/islam/3182669.stm

A website for Islamic sources etc. on Islamic philosophy: Islamic Philosophy Online: www.muslimphilosophy.com.

2 The Greek and Persian legacy

Hellenism: The encounter with Greek philosophy

In Chapter 1, mention was made of the well-known hadith 'Pursue knowledge even to China, for its pursuance is the sacred duty of every Muslim.' Muslims did not need to go to China in this case, but they did have to go as far as the city of Alexandria in Egypt.

The experience of Islam's encounter with a literary and cultural tradition referred to as 'Hellenism' is a fascinating one in its own right. People in our modern age often comment that every city looks the same these days, with the chain stores, similar planning designs and so on, but the fact is that, during the heyday of Greek culture, one Greek city looked very similar to another: this is 'Hellenism'. It is a particular way of doing things that provided the model that was copied from Elea in Italy to Alexandria in Egypt. As the Athenian orator Isocrates (436–338 BC) said in his discourse *Panegyricus*: 'The name Hellene no longer suggests a race, but an intelligence, and the title "Hellenes" is applied rather to those who share our culture, than to those who share a common blood.' Hellenic culture meant being part of a city-state, a *polis*, with its own city walls, marketplace, bath houses and town halls, as well as many other characteristic features and activities. Hellenic culture was not just its architecture, but its arts, its theatre, its religions, its festivals, its legends and, of course, its philosophies. Such a magnificent culture is bound to influence other cultures, but it was usually encountered by scholars who already knew Greek and had some kind of context when studying Hellenism. It is much more difficult – as any reader of this book who has absolutely no knowledge of Islam or philosophy will testify – to approach a text when you have little or no knowledge of Greek or the culture. And yet this, to a large extent, was actually the position Muslim scholars found themselves in. Although in many cases the Muslim intelligentsia were not coming entirely from a blank slate, knowledge of Greek philosophy and culture was extremely limited. Today, scholars of Greek philosophy argue and disagree over what the Greeks meant, although they have the luxury of hundreds, if not thousands, of years of previous scholarship to tap into, as well as a bank of resource materials that is unmatched in terms of quantity and quality by any previous generation. There is no reason to believe that differences of views were not also prevalent amongst the Muslims in the early centuries of translation, given, especially, such factors as the linguistic difficulties of translating Greek or Syriac into Arabic (not only in terms of vocabulary, but whole complex concepts that would have been unfamiliar to an audience untrained in philosophical discourse) and the absence of existing translated works that can be used to compare, contrast, verify and so on.

The great city of Alexandria was named after the one-time student of Aristotle, Alexander 'the Great' (356–323 BC), who was king of Macedon in northern Greece. His title of 'Great' is due to the fact that by the age of 30 he had created an empire that spread from the Ionian Sea to the Himalayas without a single defeat in battle. This, then, was one of the largest empires of the ancient world, and if Alexander had ever fulfilled his plans to conquer Arabia as well, Islam may never have existed. As it turns out, Alexander died young and his empire splintered. As this empire spread, so did Hellenic culture and, more significantly for our purposes, Greek philosophy. When we are talking about the influence of Greek philosophy on Islam we do not begin this journey in Greece as such, but in Egypt and the city of Alexandria.

Alexander, in fact, founded a number of cities named in his honour, but it was Alexandria in Egypt, established in 331 BC, that is significant for the spread and, indeed, the very survival of philosophy. Although Alexander himself spent only a few months in this city, Alexandria grew to be the largest city in the world within a century of its foundation. Despite being situated in Egypt, it was home to a sizeable Greek community and became the centre of Hellenistic learning, with the largest library in the ancient world. It is difficult to determine what 'large' really meant, but estimates of the number of scrolls the library contained are usually within the hundreds of thousands at its peak.

Although Alexander the Great united Greece and caused the spread of Hellenic culture to distant parts of the world, by the second century BC it was the Romans who were the dominant power in the Mediterranean and something of a fusion of Roman and Greek culture prevailed. Under Roman rule, philosophy continued to flourish and was read, debated and written about amongst scholars. For example, the work in medicine and anatomy by Galen of Pergamon (*c.* AD 129–99) and in astronomy by Ptolemy of Alexandria (*c.* AD 90–168). At first the great philosophical schools in Athens such as Plato's Academy, Aristotle's Lyceum and the Stoa and Epicurean Garden continued and, indeed, were supported financially by the Roman emperor Marcus Aurelius (AD 121–80). But, certainly after the death of Marcus Aurelius and some time before that, the religious beliefs of Christianity and Gnosticism, especially, grew in influence upon the philosophical world. The discipline of theology developed as a separate school from philosophy, concerned as it was with understanding religious concepts but with a philosophical quality. For example, the Christian doctrine of the Trinity, which defines God as three persons (Father, Son and Holy Spirit), led to a number of models and heresies, as well as puzzled comments from Islamic scholars. The philosophical influence of, most notably, Aristotle here is important: the Nicene Creed, used to this day during the Eucharist, describes God as 'being one substance with the Father', yet this notion of 'substance' has its origins with Aristotle. Another example is John Philoponus (AD 490–570, also known as John the Grammarian or John of Alexandria), who was an Aristotelian commentator and was condemned as a heretic by the Orthodox Christian Church because he saw in the Trinity three separate natures, substances and deities, which he equated with the three Aristotelian categories of 'genus', 'species' and 'individuum'. Here, then, we have two examples of philosophy lending a hand to theology, although in the latter case not welcome by some.

Alexandria came under Roman rule from 80 BC, then it fell to the Sassanian Persians in AD 619. However, in 641, after also experiencing a brief spell under Byzantine control, the city was captured by the Muslims and was to remain under their rule until Napoleon's expedition in 1798. Egypt was a logical progression in the expansion of the nascent Islamic empire: by 639 the Arabian peninsula, as well as Syria and Iraq, had been entirely subjugated by the armies of Islam. The next destination was westward, to Egypt, but this was to be a very different enterprise from military expeditions so far as it was relatively unfamiliar territory. Arabia was, of course, the Muslim heartland, and Syria and Iraq were lands the Arabs had long been familiar with through trade and settlement. It was the military governor of Palestine, Amr ibn al-'As (c. 573–664), who persuaded the then ruler of all Muslims, Caliph Umar (579–644), that Byzantine Egypt should be invaded in order to secure the southern borders of the Muslim empire from a Byzantine threat. There were other reasons; though decimated to an extent by Persian rule, plague and Byzantine rule, Egypt was nonetheless a great prize, not only as a vital source of grain, but also as the legendary land of the pharaohs, which represented wisdom. Amr was perhaps more military-minded than concerned with the philosophical discoveries that might await the conquering of such a land, however.

It is one of those twists of fate that the conquering of Egypt may never have happened, and the consequences for the nascent Islamic empire could well have been very different, for the Caliph Umar had second thoughts, concerned, quite understandably, that Amr's army was too small and ill-equipped to face a Byzantine force. From his capital of Medina, Caliph Umar wrote to Amr ordering him not to enter Egypt. According to the Egyptian chronicler Ibn al-Hakam (d. c. 870), this letter contained a postscript that read: 'If you receive this letter when you have already crossed into Egypt, then you may proceed. Allah will help you and I will send you any reinforcements you may need.' Apparently Amr had seen the messenger of the letter riding towards him while the general was in Rafah, just short of the Egyptian border. Guessing the contents, he said he would not open the letter until the end of that day's march, by which time he was just over the Egyptian frontier.

By that time, also, Amr's forces had been strengthened by Bedouin tribesmen from the Sinai, no doubt keen to acquire the spoils of war. Consequently, his army met little resistance at the fortified town of Pelusium, east of Port Said. The famed Babylon, near the site of what is now Cairo, would be a greater challenge, but Amr now had reinforcements sent by the caliph, and took the city after a six-month siege. The Arab army arrived at Alexandria in March 641. Although more heavily fortified than Babylon, Alexandria was captured after a siege that had lasted fourteen months. Occasionally one will still come across accounts of this invasion as leading to the destruction of Alexandria's library by a military general who was ruthless in the extreme, but the evidence simply does not point to this. During the invasion, Amr was often welcomed by the Egyptians because he offered them religious freedom, allowing people to practise their own religious rites and retain ownership of church property, whereas, under the Byzantines, Coptic Christians were forced to convert to the Chalcedonian branch of Christianity. On the conquest of Alexandria the Byzantine army were given an eleven-month amnesty during which time they were allowed to pack and leave the city, taking their possessions with them as they sailed out to their capital Constantinople. Further, Amr left many of the local citizens in positions of power, such as tax collectors and administrators, to continue their duties. This amount of enlightened mercy and common sense does not seem to be the act of a man often portrayed as barbaric. It is worth mentioning that, at the time Amr conquered Alexandria, not only did the great lighthouse of Pharos still exist in the harbour but, also standing, were two obelisks that were over 2000 years old. An example of Arab respect for Egyptian culture was to leave all this in place. In fact, the two obelisks were removed 1200 years later by the British: one shipped to Central Park in New York and the other, known as Cleopatra's Needle, to the banks of the River Thames in London. Given this, why should we suppose that the Arabs set out to destroy the library?

One of the classic historical works on Roman history is Edward Gibbon's *The History of the Decline and Fall of the Roman Empire*, but it is unfortunate that he states in Chapter 51 'I shall not recapitulate the disasters of the Alexandrian library' (Gibbon 1994: 285) because this is the kind of historical information we lack. One ancient visitor, Strabo, arrived in Egypt on a military campaign in 24 BC and stayed in Alexandria for some time. He says that up to a third of the ancient city was made up of royal grounds and gardens, as well as the government and public institutions and, significantly, the 'Ptolemaic shrine of the Muses' (or what today we would refer to simply as the 'Museum'). This museum, according to Strabo,

> ... has a walkway, an arcade, and a large house, in which there is the eating hall for the men of learning who share the Museum. They form a community with property in common and a priest in charge of the Museum.
>
> (Strabo 2002: 51)

Important here is that the Museum was evidently modelled on those two great centres of learning in Athens: Plato's Academy and Aristotle's Lyceum. The library, as the depository of books, was, most likely, housed as part of the Museum.

The 'disasters' of the library that Gibbon pays little attention to refer to a fire that reportedly destroyed the whole library during Caesar's Alexandrian War in AD 47/48. Caesar had only intended to set fire to the ships in the harbour, but the wind caused the library to catch fire too. How much of the library was *actually* destroyed by this event is open to scholarly debate, although the general consensus seems to be that much of it was undamaged and it was not until around the fifth century AD that the physical structure that constituted the library was largely destroyed by Christian attacks on paganism, although scholars hid what writings they could. The library, with its pagan statues and writings, would have been a prime target. Many philosophers were forced to flee the city and it was also the occasion of the unfortunate and tragic death of the female philosopher Hypatia, who was lynched by a group of monks in AD 415.[1] In addition, the city suffered from a number of natural disasters, including a tsunami in AD 365. By the time Amr arrived in the city, therefore, although much of the library no longer existed, many of the scrolls were still housed in the Museum. For an Arab people used to desert landscapes it is difficult to imagine the impression that so many scrolls, so much hidden knowledge, in one place would have had on them. By the seventh century, most of Europe was in its Dark Ages, and Greek philosophy had been long lost once the Roman Empire declined. It was thanks to the library of Alexandria, and the subsequent translation of these works by Muslims, that philosophy was able to return once more to Europe.

When the Muslims entered Egypt in the seventh century what was it like then? By this time, Alexandria was the last remaining centre of philosophy, the others having been banned as a result of Christian influence in the area and concern with what was regarded as pagan beliefs. Plato founded the Academy in 387 BC, and Aristotle formally founded the Lyceum in around 334 BC. These were two major schools of philosophy, both in Athens, that were still in existence during the first two or three hundred years of the birth of Christianity. Other philosophical schools existed in Athens such as the schools of Epicurus – possibly the first of the ancient Greek philosophical schools to admit women – and the school of Zeno (named after Zeno of Citium, not Zeno of Elea, the latter being famous for his paradoxes). As already noted, the dominant Christian empire at the time was Byzantium, also known as the Holy Roman Empire, and its tendrils also stretched to Egypt, hence the concern for philosophers in Alexandria that their fate would be that of the Athenian schools if they did not make at least some effort to 'Christianize' Greek philosophy.

There is an interesting story that when the Academy of Athens was closed, seven of its philosophers fled to the ancient and learned city of Ctesiphon in the Persian Empire (now in Iraq), where they lived for about a year before being allowed to return to Byzantium; some of them at least set up shop in Alexandria. It was the writings of these scholars, notably the names of Philoponus and Simplicius in the sixth century, that the Muslims first encountered when they entered Alexandria. Other significant commentators were Ammonius in the fifth century, and Stephen in the seventh century. These all concentrated on a Neoplatonic interpretation of Aristotle (see **Neoplatonism**). And so, in answer to the question, what is it that the Muslims encountered when they began to digest the great works of scholarship in Alexandria?, it was not Plato and Aristotle as had been taught in the old Greek schools of Athens (and how it is also taught today), but translations and commentaries of some of the writings of Aristotle with a Neoplatonic twist. The 'Greek' philosophy that existed in Egypt by the time the Muslims arrived was a very different beast from the Greek philosophy a few hundred years earlier in Athens. It had indeed survived, but it had also been transformed into a cosmopolitan and eclectic school combining Neoplatonism (itself a synthesis of philosophy and religion), Christianity, mysticism and Egyptian thought. The works that were produced by these Neoplatonists were in Greek, but this was not the only language that the philosophers were translated into before Arabic. They were also available to the Muslims in Syriac, which is a dialect of Aramaic (purport-edly the language spoken by Jesus). Classical Syriac was widely spoken as an unwritten language across much of the Fertile Crescent, and it did not become a written language until the first century AD. It became the lingua franca for many early Christians but, importantly here, it also influenced the development of Arabic. As Arabs encountered Syriac and struggled to understand philoso-phical concepts for which Arabic had no vocabulary, inevitably Syriac words were incorporated, in the same way that today many modern Anglicisms have entered foreign languages, often much to the annoyance of language purists.

The Arabs conquered Syria and Iraq in the seventh century and encountered a number of ancient Greek schools of philosophy there; the most famous worth mentioning were Antioch, Harran, Edessa, Nisibis and Qinnesrin. These are examples of people of different faiths working together as these centres on the whole were Christian, with the exception of Harran in Northern Syria, which was the home of a group referred to by the Arabs as Sabaeans, a now extinct nature-cult who are mentioned in the Quran as worshippers of the Sun. What these schools did was to translate Greek works, many deriving from Alexandria, into Syriac, and so when the Arabs conquered these lands they were confronted with the task of translating into Arabic works that had been translated into Syriac from the Greek! Inevitably perhaps any translation also results in a certain degree of interpretation, and so the Arabs were, on the one hand, confronted with a Neoplatonic Aristotle in Alexandria and, on the other, a Christian Aristotle in Syria; the latter translators not being particularly enamoured of Plotinus' criticism of Christians. The **Umayyad** caliph Yazid (d. 704) is credited as the initial sponsor of this task, although the main impetus seems to have come from the **Abbasid** dynasty of Baghdad, notably the caliphs al-Mansur, Harun and his son al-Ma'mun, who founded the House of Wisdom (see below).

Neoplatonism

So the conflict between religion and philosophy that was to come about in Islam has its precedent in Christianity, especially with the death of the last non-Christian emperor Julianus Augustus (Julian the Apostate) in AD 363. In Western Europe, the Roman empire collapsed and the Dark Ages ensued; while Eastern Europe became an empire ruled by Christian ideology, which resulted in the closing of the philosophical schools in Athens in the fifth century under the order of the Christian Roman emperor Justinian, and the scholars fleeing further east to Egypt and Persia. Perhaps, then, what we may call the last great classical philosophical school (albeit imbued with religious mysticism) is Neoplatonism.

Little is known about the supposed founder of Neoplatonism, the philosopher Plotinus (*c.* AD 204/5–270). He may well have been a native Egyptian of Greek origin (although this remains speculative). It is known that he took up the study of philosophy at the age of 27, and this compelled him to study at Alexandria for some eleven years until he then decided to travel to Persia to learn about Persian and Indian philosophy. At the age of 40 he went to Rome to teach and spent the rest of his life there, although he did make a failed attempt to get the Roman emperor to build a 'city of philosophers' that would live under the constitution set out in Plato's book *Laws*. Plotinus is historically important not only for Islam, as his writings also influenced the Christianity of the Middle Ages, and the school of Neoplatonism cites Plotinus as its founding father. Whilst Plotinus seemingly considered himself merely an interpreter of Plato, his writings possess a more mystical and religious quality that made his understanding of Plato more appealing for the more religiously inclined.

Plotinus does not appear to have written anything until he reached the age of 50, and the works we now have are 54 essays that together present his understanding of Plato. Alexandria was not just the home for Greek thought, however, for it also housed a large Jewish population and the city was a melting pot of ideas in not only philosophical, but religious and mystical traditions from numerous cultures. These attempts to combine philosophy with religion would have had an immediate appeal to Muslim scholars, given this concern with the relationship between these two seemingly diverse and irreconcilable schools of thought. It is, therefore, of little surprise that one of the first major philosophical works (and, afterwards, one of the most popular) that was translated into Arabic was parts of the metaphysical work *Enneads*, for which Plotinus was credited as its author.

In actual fact, much of what we know of Plotinus comes from his disciple Porphyry (234–*c.* AD 305), who was born in the ancient city of Tyre (now in Lebanon) and who edited and published Plotinus' *Enneads* in about AD 300. Porphyry is worth more than a mere mention, however, for he was not only Plotinus' disciple, but a hugely influential writer and thinker in his own right. His work *Isagogue* (translated as 'Introduction') was translated into Arabic (*Isaghuji*) from Syriac, thus becoming the standard introductory text on logic in the Muslim world and a primary source for considerable philosophical debate amongst Muslim scholars. Both Plotinus and Porphyry considered themselves philosophers and rejected Christianity because of what they saw as its reliance on faith rather than reason. Porphyry's work *Against the Christians* – a contentious title if ever there was one – was, not surprisingly, burnt by Christians, and no copies have survived. Neoplatonism, however, was incredibly influential: many of the last scholars to flee from Athens in the fifth century were Neoplatonists, and there were a number of Neoplatonist schools elsewhere. As we shall see, much of its teachings have been incorporated into Islamic philosophy and theology, and it has been very influential upon Christian thought too, even as recently as the Cambridge Platonists in the seventeenth century, the English artist and poet William Blake (1757–1827) and the French philosopher Henri Bergson (1859–1941).

Early struggles by Arab Muslims to get to grips with what must have been a vast amount of new literature by thinkers whose significance would have been little understood at the time resulted in something of a scatter-gun approach at first, with confusion over what works were Platonic or Aristotelian in nature, and even who the correct authors were. As just one example, Plotinus' *Enneads*, which was titled in Arabic as *Athulugia* (Theology), was mistakenly thought to be a work by Aristotle. It is quite understandable for Muslim commentators to be confused by authorship. At the insistence of the Christian overlords, those scholars that remained in Alexandria would have had to make compromises, one being that they were forced to turn away from Plato – who was regarded as a typical pagan polytheist – and, if one wished to study Aristotle, he was to be interpreted in a Neoplatonic way that would be more amenable to the Christian patriarch of Byzantium. This complicated picture will be elaborated upon later in this book, but for now it is sufficient to know that Aristotle's 'God' – or, rather, the Unmoved Mover as it is better translated – does not possess the same characteristics as Plato's 'God' (or Demiurge, as it is often translated), nor, for that matter, the God of Christianity and Islam, particularly in relation to issues involving causation. When Muslims encountered the Greek works it is this Neoplatonic Aristotle that they were faced with, and so no wonder they were confused.

We will not get far in our appreciation of Islamic study if we do not have some familiarity with what Neoplatonism is, given its importance in the Muslim understanding of ancient Greek philosophy. It is rather unfortunate to start a book on what is essentially an introduction to Islamic philosophy by detailing the somewhat complex and abstract nature of Neoplatonism, but some basic understanding here will go a long way. When the Arab general Amr entered Alexandria he was encountering what was then the cultural centre of the world. It was the meeting place for not only various schools of Greek philosophy, but Jewish, Christian, Egyptian, Persian and Phoenician traditions. Put all these religious and philosophical ingredients together in a melting pot and one result is what is called Neoplatonism. The term itself was not invented until the nineteenth century and, to make matters more complicated, Neoplatonism – despite its '-ism' – was not so homogenous, and so it is difficult to categorize what Neoplatonism essentially is, what features are common to all its forms. Having said that, what has been noted so far is that a key reason why it appeals to those of a religious bent, particularly monotheistic beliefs such as Islam, is this emphasis on the 'One', the absolute unity that is summed up in the key principle of Islam: ***tawhid***. This emphasis on 'oneness' is in contrast with Plato's dualism: the view that there are essentially two realms, one being the world of shadows – this world of fallible sense perception – and the other the perfect realm of the Forms. Plotinus, however, did not interpret Plato this way, while also not going down the road of the more pragmatic, almost empirical approach adopted by Plato's one-time student Aristotle. Plotinus' 'One' is ultimate reality: it is self-caused, incorporeal, all-good and absolutely free. The One has no beginning and no end, and all other things emanate from it as a series of descending, lesser realities. The first stage below the One is Nous, or Intellect or World-Mind, which emanates like light from the Sun and which Plotinus calls 'vision that has not yet achieved sight' as it becomes more fragmented. This fragmentation and separation from the One continues to the next stage of **emanation**, the Psuche or World-Soul, which includes within itself all individual souls. From this Psuche comes the next stage, matter itself, which includes our physical bodies.

The appeal for Muslims is unsurprising for, certainly, reference to one supreme principle or being fits within the monotheistic worldview as opposed to Plato's polytheism. However, delving too deeply into Plotinus would not provide too much of a correlation with Islamic doctrine. Plotinus' 'One' lacks personal attributes that would be worthy of worship, and, although the source of creation, this is the result of what is called 'emanation': things come into existence merely as a *consequence* of the existence of the One, rather than the One *willing* existence as such. Plotinus provides a very good analogy of the Sun, which emanates light indiscriminately without it being affected in any way. This 'god of philosophy', while having some attraction in terms of oneness and creation, is nonetheless far removed from the more personal God depicted in the Quran. Despite the difference, the fact that there was some common ground from which Muslim thinkers could work is a starting point.

It is worth reflecting here for a moment on why Muslims would actually make any effort at all to understand philosophical works, other than the rather general notion that it is a religious duty to seek knowledge. In other words, given that presumably followers of Islam have faith in their religion, why devote time and effort to translate and debate works that are at variance with this belief? Or, even if it were the case that these works had common views with Islamic teaching, then what is the point of studying them if these views can be found within Islam already? Various reasons can be given for this: for one, Plotinus' *Enneads* was translated by 'Abd al-Masih Ibn Na'imah of Emesa, who died in 835, and so this translation occurred within two hundred years of the death of the Prophet Muhammad. In terms of the development of a sophisticated religious doctrine this is not a great deal of time, and so Islam would still have been a relatively 'new' religion, certainly in comparison with Judaism, Islam and Zoroastrianism (the religion of Persia, which had existed in some form or other since the third millennium BC at least). All these great world religions had bedded themselves in with highly sophisticated, rational, philosophical justifications for their religious beliefs to a much greater extent than Islam. No doubt a need was felt amongst Islamic scholars for their own religion to be supported by a philosophical tradition. Another reason is that, while perhaps there was some confusion in terms of distinguishing individual Greek philosophers, at least to begin with, the Arabs nonetheless had an awareness of being in the presence of great minds. Any intelligent person would naturally want to know what it is that makes someone a thinker of great repute. In other words, these ancients had something to say, and to ignore it is to devalue one's own worth as an intelligent human being. Over time, Muslim thinkers took great pride and interest in their diligent study of the ancients as they sought out commonalities, evaluated strengths and weaknesses of philosophical discourse and gradually familiarized themselves with the distinctive works of Plato, Aristotle and other philosophers. As an additional motivation, of course, as the old saying goes, knowledge is power and may be of considerable use to any civilization.

India and Persia

When the Arabs had conquered Alexandria, most of the Near East was now under Islamic rule. In terms of philosophy, this meant the schools of Alexandria as well as the Syriac schools mentioned above, but conquests did not end there. In 651 the whole of Persia was under Muslim control, and in 713 this was extended to Sind in India, and Transoxiana, which was the ancient name used for the portion of Central Asia corresponding approximately to modern-day Uzbekistan, Tajikistan, southern Kyrgystan and southwest Kazakhstan. Such an incredible mix of cultures and ideas was bound to impact upon Islamic philosophy. Perhaps most important was the school of Jundishapur in southern Persia. If you were to visit today you would encounter a desolate place, but at one time it was one of the most important centres of learning; the House of Wisdom that was to be built later in Baghdad (see below) was in fact established by Jundishapur scholars. This city was founded in 260 by the Sassanid (Persian) emperor Shahpur I and, for a short time, was the capital of the Persian empire. Descriptions of the city picture a remarkable place that was thriving in terms of science and culture, and, like Athens during its days of democracy, its governors were elected by the city's residents. It is not surprising that with the closing down of Hellenic schools elsewhere, Greek and Roman scholars made their way to Jundishapur as a haven. The city also contained a number of Syrians (most of whom would have been Christians), Nestorians (a Christological belief) and, so it is reported, a small Indian community, which, given the trade route between Jundishapur and India, should not come as a surprise.

It is not known when the Jundishapur school itself was founded, although it started to become known as a centre for science and philosophy when the Greek philosopher and medical doctor Theodoras took residence there during the reign of Shahpur II (AD 309–79). In ancient times, there was no clear-cut distinction between philosophy and medicine: the belief maintained by such philosophers as Galen − that a medical doctor should be a philosopher at the same time − was quite common. It is reported that under Shahpur II the school, which had taken seven years to build, had about five thousand students from Persia, Rome, Greece, Syria, Arabia and India. It is a very complicated picture, involving as it does Hellenic learning mixed with Persian, Christian, Indian and so on; and so it is difficult to outline in any clear sense what the influence of Persian and Indian philosophy on Muslim philosophy actually was, given that Persian and Indian thought was, in its turn, already influenced by other Greek and Roman philosophies before the arrival of Islam. The Persian emperor Khusraw I (r. 531−79) had a strong enthusiasm for philosophy and encouraged philosophers from Hellenic schools to come to the Jundishapur school, where he would engage in philosophical debates with them. These were then published, and conferences were even held where scholars from around the world would congregate.

Even before the coming of Islam, the Jundishapur school was well-known amongst many nomadic Arabs of the time, and students would travel from the Hijaz (the region in the west of present-day Saudi Arabia and essentially the birthplace of Islam) to study there. One of the best-known pre-Islamic Arab philosophers was Harith bin Kalada (who was born in the middle of the sixth century and so may well have converted to Islam), and he was followed by his son Nadr bin al-Harith who became a renowned scholar of medicine especially. After the Arab Muslims conquered Iran they preserved all of Jundishapur's institutions, for example its hospital, medical school, library and temples, and encouraged scholars to continue their studies there. In fact, one of its physicians became the royal doctor for the Umayyad caliph Muawayia. In time, however, as scholars migrated to the House of Wisdom in Baghdad, the school declined and disappeared.[1]

While Indian scholarship generally speaking − in astronomy, mathematics and medicine, for example − certainly contributed to Islamic thought, the influence of Indian philosophy specifically is very difficult to determine, and there is considerable scholarly debate and disagreement on the extent of the impact of Indian philosophy on Islamic philosophy and theology. For example, there are in Arabic writings that reference an Indian philosophical school called 'Samaniyyah', but it is inconclusive as to who these Samaniyyah were and the extent to which they had any direct influence on Islamic thought. Also, there are references to another school referred to as 'Brahmimah', but it may be too simplistic to suggest that this is a comment on the Brahmin, and, even if it is, again it is not clear whether their views had any significance for Islamic philosophy. Having said that, early Arabic thinkers were familiar with the work of a first-century philosopher by the name of Appollonius of Tyana (*c*. 3 BC−97 AD), who was a Greek Neopythagorean: a contemporary with Jesus Christ, he was born possibly in the Roman province of Cappadocia in Central Anatolia and travelled to Mesopotamia and Iran. In Arabic he was known as Balinas and a book attributed to him was translated into Arabic as *Kitab Sirr al-khaliqah* (The Book of Causes). In this book, the author refers to the Brahman and to 'al-Budd', the Buddha. From this text it seems likely that early Muslim scholars had some familiarity, limited though it may be, with Vedic philosophy. In the Hindu texts the Upanishads, there is a move from the various anthropomorphic gods to a non-dualistic God as Light. Again, this more 'monotheistic' strand of Indian philosophy would have an attraction for Muslims.

What was considerably less accommodating towards the key Islamic doctrine of tawhid, of 'Oneness', was the dualism of the Persian religion of Manichaeism. This is named after the prophet Mani, who lived around AD 216–76 in Babylonia, which was then part of the Persian Empire. By the time of the Arab conquests, however, Manichaeism was one of the most widespread religions in the world, stretching from Europe in the west to China in the east, and was for a time a serious rival to Christianity. Manichaeism built upon earlier religions, notably Christianity, Zoroastrianism and Buddhism, and claimed to be the complete and uncorrupted teachings of the prophets of these religions, not unlike the claim made in Islam that Muhammad was the 'seal' (as in 'final') of the prophets; consequently, Muslim scholars, notably al-Biruni (973–1048), denounced Mani as a false prophet. The religious teachings are fascinating and complicated, but in general they are dualistic in that a key belief in a powerful, though not omnipotent, god is opposed by an evil force. This is certainly one way of getting around the problem of evil, but inevitably this can only be achieved by limiting God's power. Manichaeism may well have influenced Christian thought such as St Augustine's views on good and evil, as well as various sects such as the Cathars in southern France, but this is speculative. That Muslims were aware of the religion is undoubted, however, as they encountered Manichaen populations in their conquests, but its influence on Islamic thought is more uncertain. One syncretic religious group called the Yazidis may well incorporate Manichaen beliefs, though not all Muslims accept the Yazidis as Islamic and they have consequently been oppressed throughout much of their history.

The House of Wisdom

Whilst the Umayyad caliphs did their bit in promoting the translation and understanding of philosophy during the first two centuries of Islam, it was given a much greater impetus under the Abbasid regime during the eighth and ninth centuries, especially under the caliphs al-Mansur (714–775, henceforth Mansur), Harun (c. 763–809) and his son al-Ma'mun (786–833, henceforth Mamun). The capital moved to Baghdad and it was Mamun who founded the famous House of Wisdom there.

Mamun, especially, is important for it was during his reign that official support was given for the translation of philosophical texts from the Greek and Syriac into Arabic. Notable translators include Yahya ibn al-Bitriq (d. 835), who is responsible for Arabic texts of Plato's *Timaeus* and Aristotle's *On the Soul*, amongst others. Also, mention should be made of Hunayn ibn Ishaq (d. 873), a Nestorian, who, together with his son and nephew, was responsible for the translation of so many of Plato's and Aristotle's works. Hunayn was particularly enthusiastic about the works of Galen, however, and it is due to this translator that the Greek philosopher-physician became so important in the development of Arabic thought, for he translated not only his 16 books on medicine, but also much of his logical and ethical writings. For a reason that has never been understood, Aristotle's *Politics* remained untranslated and unknown to the Arabs.

Whilst the focus was primarily on Plato and Aristotle, or works that were believed to be written by them, what of the pre-Socratics? Accounts of the writings of those philosophers who preceded Socrates, such as Thales, Anaximenes, Anaximander, Democritus, Pythagoras and Heraclitus, were given brief attention by Arabic scholars but, of course, to this day we only have fragments of the actual writings of the pre-Socratics in most cases, and so it should hardly come as a surprise that Arab translators came across little of their material then. Not much attention is given to philosophers post Aristotle either, with of course the exception of Plotinus. Why this should be so is probably due to the high status Aristotle had amongst Muslim thinkers. For example, the Andalusian Muslim philosopher Abû Bakr Muḥammad Ibn Yaḥyà ibn aṣ-Ṣâ'igh at-Tûjîbî Ibn Bâjja (*c.* 1085–1138), or Ibn Bajja for short, though henceforth referred to by his Latinized name **Avempace**, completely ignores the pre-Socratics because, he argued, Aristotle had refuted their views and so there was no need to spend any time or energy on them. This view was echoed by famous philosopher and theologian **Ghazzali** (*c.* 1058–1111), who, in his *Incoherence of the Philosophers*, states that Aristotle, 'had refuted all his predecessors, including his teacher, whom they nickname Plato the Divine' (we will have a lot more to say about Ghazzali later).

It was the second Abbasid caliph, Abu Jafar al-Mansur, who founded the new city of *Madinat al-Salam*, the 'City of Peace', although the local people called it by the name of the original settlement there: Baghdad. In the design of the city, Mansur was also influenced by the Greeks and Alexandria, in this case the mathematician and 'father of geometry' Euclid of Alexandria (*c.* 300 BC), and so Mansur insisted that his new city should be the closest one could get to achieving a perfect circle. This ringed city, with two sets of walls, was completed around 765, and the caliph's intention was that it would be the start of a new age for Islam under the new Abbasid dynasty, with Baghdad as the intellectual and culture centre of the Islamic empire; for some centuries it was indeed the centre for scientific and intellectual exchange, as well as commerce. The city became incredibly wealthy and could lay claim to being the largest city in the world, with a population of over a million, until that title was acquired in the ninth century by another Muslim city, Córdoba in Spain. The Muslim geographer al-Yaqubi (d. *c.* 897/8) wrote of Baghdad a hundred years after it was built:

> I mention Baghdad first of all because it is the heart of Iraq, and, with no equal on earth either in the Orient or the Occident, it is the most extensive city in area, in importance, in prosperity, in abundance of water, and in healthful climate … No one is better educated than their scholars, better

informed than their authorities in tradition, more solid in their syntax than their grammarians, more supple than their singers, more certain than their Quran readers, more expert than their physicians, more competent than their calligraphers, more clear than their logicians, more zealous than their ascetics, better jurists than their magistrates, more eloquent than their preachers …

(Yaqubi 1892: 17)

While Yaqubi waxes lyrical about the cultural and intellectual achievements of Baghdad, he is less enamoured of its moral standards, however. Other tales have been written depicting the city as a den of iniquity, with drunken brawls and decadent displays. Baghdad, whilst the capital of the Islamic empire, also recognized its Persian heritage, which, like Greek philosophy, did not always rest well with Muslim orthodoxy. Caliph Mansur, though the leader of Muslims and, therefore, regarded as the best living Muslim amongst the community – considered a prerequisite for any Muslim ruler – looked to Zoroastrian astrologers for guidance as to the best time to build his city, and he was also a strong adherent of Hellenic wisdom, which as already noted was such a prevalent culture of the time.

The importance of the patronage of Mansur for philosophy in Islam cannot be underestimated. According to the Arab historian Said al-Andalusi (1029–70), Mansur was 'in addition to his profound knowledge of logic and law very interested in philosophy and observational astronomy; he was fond of both and the people who worked in these fields'. The caliph populated his court with scholars to translate, copy, study and collate Persian, Greek and Sanskrit texts, and to house all this a library called *Bayt al-Hikma*, the 'House of Wisdom', came to be formed. Like the Library of Alexandria, this was much more than a library: it was a translation bureau and a university. Enormous sums of state funds were ploughed into this project, as delegations were sent out to bring back copies of Plato, Aristotle and other great thinkers. Over time, Greek was replaced by Arabic as the universal language for scholars, hence we have such Arabic words as algebra and alchemy.

The next great patron of Islamic philosophy is the seventh Abbasid caliph Mamun, who reigned from 813 to 833. He was regarded as an expert in science and philosophy, and he was an enthusiast for astrology, which at that time was considered as scientific as any other science; indeed, it was not unusual for an astrologer to be also a physicist, astronomer, translator and so on. One discipline did not exclude another, and what united all the disciplines was a curiosity about the workings of the world.

Here we end this very brief history of the beginning of philosophy in the Islamic world for, alas, the House of Wisdom, along with the city of Baghdad itself, was destroyed by the Mongols in 1258.

Note

1 The story of Hypatia, probably the earliest female philosopher we know to have existed, is retold in the film *Agora*.

Further reading

Lyons, J. (2010), *The House of Wisdom: How the Arabs Transformed Western Civilization*, London: Bloomsbury.
MacLeod, R. (ed.) (2004), *The Library of Alexandria: Centre of Learning in the Ancient World*, London: I.B. Tauris.
Remes, P. (2008), *Neoplatonism*, Ancient Philosophies, Durham: Acumen.

3   The first Muslim philosophers

Early theological disputes: What does it mean to be a Muslim?

We have already noted the suspicion and conflict that can exist between philosophy and theology, yet the issues that arise from these two disciplines frequently overlap with each other, so that it is not always easy to distinguish a philosophical question from a theological one; at best, a theological question may well have philosophical implications. One such scenario where this occurred was in Islam's very early days when it was experiencing the birth pangs of religious and philosophical questioning. These early disputes that begin in the very first hundred years from the time of the Prophet Muhammad have traditionally been regarded as 'theological' in nature as they do, on the whole, concern themselves with topics such as the nature of religious belief and the nature of God. However, what makes such issues 'philosophical' is that they also raise concerns regarding the freedom of the individual, what constitutes a good Muslim (and, by implication, what constitutes a good human) and ethical questions concerning the right way to live.

To be a Muslim, to submit to the will of God, is no different from being fully human. The philosophical question, 'What does it mean to be human?' is a question the ancient Greek philosophers such as Plato and Aristotle struggled to answer, and it continues to be a prevalent concern for philosophers to this day. For the Muslim the answer means, quite simply, to be a Muslim! Yet the follow-on question is not so easy to answer: What does it *mean* to be a Muslim? Here arises the first sticking point, but it is incredibly important: if Islam were to survive at all during those painful birth pangs, then it needed to establish a clear identity, a confidence in itself when confronted by other, more firmly established religions. There is a famous hadith which recounts an incident reported by the Caliph Umar that the Prophet Muhammad came upon a stranger one day who asked Muhammad what Islam means. The Prophet answered with the following: 'Islam means that you should testify that there is no God but God and that Muhammad is the Messenger of God, that you should observe the prayer, pay the **zakat** [alms-giving], fast during Ramadan, and make the pilgrimage to the **Kaba** [the large, cube-shaped building that is the centre of pilgrimage in Mecca] if you have the means to go.' The stranger agreed with this, but then went on to ask Muhammad to tell him what is meant by *belief* (**iman**). The Prophet responded by saying that you should believe in God, his angels, his Books, Prophets and so on, but what is particularly interesting about this hadith is the fact that the stranger, who turns out to be the angel Gabriel, made a distinction between 'Islam' as 'submission' and 'iman' as 'faith': the two are not the same thing. This comes back to our question: What does it mean to be human/Muslim? That is to say, is it enough simply to 'submit', or is something much more than that required?

Evidently it is not sufficient to simply declare oneself a Muslim and to go through the motions as it were, any more than it is sufficient to say, 'I am a human' and, by the mere utterance, be fully human. For Plato, to be human required you to exercise reason; to choose not to do this means you are human in name only. Being Muslim is in some ways very simple, but many Muslims would dispute that simplicity is enough. This is also a deeply moral question: what constitutes a good Muslim? How can we be better people? Again, if we look to Plato, to be fully human is to have knowledge of the greatest form of all, the Form of the Good, and to know what is Good is to *be* Good. Similarly, to know the will of God and to submit to the will of God is what constitutes a good Muslim. The complication arises in, first, knowing what the will of God is and, second, how 'submission' is to be understood. If 'submission' is something different from belief, then it is not enough to merely submit; there is much more to it than that.

The Kharijites

It is this very question of what it means to be a good Muslim that led historically to the first divisions within Islam. There is little disagreement amongst Muslims that the Prophet Muhammad signifies the best Muslim, given his honorific title **al-insan al-kamil** ('the person who has reached perfection', or 'the Perfect Man' for short, to be explored in much more detail in Chapter 6). However, this status is not always so willingly applied to the Prophet's successors. The first four leaders, or caliphs, that came after Muhammad are certainly regarded in high esteem, at least amongst the majority **Sunni** Muslims, hence the honorific title of **Rashidun**, the 'rightly-guided'. The first four caliphs were Abu Bakr (r. 632–34), Umar (r. 634–44), Uthman (r. 644–56) and Ali (r. 656–61). What gives these four the status of 'rightly-guided' – a term not given to them until the time of the Abbasid dynasty incidentally – is that they are considered as models of righteous rule, given especially that they were all close companions of the Prophet and, hence, were subject to his guidance. It should be noted, however, that **Shia** tradition does not recognize the first three caliphs as rightly-guided at all, and, in fact, they were regarded as usurpers. For the Shia it is Ali, the cousin and son-in-law of Muhammad (and fourth rightly-guided caliph for Sunni Muslims), who is the rightful heir to the leadership of the Muslims. Here, then, we have the beginnings of differences as to who or what qualifies as the best Muslim, but it is complicated further so early on in Islamic history by a notorious group called the **Kharijites**. The Arabic word *khawarij* literally means 'those who went out' and is an appropriate reference to a group of Muslims who rejected the status of Ali as the 'best Muslim' and, therefore, 'went out' of the community to, effectively, form their own fellowship of like-minded people. The reason for their rejection of Ali's authority is due to the latter's dispute with his governor of Syria, Muawiya (602–80). The governor reproached Ali for not seeking revenge for the murder of the third caliph, Uthman, who was also Muawiya's uncle. This led to military conflict between the governor and the caliph and, during the Battle of Siffin in 657, Ali agreed to arbitration in an effort to end the conflict. Whilst this action may well be a common tradition amongst the Arab tribes of the time, it was nonetheless seen by some of his followers as a loss of authority: the best Muslim is seen by the Kharijites as effectively God's 'shadow on earth', His caretaker, and so to seek *human* arbitration is to supplant God's authority as well as demonstrating human fallibility. They therefore rejected Ali and his supporters as true Muslims and, in fact, withdrew any support for the Umayyads as well, and so effectively became an outlaw community.

Consequently, Ali was condemned by the Kharijites as an unbeliever and therefore sinful (Ali was most likely killed by a Kharijite). The doctrines of the Kharijites, who referred to themselves as the 'people of paradise', were extreme in their quest for a perfectionist ethic, and may well be regarded as the first Islamic 'fundamentalists'. In particular, they advocated a radical approach to the notion of **takfir**; the practice of declaring someone an unbeliever, or **kafir**. *Takfir* raises important issues as to what constitutes a good Muslim, or a Muslim of any kind for that matter, and also who has the right or authority for one Muslim to declare another Muslim to not be worthy of being called a Muslim at all. It is not, therefore, some abstract theological nitpicking going on here, but a serious issue of correct ethical behaviour in the right social-political order. The strictest Kharijite faction, the Azraqites, regarded sinners as the 'people of hell' and were not averse to executing sinners, or at least banishing them, so that they would not contaminate the rest of the community. There were more moderate groups, such as the Najdite Kharijites, who would discipline sinners only after a series of warnings and if they persisted in such sinning activities as adultery or theft.

Remember that to accuse someone of being a sinner, and therefore a non-Muslim, or non-believer (whatever that person may declare to the contrary), is tantamount to one human being declaring another to be 'inhuman', not worthy of the assignation 'human', and, hence, it is both a statement of a being's worth as well as a comment on their ethical make-up. The Kharijites put themselves in the position of being able to expel or even kill anyone they determined to be unbelievers. More significantly, the worst unbelievers were those who hid under the façade of Islam, that is, those who 'submitted' to Islam but lacked true belief. It is not sufficient to simply make the declaration of faith, for you are to be judged by your actions. This view was counter to many other traditions, which suggest that it is not up to humans to determine who is or is not a good Muslim and also that it is enough to simply state that there is no God but God in order to qualify as a Muslim. Whilst the Kharijites were hugely idealistic and, therefore perhaps inevitably, never achieved huge support, they were, nonetheless, quite egalitarian in other ways, for the selection of who should lead their community was based purely on the qualification of who was the best Muslim amongst them, regardless of ethnicity or family line. In fact, one Kharijite group, known as the Haruri, extended the imamate (spiritual leadership) to women, which is something neither Sunni nor Shia are prepared to tolerate to this day.

The Murjites

Despite the short-lived existence of the Kharijites, the question of self-definition had gained its own impetus in theological and philosophical discourse. As we have noted, many Muslims believed that it was not the position of human beings to decide who is or is not a Muslim, and this sympathy developed into a somewhat broad collection of scholars referred to as the **Murjites**. The Arabic term *murji'ah* has its linguistic derivation from 'putting off' or 'suspension' and so they advocated that judgement of a person's belief be 'put off' until the time that God determines. Consequently, it was sufficient for someone to make the outward declaration of faith to be a member of the community, regardless of that person's actions or genuine beliefs. Needless to say, this resulted in a number of the community who seemed somewhat half-hearted in their commitment, but this was considered to be something their conscience would have to grapple with, as they would suffer the consequences in the after-life. It is also obvious why such a view should be considerably more popular than that adopted by the Kharijites as it allowed for a much greater degree of laxity amongst its members. Effectively it was quite easy to be a Muslim and one could even commit a grave sin and enter paradise provided one remained faithful in his heart. That is to say, how one acted was not necessarily a reflection of what one believed.

The Qadarites

The Kharijites felt justified in punishing sinners because they believed that the individual chooses freely to sin. The issue of free will and predestination, which we shall return to later, is certainly an important philosophical issue but, again, has serious political, social and ethical implications that the political authorities were only too aware of. If humans are considered to be free agents, then they are responsible for their acts, and hence deserve reward or punishment. This view of free will was also adopted by a group referred to as the **Qadarites**, which possibly derives from the Arabic *qudra*, which means 'power' or 'capability', for, essentially, they believed that human beings have within themselves power over their own actions. However, this stance was strongly opposed by the Umayyad authorities of the time, who had a much greater sympathy for the **Jabarites**, an umbrella term for a tendency – rather than a school as such – that defended predestination. The reason for state support for the predestination position is that whereas the Qadarites believed that political leaders are responsible for their actions, the Umayyad caliphs preferred the notion that they are God's caliphs, preordained to rule by God and, therefore, in no way responsible for what they do. Perhaps the best-known Qadarite is al-Hasan al-**Basri** (d. 728). Although born in Medina, he lived much of his life in that philosophical breeding ground, Basra, and he argued for free will on the basis of Quranic scripture, in which God sets out certain prohibitions and permissions. For this reason, Basri argues, Man *must* have free will, otherwise why would God set out in the Quran what Man can and cannot do, for this implies that human beings have the freedom to obey or disobey.

The Mutazilites

The concern over moral laxity and, more generally, a lack of a strong Islamic identity was an accusation levelled against the Umayyad dynasty by its enemies. The political pragmatism of the Umayyad is certainly one reason for its success and its ability to spread an empire with relative ease; non-Muslims were allowed to continue practising their beliefs largely unmolested, while Muslims were not given a hard time if they were not as strict in their own practices as they should have been. One such enemy of the Umayyad was the Abbasid clan that came to power from 750 and had its capital in Baghdad. The Abbasid dynasty laid claim to power on the basis that they were the true successors of the Prophet Muhammad and that the Umayyads were not only usurpers, but also lacked moral character. Therefore, the Abbasids, upon coming to power, had to demonstrate a much greater ethical responsibility, whilst at the same time not wishing to be quite as radical as the Kharijites. As often occurs in history, political reality can conflict with idealism, and we see a kind of compromise emerge with a group called the **Mutazilites**.

On the question of what constitutes a good Muslim, the Mutazilites took the stance that the person who had sinned was neither an unbeliever (*kafir*) nor a believer (**mumin**) but was in an intermediate state between the two. However, unlike the Kharijites, the Mutazilites did not excommunicate the sinner from the community of believers. This form of communal pragmatism had its appeal for the Abbasid rulers, and indeed the Mutazilite doctrine became the official government doctrine during the reign of the Abbasid caliph Harun al-Rashid (d. 809), of the *Thousand and One Nights* fame, and continued to have caliphal sympathy until the reign of Caliph al-Mutawakkil (r. 847–61). As the state ideology, pressure was put on the religious establishment, the ulama, to conform to Mutazilite doctrine.

The Mutazilites, originating in the eighth century, are an example of the crossing of lines between theology and philosophy. The main centres of the school were to be found in the two Persian cities of Basra and Baghdad, and we have already noted the long philosophical tradition that existed in this region. They called themselves *Ahl al-Tawhid wa al-'Adl* ('People of Divine

Unity and Justice') and they were sometimes referred to as the 'rationalists' for they made full use of logic and philosophical reason to defend their views. The term 'Mutazilite' seems to derive from the Arabic *i'tazala*, which means 'to withdraw', and may be a reference the withdrawal of certain scholars from a theological debate on the place of the sinning Muslim, hence their name. Whilst they may have lost political influence by the middle of the ninth century, their views continued to have intellectual power for some centuries to come, and indeed they remain influential in Islamic philosophy to the present day.

The theological flavour of the Mutazilites is a result of their primary concern with such religious issues as the nature of God, of the Quran and the subject of sin. Nonetheless, the methodology rested with primarily Greek reasoning as a starting point. Whilst the Mutazilites have often been described as 'rationalists' they should not be regarded as liberal freethinkers. In fact, they supported quite a strict and militant Islam in an effort to impose religious uniformity. They even engaged in an Islamic 'inquisition', or **mihna** ('ordeal') as it was called, in which religious scholars were imprisoned and tortured if they did not sign up to Mutazilite – and by implication, state – doctrine.

For the Mutazilites, reason and revelation were regarded as complementary; reason did not supersede religion. Having said that, the Mutazilites were quite prepared to question tradition, which they often regarded as lacking intellectual credibility and, consequently, unable to defend itself against theological and philosophical attack. The reason they called themselves 'the people of unity and justice' is to lay emphasis on their religious credentials, and it is also because this refers to their two central beliefs. It is worth considering in some more detail what these beliefs entail.

The first one, then, is the belief in God's unity or tawhid ('Oneness'). Given that the Mutazilites would use the tools of reason to question tradition, their view on Oneness is a response to a number of hadiths that state that God could be seen by the faithful in the after-life. It was also a response to certain Quranic verses that seem to portray God in an anthropomorphic way. For example, 'Those who pledge loyalty to you [Prophet], are actually pledging loyalty to God Himself – God's hand is placed on theirs' (48:10, see also 3:73 and 36:71), or references to God's eyes (11:37) and face (2:115). In addition, in an effort to establish a clear identity for Islam and to distance it from other religions, God's Oneness was seen as distinct from the trinity in Christianity or the dualism of Persian Manichaeism, both of which were regarded by the Mutazilites as blasphemous and akin to polytheism. For the Mutazilites, God does not have a body, for this would imply that God has body parts, which conflicts with divine unity. As he does not have a body and, in fact, is not like material creatures in any way, it is not conceivable that believers could 'see' God in Paradise, for to see Him is to limit Him. We can note here that the Muatazilites use a number of negatives in relation to God: he *cannot* be seen, he does *not* have a body, he does *not* have actual hands, but this is because, as God is so different from His creation, it is not possible to make use of the limits of human language to describe Him in any positive way. This approach to understanding God would not be unfamiliar to the Christian approach of *via negativa* (negative way) adopted by, for example, **St Thomas Aquinas** (1225–74) or, indeed, the Hindu concept of *neti, neti* ('not this, not that'). The best one can do is to say what He is not. Reference to God as having hands or a face and so on are to be understood as metaphors for God's grace and knowledge, rather than a literal interpretation. One can perhaps understand why the Mutazilites came into conflict with the traditionalists and why the ulama, who were on the whole very traditional and literal in their beliefs, resisted attempts by the Caliphate to convert them to Mutazilite doctrine.

This is the appropriate moment to highlight a particularly contentious issue that was debated amongst the Mutazilites and their opponents: Was the Quran created in time or is it eternal? The necessary truth of God, as existing in the Quran, might suggest that the Mutazilites believe the holy scripture to be eternal, but not at all. In fact, the Mutazilites were strong supporters of the view that the Quran was created in time. To suppose otherwise is to conflict with tawhid, the unity of God, for an eternal Quran suggests two coexisting eternal things, God and His Word. Whilst the Quran is the word of God, and therefore it is necessarily true, it is the created word and not in any way an attribute of God or a separate eternal substance. To the modern reader, such concerns may seem trivial, but it got at the very heart of how God was to be understood and was important in Islam's effort to distance itself from any form of polytheism, dualism or the Christian trinitarianism. Further, as the Quran makes a number of references to historical figures and events that existed prior to Islam, an eternal Quran would conflict with the possibility of free will, for the fate of all these figures would have been predetermined. The mihna, or 'inquisition', required scholars to sign up to the doctrine of a created Quran and resulted in some opposition until, with the decline of the Mutazilites' influence, the concept of the eternal Quran became official Sunni doctrine. One famous opponent was Ahmad ibn **Hanbal** (780–855), who believed that there was scriptural evidence for the existence of an eternal Quran in 85:21 where it speaks of a 'heavenly tablet'. Hanbal spent a number of years in prison as a result of his opposition to Mutazilite doctrine. The followers of Hanbal were referred to as **Hanbalites**, or Traditionalists (*ahl al-hadith*), of whom the greatest proponent was Ibn Taymiyya (1263–1328), who argued strongly for a strict adherence to Islamic sources rather than the engagement in philosophical discourse.

The second central belief, as their name implies, is in the justice of God. The Mutazilites shared a view of free will that was in line with the Qadarite view, although more for the reason of defending God's good nature as a just divinity, rather than a concern with the moral status of His creation; for surely, the Mutazilites argued, God would be unjust if He were to punish humans for acts they had no control over. God, by His nature good, always wills what is good for His creations. In fact, God could not do otherwise; it is His nature to be just, as in rewarding those who are good and punishing those who are sinful. The way of explaining the existence of evil in the world was to see it as human in origin. This protects God's goodness and it also explains why there was such a militant fervour for promoting the doctrine of tawhid for, logically (and here is the rational element also), if the people of society embrace God as 'One', then society itself will be one and also inherently good. There is a Platonic parallel here that raises problems for the Mutazilites' concept of God: God was bound by His nature to be just. That is, it is not that the acts of God are good and just because God wills them, but God wills them because they are good and just. Any reader out there familiar with Plato's dialogue *Euthyphro* and the famous dilemma will immediately recognize the problem here for, as Plato points out, if God does what is good and just by necessity, then goodness is something separate from God. It follows that the individual can determine what goodness is independent from God: goodness is just 'out there'. It also, of course, places a limitation on God's power and raises that old philosophical chestnut concerning what God can and cannot do; to say that God by necessity must do good is to say that God cannot possibly do bad but, surely, an all-powerful God can do whatever He likes. This reveals the rationalist element of Mutazilite belief: justice is an ideal and is essential to God's nature, for God is essentially rational. Mankind, sharing God's nature, is also rational or, at least if Man wishes to embrace tawhid, also embraces reason. This is a view not unfamiliar to philosophers from Plato, Descartes and beyond.

These two central views of the Mutazilites, then, are the reason for their preferred title of 'the people of unity and justice', but these are the two primary tenets of what are famously referred to as the 'five points' of the Mutazilites, so let us briefly consider the other three.

The third tenet concerns God's 'promise and threat' (*al-wa'd wa'l-wa'id*), which is essentially synonymous with heaven (God's promise) and hell (God's threat). This relates closely, and follows on logically, from the view that God is necessarily just, for if God did not fulfil his promises and carry out his threats then He could hardly be described as just! The conception of such a logically rational and necessary God, then, means that the actions of God are likewise rational and necessary; this is not a divinity that is subject to whim, that gets angry or feels pity and is therefore able to change His mind concerning His decisions. Constrained as God is by this 'promise and threat', it is therefore possible to know through the faculty of human reason whether someone is destined for heaven or hell by considering their actions in the world. However, while emphasizing the importance of reason, the Mutazilites also asserted the importance of the Quran as the best guide in determining God's will: God's punishments and rewards are everlasting and irreversible and these are stated clearly in the Quran, which is also everlasting and irreversible. It should be pointed out, however, that the attack upon tradition, for the Mutazilites, is not an attack on the veracity and authority of the Quran, but there is certainly more questioning of hadith.

The fourth tenet is a topic we have devoted quite some space to so far, rightly so given its implications, and that is what constitutes a sinner. Recall that the Kharijites were very clear as to what makes a person a sinner and, also, that they believed that they were in their rights to punish, even to execute, such a person. In reaction to that we have the Murjites, who 'distanced themselves' from such extremism by declaring that only God could decide who had sinned or not and, hence, a Muslim remained a member of the community regardless of his or her actions. The Mutazilite position did not differ greatly from the Murjites' for, although they adopted what was called the 'intermediate position' (*al-manzila bayna al-manzilatayn*), this effectively also meant that Muslims remained unpunished (in this life anyway, and also keep the fifth tenet below in mind) for they were to be regarded as neither infidels nor believers but in an 'intermediate position'. Whilst this may seem unsatisfactory, it was nonetheless pragmatic in the Mutazilites' determination to maintain the unity of the **umma**.

The final, fifth, point is the doctrine of 'enjoining the right and prohibiting the wrong' (*al-amr bi al-ma'ruf wa al-nahy 'an al-munkar*). It is one thing to adopt an 'intermediate position' in terms of who is and who is not a good Muslim, but the question still arises as to the extent to which the community of Muslims have a responsibility towards ensuring their fellow Muslims' aim to be virtuous, rather than to simply step back and let people do as they wish. For the Mutazilites, Muslims are obliged to 'enjoin the right and prohibit the wrong' and so they should, when opportunities arise, do their best to enforce good practice. This, again, is in line with the concern for communal solidarity.

The decline of the Mutazilites and rationalism

Ashari

The Mutazilites are relevant to this book because, although they may well come under that very broad umbrella of 'theology', they engaged in a kind of theological rationalism that was not only influenced by previous philosophical traditions, but their methods and beliefs continued to have a lasting influence on philosophical traditions after their decline in political influence. In fact, the waning in their power was precisely because they were regarded as too abstract and 'philosophical' to have mass appeal, in opposition to an increasing Sunni concern for orthopraxy and the science of fiqh (the law).

One particularly strong opponent of the Mutazilites, and generally regarded as the chief representative of what came to be regarded as orthodox Sunni theology, is the Basra-born Abu al-Hasan al-**Ashari** (874–936). In fact, with the decline of the school of the Mutazilites came the rise of a new theological school called **Asharism**. Ashari, however, was not quite within the camp of figures such as Hanbal (though Ashari greatly respected this traditionalist), for he was himself originally a Mutazilite before rejecting them at the age of 40 and still made use of the logical, philosophical skills of the Mutazilites for his own arguments. In his work *The Vindication of the Use of the Science of Kalam*, Ashari supports the use of logical deduction, but on the grounds that it is recommended in the Quran and that the Prophet Muhammad himself was not averse to such methods. As Ashari says, '[T]he Prophet was not unaware of these matters and knew them in detail, but as problems about them did not arise during his lifetime, there was no question of his discussing or not discussing them' (Ashari 1905: 4). Consequently, Asharism can be seen as treading a middle way between Mutazilite rationalism and Hanbalite traditionalism, and his main arguments follow.

On the topic of God's unity (tawhid), Ashari is in agreement with the Mutazilites in upholding the view of God as one, single and eternal, and therefore very different in nature to His creation. However, Ashari disagrees with the Mutazilite view that descriptions of God's attributes (hands, eyes etc.) are not of Him at all, but are allegorical. For Ashari, to say, for example, that God has 'hands' is not synonymous with 'grace', but nor is it to mean 'hands' in the same way as you or I have hands. Rather, God's 'hands' are so different from human hands, it makes no sense to even *attempt* to understand what is meant by them. The expression Ashari uses here is *bila kayfa*, 'without questioning how', and so we must simply believe God 'has hands' but we do not know *how* he has hands.

The Mutazilites, we recall, had a major concern for upholding the justice of God and, related to that, the emphasis was placed on human responsibility, on free will, to determine why evil and injustice exists in the world. However, this does conflict with the notion of God's omnipotence, which was of much greater concern for Ashari. Here, Ashari once again appeals to *bila kayfa*, for although it may not make rational sense for there to be injustice in the world and yet for there to be an all-powerful God, it is something we must take on faith, not on reason, and this, for Ashari, is the problem with the Mutazilite view of God, imposing on the divine a rational purpose. However, the problem then arises that if, indeed, God is all-powerful, then human beings are not responsible for their actions, and the implication of this view is that human beings cannot be blamed for what they do, nor should they strive to be anything other than what God made them: humans have an essence that precedes their existence and there is nothing you can do to change the way you are and will be.

Giving Ashari credit here, he does not simply adopt the traditionalist standpoint of a faithful adherence to tradition without any attempt to reason whatsoever, although one may wonder over the extent to which his reasoning here lets him down for, at the very least, it is rather complicated and inadequate. Here Ashari presents his somewhat perplexing thesis known as 'acquisition' (*kasb*): we are conscious of certain actions that we do which we nonetheless have no control over, for example, shivering when it is cold, or sneezing when there is dust in the air, or having a fever when we are ill. We are also conscious of other kinds of actions over which we do seem to have control: for example, I have the power to get up from my chair at my desk right this moment and make myself a cup of tea. In the latter action there is a power created in us and so our ability to engage in these acts is 'acquired' by us and we are responsible for them. Nonetheless, the possession of this power to act is acquired *from* God (as, of course, are the involuntary acts). In this way, we are responsible for our acts because they are voluntary, but we are not limiting the power of God, because he provided us with the power to act in the first place. This may still suggest that God's power is limited if it is the case that human beings can initiate acts of their own accord, but Ashari makes a clear distinction between 'acquisition' and 'creation' (*khalq*). As God is the creator of everything, the actions of human beings are also created by God, because the power human beings possess is derived power (from God) and, in itself, cannot create anything. God creates in human beings the power and the ability to perform an act, and also gives humanity the power to make free choices between doing right or doing wrong, *but* – curiously – this free choice is not able to produce the action, for this is created by God! Humans, then, have no free will in the sense Mutazilites (or Qadarites) understand it, for human beings have no real or effective power, but they do have some derived (acquired) power in the sense that the production of an action is shared. As the Persian philosopher 'Abd al-Karim **Shahrastani** (1086–1153) explains:

> God creates, in man, the power, ability, choice, and will to perform an act, and man, endowed with this derived power, chooses freely one of the alternatives and intends or wills to do the action, and, corresponding to this intention, God creates and completes the action.
>
> (Shahrastani 1923: 53)

People are morally blameworthy, nonetheless, because the completion of an act is at least *partially* due to the intention of the agent to commit a right or wrong act.

As I warned, this is complex and somewhat unsatisfactory, and it is a topic that has puzzled and been debated amongst scholars over the years. Those students who have studied free will versus determinism in relation to Western philosophy, however, may not be totally unaccustomed to such obtuse reasoning, as it is not too dissimilar to the doctrine of Occasionalism proposed by the eighteenth-century French rational philosopher **Nicolas Malebranche** (1638–1713) and the debate with his harshest critic, the Scottish empiricist philosopher **David Hume** (1711–76); the latter – who also perhaps presented an unsatisfactory explanation of free will with his compatibilism – calling Malebranche disrespectfully the 'Occasional Philosopher'!

Alkindi

As we are starting to drift into the tenth century with theological and quasi-philosophical debate, it is best to take a step back in time to the beginning of the ninth century to determine when systematic Islamic philosophy really properly begins. We have noted that early philosophical discussion seems to stem largely from Persia. However, perhaps the first systematic Islamic philosopher is also quite possibly the only highly regarded philosopher to be Arabian, Abu Yusuf Ya'qub al-Kindi (*c.* 801–73), henceforth referred to as '**Alkindi**'.

Indeed, he has the title 'the philosopher of the Arabs'. In actual fact, the Persian connection is very strong, for Alkindi – in Latin known as Alkindus – was born in Kufa (now in southern Iraq), studied and lived in Baghdad, and became a prominent figure at the House of Wisdom where he received state patronage. The Arabian connection is because he claimed descent from the noble Arabian tribe of Kinda, hence 'al-Kindi' ('of Kinda'). Alkindi came from an influential family, indicated by the fact that both his grandfather and father respectively were governors of Kufa, although Alkindi's father died shortly after his birth. He received his early education in his hometown and he later moved to Basra.

What do we mean when we say he was the first systematic Islamic philosopher? As we have already elaborated, philosophical ideas, as well as a knowledge of Greek philosophy especially, were around before Alkindi, particularly with the Mutazilites. In fact, the early part of his career coincided with the ascendancy of the Mutazilite movement, and, because of his own rationalist tendencies and sympathy for Greek logic (as well as his emphasis on tawhid), he has sometimes been identified, wrongly as it happens, as a Mutazilite sympathizer, although it is more accurate to describe him as a sympathizer for ancient Greek philosophy. However, none of the Mutazilite scholars developed a philosophical system of thought, largely, perhaps, because this was not their intention, but also this may be partly due to the fact that an understanding of Greek philosophy for the Arabs was still in its infancy. Alkindi, being the 'first' then, was also subject to such problems in his struggle to relate complex Greek philosophical concepts with the Arabic worldview of the time, but the effort was certainly made and was to pave the way for future philosophers (most directly, Alfarabi, see Chapter 4) to build on the system he had initiated.

Alkindi was a philosopher in the classical sense of the term in that he seems to have put his hand to just about every form of knowledge there was, not unlike, for example, Aristotle. There are some 260 works attributed to him covering such topics as philosophy, logic, astronomy, astrology, medicine, cosmology, geometry, music and so on. Unfortunately, the majority of his works are now lost, most as a result of the Mongol invasions that sacked Baghdad in 1258. Only around 40 of his works have survived and so it is difficult to evaluate the importance of his overall contribution, which is not helped by the fact that his work was soon superseded and, consequently, later authors rarely refer to him. His extensive library was for a short period confiscated and removed to Basra, and Alkindi spent his old age in seclusion as he had made a number of enemies in the courts, partly because of his own intellectual arrogance, and, apparently, he had a reputation for miserliness that alienated many.

Alkindi seemed to be particularly fond of Neoplatonism, although he had to employ translators, as he had no knowledge of Greek or Syriac himself. He was fortunate in that he had the support of the Abbasid caliphs during his lifetime, although the loss of much of his oeuvre may well be a result of future political authorities having less sympathy for such philosophic rationalism. The support of the caliphs was crucial, as Alkindi pitted himself against the traditional theologians who saw the Greeks as un-Islamic, although Alkindi was no doubt helped by his own sympathies for Neoplatonism, which, as we have seen, has more in common with monotheism than early Greek philosophy. Having said that, Alkindi is responsible for commissioning translations of a number of important works by Plato and Aristotle. As Alkindi was from a wealthy and aristocratic background he was able to employ a large number of mostly Christian translators to engage in the task of translating ancient Greek works into Arabic, translations that proved to be an important contribution to Islamic knowledge.

Aside from Alkindi's contribution to the philosophical understanding of the ancients in Islam, what unique contribution did Alkindi himself make? Perhaps his best-known work is *Treatise on the First Philosophy* (it is also the longest of his texts that has survived) and in his introduction he states the following:

> The noblest in quality and highest in rank of all human activities is philosophy. Philosophy is defined as knowledge of things as they are in reality, insofar as man's ability determines. The philosopher's aim in his theoretical studies is to ascertain the truth, in his practical knowledge to conduct himself in accordance with their truth.
>
> (Alkindi 1974: 97)

To state that philosophy is the 'highest rank of all human activities' would inevitably outrage the theologians and ulama especially, and, in an attempt to pre-empt such criticism, Alkindi writes in the same work:

> We should never be ashamed to approve truth and acquire it no matter what its source might be, even if it might have come from foreign peoples and alien nations far removed from us. To him who seeks truth no other object is higher in value. Neither should truth be underrated, nor its exponent belittled. For indeed truth abases none and ennobles all.
>
> (Alkindi 1974: 103)

Alkindi saw no conflict between theology and philosophy, for they are both aiming towards truth and, he argued, both methods are able to attain truth; although he also argued that theologians should make use of the tool of philosophical logic in their argumentation rather than rely on literalism. For Alkindi, a philosopher and a religious prophet have equal standing in terms of the truth they possess, although he was careful to stress that in terms of status a prophet is greater than a philosopher because prophetic knowledge is spontaneous and infallible, whereas the philosopher must struggle through the application of logic and demonstration and is liable to error. Nonetheless, given that a philosopher, if sufficiently skilled, can achieve the same truth as a prophet, this still begs the question, Why the need for revelation?

Alkindi's purpose in writing *First Philosophy* was to use philosophical method to demonstrate the nature of God. He accepted the orthodox doctrine that

God created the universe ***ex nihilo*** ('out of nothing') and therefore, matter being finite, it requires an infinite being to bring it into existence. This infinite, Alkindi argued, is God. God is both creator and sustainer, the Prime Cause. While Alkindi is sympathetic towards the ancient Greeks and Neoplatonism, he does sometimes disagree with them if they conflict with his understanding of the nature of God in Islam. For example, arguing that the world was created by God *ex nihilo* conflicts with Aristotle's positing the origins of the world as eternal. For Alkindi, all matter and time are finite; only God, the Eternal, is infinite and unchanging. However, Alkindi, interestingly, does not refer to 'God' as 'God' as in the Arabic 'Allah', but uses such terms as '*al-bari*' ('the Creator') or '*al-illat al-ula*' ('the First Cause'). While this may seem trivial, the term 'First Cause' is particularly irksome for traditionalists, for not only is this expression absent from the Quran, but it also suggests a form of polytheism by seeing God as the first of a series of causes, rather than the one and only cause. Also, Alkindi betrays his Neoplatonic sympathies by describing God's creation as 'emanating' from Him, as an outflow from the ultimate source that is God, which again annoyed many traditionalists who could not find such a description of creation as 'emanation' in the Quran. In relation to the soul, Alkindi stated that it is simply an entity emanating from God in the same way the rays emanate from the sun. Therefore, it does not have material substance but is spiritual and divine in origin. With the death of the body, the soul returns to the Divine Light and shares in the supernatural.

Aside from Alkindi's more abstract and speculative philosophical works, we have other writings that are of a more practical and ethical nature, among them *On the Art of Avoiding Sorrows* (*Fi al-hila li-daf al-ahzan*), though the attribution of this work to Alkindi has been questioned by some. If this is the work of Alkindi, then it is a demonstration of the influence of Stoicism in his thought. Like many Stoics, Alkindi here advises his readers to focus on the life of the spirit rather than that of the body, and warned against the excessive development of attachments to worldly goods.

Alkindi's reputation spread across Europe largely as a result of his scientific output, rather than his philosophical works. His contribution rests more in his style and presentation than in his originality, and it is to his credit that he was the first Arab writer to provide a systematic and comprehensive classification of the sciences. He served as a court physician and wrote a number of medical works. In addition, works on mathematics and astronomy proved popular in the West, and especially a work on optics in which he argued that light takes no time to travel, and vision is achieved through rays sent from the eyes to the object. Whilst not always correct, his writing introduced the science of optics into Europe, which influenced the work of the English philosopher-scientist Roger Bacon (d. 1294), amongst others. Alkindi was also something of a music theorist, and he borrowed heavily from neo-Pythagorean and Neoplatonic theories of music, although he was original in introducing a theoretical fifth string to the lute and therefore reached the double octave without resorting to the shift. Many of these works were translated into Latin and Hebrew, and he was particularly popular in Muslim Spain. Whilst his notoriety as a philosopher was soon overtaken by the likes of Alfarabi (who was born a year before Alkindi's death) and Avicenna, his particular approach helped to open the door to further philosophical speculation by his successors, not to mention the fact that the Latin translations of his works were to have a major impact on later generations of European philosophers and scientists.

Alrazi

Abu Bakr al-Razi (*c.* 864–925), henceforth **Alrazi**, was known in Western Europe by his Latinized name 'Rhazes'. In the same way Alkindi's name is due to his links with Kinda, Alrazi is named because his birthplace was Rayy, which today is near the city of Tehran in Iran, and so, like Alkindi, was Persian in origin. Also, like Alkindi, he had considerable wealth, which allowed him to indulge his interests in a number of intellectual fields, including musical theory and alchemy, before receiving a formal training in medicine. He gained the reputation of being the unequalled physician in Islam according to a number of sources, and this reputation remained unsullied. His medical works continued to be used in Western Europe up until the late sixteenth century, including the first work devoted to the topic of smallpox, which was translated over a dozen times into European languages. In his own work, *The Philosophical Way of Life*, he describes himself in this way:

> In love of learning and dedication to knowledge, those who have spent time with me and know me personally know that from my youth until today my commitment has been unabating. So much so, that I have never come across a book I had not read or a man I had not met without dropping everything – even at significant harm to my interests – and getting into that book or taking the measure of that man's thinking. My perseverance and dedication reached such extremes that in a single year I wrote over twenty thousand pages in a hand like an amulet maker's.
>
> (Kraus 1973: 109, 110)

His philosophical output, however, was to cause considerable concern and controversy. Again, like his predecessor, he had a prodigious output of over 200 works, covering numerous subjects, although only a small percentage of his philosophical works survive now. It is unfortunate that so many of his works have been lost, but we know the titles of many of these, including *Metaphysics According to Plato's View*, *Metaphysics According to Socrates' View* and *Commentary on the Timaeus* (*Timaeus* is a dialogue by Plato), which tells us much about Alrazi's primary interests so far as philosophy was concerned. Although his works are evidence of a love for the ancient Greeks, he also believed that the philosopher should not set out to imitate the masters, but rather to take in what can be learnt from them and then to surpass them. Alrazi had a high regard for independent thinking, but it was this that got him into trouble with the religious traditionalists, for he argued that people do not need leaders or guides to follow. As he said, 'How can anyone think philosophically while committed to those old wives' tales [religion], founded on contradictions, obdurate ignorance, and dogmatism?' Here we have a contrast to some extent with Alkindi and, indeed, with most of the Islamic philosophers we will be looking at, for, keeping with Alkindi for the moment, he at least made use of philosophy to support his religious beliefs in terms of creation *ex nihilo* and tawhid. Alrazi, on the other hand, seemed to have little time for religion whatsoever, which makes us wonder to what extent he may even be deserving of the title 'Islamic' philosopher.

But this would be unfair, for Alrazi is no secularist, as he did believe in God and in the soul. He merely had little patience for the kind of blind obedience to Islamic law that was typical of the traditionalists. Alrazi believed that everyone was capable of being a philosopher and that there was nothing special about him, other than that he had devoted more time and energy to philosophy while many others chose to ignore it.

Briefly, then, let us consider what Alrazi has to say on the two central concepts of God and the soul. In fact, Alrazi postulated five eternal beings or principles, which are 'God', 'soul', 'time', 'space' and 'matter'. These five principles coexisted and interacted with each other to create the world we live in. Only God and the soul are beyond time and space, and the world was set in motion when the soul mixed with matter in an attempt to achieve a material form. Alrazi's concept of the soul is very Platonic: he saw it as the source of erotic passion and desirous of a union with matter. This blending of a passionate soul with matter caused confusion and disorder in the world, however, and so the role of God was to bring order into this chaos and to enlighten the soul into an awareness that matter is not its natural home. Although not the cause of it, God had allowed the soul to fall because knowledge can only come from experience, and so now the ultimate aim of the soul is to return to the spiritual world where all souls are combined, but this can only be achieved through God's grace. Whilst all this was going on, God also created mankind and gave them the power of reason (philosophy) to counter the passions of their own souls. Hence we have the individual soul – which is emotive and desiring of physical pleasures – and reason – which fights against emotion and desire – for, as long as individual souls engage in the pleasures of the physical world, they shall remain within it through a series of reincarnations.

Now, although Alrazi writes of God and the soul, we can see there is much for the more orthodox Muslims to feel uncomfortable with in this cosmological picture. First, the very idea of five eternal beings conflicts with tawhid and, even if only God and the soul are beyond space and time, that still leaves us with two entities instead of one, suggesting a Platonic dualism. Second, what becomes an important and contentious debate is the concept of the soul, and here Alrazi is again demonstrating his Platonic influence in talking of the reincarnation of the soul, an idea which is not to be found anywhere in Islamic scripture.

Not all of Alrazi's philosophical outpourings were quite so complex. At a more practical level, he was concerned with what constitutes the ethical life. Here, Alrazi seems most influenced by Epicurean philosophy. **Epicurus** (341–270 BC) was the ancient Greek philosopher who founded the school of Epicureanism, and Alrazi followed in his footsteps in terms of the emphasis on empirical method: that one should not believe something unless it can be tested through experience. Alrazi is also Epicurean in stating that pleasure was achieved by living a moderate life, rather than engaging in excess:

> You need to know that those who consistently give precedence to their appetites, feeding and fostering them, reach a point, as a result, where they are no longer able to enjoy them, or to give them up. Thus those who are addicted to orgasms with women, or to drinking wine, or listening to music, do not enjoy these things … as do those who are not addicted to them.
>
> (Kraus 1973: 22, 23)

Alrazi, then, is critical of an addiction to pleasure, but does not deny the importance of pleasure in moderation, and that to deny oneself pleasure can be just as harmful. In this respect, Alrazi also resembles Aristotle's ethics in promoting a middle way, or golden mean. Plato can also be seen here in his view of a life of pursuing pleasures as inevitably a life of dissatisfaction and misery, and his belief that it is the role of the rational part of the soul to rein in the passions. The strongest and, therefore, the most dangerous passion is sexual desire ('ishq), which enslaves the human and, as lovers will often undergo such negative feelings as anxiety and sickness in their quest for a loving relationship, the results can be neurosis or madness if their love remains unsatisfied. Alrazi's recommendation for the avoidance of this state is to imagine your loved one as already lost to you, hence avoiding disappointment later on when you will lose your lover as a result of a break up or death! The other option, of course, is to try to keep your passions in check through reason, although Alrazi realized how difficult this could be.

Alrazi had a genuine concern for what it meant to be human and how a person could live a life in, in more modern terminology, a state of 'well-being', although, ironically, he saw himself as also suffering from excess. As the quote above on Alrazi's obsessive passion for intellectualism demonstrates, he was self-critical and recognized that such an obsession was bad for one's health both physically and mentally. Whilst sexual desire was, Alrazi argued, perhaps the most serious vice if it remained unchecked, another condition that caused anxiety and despair for human beings was the fear of death. Alrazi, in his following of Epicurus, argued that death is nothing to fear for, in death, there is no pain. Alrazi did not entirely dismiss the possibility of an after-life and, if such was the case, then those who have followed sharia should have nothing to worry about for they can expect to go to a much better place. However, this would be of little consolation for those who have sinned!

Further reading

Adamson, P. (2007), *Al-Kindi*, Great Medieval Thinkers, Oxford: Oxford University Press.

Vasalou, S. (2008), *Moral Agents and Their Deserts: The Character of Mu'tazilite Ethics*, Princeton, NJ: Princeton University Press.

Watt, W.M. (2008), *Islamic Philosophy and Theology*, Piscataway, NJ: Aldine Transaction.

4   God, the soul and the after-life

Alfarabi and emanation

Quite possibly the greatest of all Muslim philosophers is Abu Al-Walid Muhammad Ibn Rushd (1126–98), better known in the West by his Latin name **Averroes** (henceforth referred to by his Latinized name). We will be looking at Averroes in more detail later on in this chapter. To put his works into context, we will also need to consider the views of some of his philosophical predecessors and, importantly, the attack against these philosophers by the theologian and philosopher Abu Hamid al-Ghazzali (1058–1111) – his Latinized name is 'Algazel' but this is not commonly used, so henceforth referred to as 'Ghazzali' – who has gone down in Islamic history as perhaps the most influential figure aside from the Prophet Muhammad himself. Averroes was, of course, a philosopher, a true philosopher, a *falasifah*, which in itself has been a discipline subject to much distrust since Ghazzali's *Incoherence of the Philosophers* planted its damaging seeds in Islamic enlightenment thought.

As we have seen in the previous chapter, the topic of God, the soul and the after-life was of concern to the very earliest Muslim philosophers; and, as we have also considered, these topics have proven to be highly contentious in the seemingly intractable conflict between theology and philosophy. Averroes was faced with the somewhat daunting task of defending the use of philosophy in Islamic thought in response to the accusation by Ghazzali that philosophy has nothing to offer in the quest for knowledge and truth. Ghazzali, however, was not merely echoing the views of traditionalist theologians by stating that we should look only to the literal understanding of the Quran and hadith, but he interestingly demonstrates a familiarity with philosophical method and is not averse to using it to attack what he considers the over-reliance of philosophy that results in sacrificing or undermining the importance of scripture. Ghazzali was fully conversant with Aristotle, and his primary aim of the first two parts of his great work *Incoherence* was to attack the perceived Aristotelianism of his philosophical predecessors Abu Nasr al-Farabi (*c*. 872–951), henceforth '**Alfarabi**', and Ibn Sina (*c*. 980–1037), henceforth '**Avicenna**', the Latinized name by which he was known. Ghazzali, therefore, does not attack Averroes or his views personally because, chronologically, Averroes comes after Ghazzali. However, as an interpreter of Aristotle, Averroes is likewise subject to the same refutations, as his contemporaries were fully aware. For this reason, Averroes composes his work *Incoherence of the Incoherence*, which as the title evidences is directly targeted at Ghazzali's major work.

Keeping this in mind, then, we can begin by considering the views of Alfarabi on the nature and power of God, before moving on to Avicenna. Alfarabi was known in the West by his Latinized name al-Farabius or Avennasar. He was also a **Sufi** (Muslim mystic) and something of a musician. Alfarabi's full name was Abu Nasr Muhammad ibn Muhammad ibn Tarkhan ibn Awzalagh (or 'Uzlugh'), although he was known as 'al-Farabi' as he was most likely born in the town of Farab in Turkestan. There is, alas, little information about the life of Alfarabi and what there is cannot be entirely relied upon. His father was said to have been a military officer in the Persian army, although the family seems to originate from Turkey. While the details of his early education are unclear, Alfarabi seems to have spent his early years learning Arabic as well as Persian and Turkish and to have studied jurisprudence, the tradition of the Prophet Muhammad (hadith) and interpretation of the Quran. He then, at the age of 40, travelled to that centre of intellectual and philosophical discourse, Baghdad, where he lived for 20 years. During his time in Baghdad Alfarabi wrote such works as *Survey of the Branches of Knowledge*, *The Achievement of Happiness* and *A Summary of Plato's Laws*.

From what can be ascertained, Alfarabi went on to become a teacher, preferring to distance himself from the royal court for much of his life. However, in 942, by then probably around 70 years of age, he chose to travel from Baghdad to Aleppo in Syria to join the royal court of Saif al-Dawla of the Hamdanid dynasty. What Alfarabi's role there was is open to question, though it was not unusual for a ruler to surround himself with people he considered to be wise and cultured. Alfarabi may well have had an official title such as 'court musician' for he invented and played a variety of musical instruments and wrote a renowned work called *The Book of Music*. The Hamdanid dynasty was Shia, and Alfarabi himself was, in fact, a Shia Muslim. His major works, particularly in the field of political philosophy, were written during this time at the court. He died in Damascus in 950, said to have been killed by robbers while travelling. Over 100 works have been accredited to him, but only a small number have survived. What we do know is that he wrote a considerable amount on topics such as logic and the philosophy of language, and this includes commentaries on Aristotle's works on logic. However, Alfarabi does not restrict himself to mere summary and explication of Aristotle's philosophy, for he goes one step further by offering his own interpretations of the writings of the great Greek thinker, and his elaborate commentaries resulted in Alfarabi being referred to by the philosopher of history Khaldun as the 'Second Teacher', with Aristotle being the 'First Teacher'.

One of Alfarabi's concerns was to mark out as precisely as possible the relationship between philosophical logic and the grammar of ordinary language. It was an interest that Alfarabi shared with other Arabic scholars who struggled to understand Greek philosophical logic in the context of Arabic thought and language. Alfarabi's view here was to see logic as universal in nature – unlike grammar which was particular to a language – and not a foreign import, so that it could provide the ground rules for reasoning no matter what language one spoke. In this way, grammar and logic are distinct sciences, one universal and one particular, although Alfarabi recognized that an understanding of logic is dependent upon how it is interpreted through the medium of one's chosen language. Following very closely in the footsteps of Aristotle (it is recorded that he read Aristotle's *On the Soul* 200 times and the *Physics* 40 times), Alfarabi argued that logic helps us to distinguish truth from error by giving us the thought processes to think things through and reach solid conclusions. While Alfarabi had much to say on logic and its importance in terms of being a 'universal language', he also believed that the arts of rhetoric, poetics and dialectic, though not universal in the way logic is, are nonetheless essential elements of philosophy for they are the means by which the philosopher communicates with the vast majority of the people.

However, while the influence of Aristotle is evident here in terms of his writings on logic and the natural sciences, in his works on the 'divine sciences', or metaphysics, we can detect a strong Neoplatonic flavour. In terms of what Alfarabi describes as the 'divine science', then, his particular focus is on the nature of being. This is the field of philosophical study referred to as ontology, which raises such questions as 'What can be said to exist?' and 'What is a physical object?' Such questions are inevitably bemusing for many readers, and Alfarabi can be extremely obscure at times, but his ontology, which considers the nature of all being, does ultimately relate to the nature of God as the *absolute* (and, indeed, perfect) being. Alfarabi is hugely influenced by Neoplatonic philosophy through his study of the theory of emanation and how this acts as a connection between the seemingly separate divine being and the material world. His fascinating cosmology blends elements of Aristotle with Neoplatonism. Like Aristotle's Unmoved Mover, God is seen as one, eternal, immaterial and necessary. However, for Aristotle, his 'God' is the 'causer' in the sense of putting the universe into motion. That is, God is the First Cause of all other things but He is not the creator (efficient cause) of all other things. For Alfarabi, and for Islamic theology for that matter, it was unacceptable that there could be a separate substance from God: before God there was nothing and God created the universe *ex nihilo* ('out of nothing').

To understand Alfarabi and other Muslim philosophers we will be considering, some familiarity with not only Neoplatonism, but Aristotle can go a long way. Aristotle saw his philosophy as the culmination of what had come before him in terms of Plato and the pre-Socratics, and as an intellectual effort to fill the gaps left by his predecessors. For Aristotle, it was important to present a picture of the universe as orderly, as all things having their proper place. For example, there are four elements (although he does refer to a fifth element, which is the heavens), which all move to their proper place: fire goes upwards, earth goes downwards etc. They have a *purpose*. There is structure and hierarchy in the cosmos and also in the world, with plants, then animals, then humans at the top of the tree. All beings have function, or purpose, and in the case of humans – who are unique in possessing reason – their purpose is to act according to their reason. As humans we must transcend our animality and strive towards what is best within us, for our reason is also what is divine within us. Within this hierarchical structure, Aristotle argues that there must be a highest being: if there is movement, then there must be a mover and, unless one is prepared to accept an infinite regress, then there must be a First Cause, an Unmoved Mover, to explain why things move in the first place. Recall that for Aristotle the universe must make sense, an infinite regress does not make sense, and so the need for an Unmoved Mover follows rationally and logically.

Equally, Aristotle uses logic to demonstrate that God must be eternal because time is eternal. He defines time as the counting of moments, and because time involves the past, present and future, there could not be a first moment because then there would be no past, which is a contradiction! Hence, Aristotle gets around (or some would say, skirts) the infinite regress problem by intro-ducing an eternal being. And so we have an eternal being, but this being did not create the universe. How can an Unmoved Mover move something (the universe) without being moved itself? Aristotle is vague here, but says it is like an object of desire which, similarly, can move us even if it does not itself move. This Unmoved Mover is also immaterial, because matter is by definition an active thing, involving movement and parts. The Unmoved Mover is Pure Actuality in that it can be nothing other than what it is (other beings are moving from one potential thing to another). Curiously, this God cannot move, but there is activity, which is pure ***logos***, the highest activity there is: pure intellect. Pure thought is self-sufficient, for it does not rely on others in the sense that it does not think about other things and, so, the only 'thing' it can think about is itself!

It must be emphasized how Aristotle's God is so different from the God of monotheism and, hence, the God of Islam. God cannot be moral because to exhibit moral virtues is to express a deficiency. For example, God cannot have courage because in order to have courage, you have to overcome a fear of something. God cannot have self-control, because one must have a desire that is bad and resist it. God cannot keep a promise, because one would need the other contracting party; and God cannot love because Aristotle equates this as desire, which again is a lack of something (that which is desired). And, as we have said, God is also not the creator of the universe.

The view that God is not the creator of the universe is a serious contra-diction of the Islamic view of God and not a view – despite his fondness for Aristotle – that the Muslim Alfarabi is prepared to subscribe to. Therefore, in maintaining that God *is* the creator of the universe, Alfarabi goes on to explain *how* God created the universe. Here, Alfarabi's particular contribution to both Islamic philosophy and theology comes into play, for he borrows heavily from the Neoplatonic notion of emanation, which we have touched upon in

Chapter 2. It is important to understand why Alfarabi felt that Neoplatonism could assist here, and this was due to one of those perennial and thorny problems that philosophers of religion and theologians equally have struggled to alleviate: How can you maintain a concept of God that is Perfect (and by 'Perfect' we mean immutable, eternal, immaterial and so on) and then state that God engaged in the act of creating the material universe at a specific time? Whilst one response might well be to simply say that God can do whatever He likes, this is unsatisfactory for the more philosophically inclined thinkers because of the irrational contradiction between declaring a Being that cannot change and is immaterial and yet must change in order to act, for the very concept of 'acting', of *doing* something, implies changing from one state to another, which perfection cannot do. Alfarabi attempted to get around this problem by proposing 'emanation'. Perhaps not surprisingly, Alfarabi's starting point is actually Aristotelian in that he agrees with Aristotle that God's activity is 'thinking of thinking' (*noesis noeseos*): God thinks only of himself and is therefore characterized as an intellect concerned with reflecting upon Himself. However, Alfarabi then moved into the works of Neoplatonists such as Plotinus and Proclus by considering the somewhat accidental consequences of divine self-contemplation.

In his work *Principles of the Opinions of the Inhabitants of the Virtuous City*, Alfarabi also presents what, at first, bears some resemblance to Plato's *Republic* by starting off with the 'macro' of the First Being and ending up with the 'micro' of the best, most virtuous city in the same way that Plato looks at the Form of the Good in order to determine what the best city-state would be. We will leave aside Alfarabi's political motives, but let us look more at this 'First Being' and the relation to emanation. As we have already noted, Alfarabi's God is, first of all, perfect. That is to say, nothing is greater (*more* perfect) than God for then that 'more perfect' being would be God, so we have here something of an ontological argument; God, by definition, must be the Perfect Being. God's perfection also implies that He cannot become anything other than what He is, for to do so would mean he is not perfect, and so God does not have the potential to become something other. This is what Aristotle means when he says the Unmoved Mover is 'Pure Actuality', whereas us mere material mortals are moving from one potential thing to another, i.e. a baby becomes a child, a child becomes an adolescent, an adolescent becomes an adult, an adult becomes dust and bones. All material things are in states of a kind of temporary actuality because they will at some time or other (or, as some would argue, constantly) change from one state to another. God simply does not do that. Importantly, because God does not change from one state to another, He cannot have any purpose. Again, this is Aristotelian, for the Greek philosopher saw purpose in all living things, the purpose of an acorn is to become an oak (i.e. an *actual* acorn has the *potential* to become an oak), but God – being Perfect Actuality – cannot become anything other than what He is and so there is no purpose to his existence other than Himself. Hence, all that God 'does' is to reflect upon Himself and this is an intellectual activity because intellect is understood as being immaterial, and God is immaterial.

Given this concept of God, it is inconceivable for the divine to engage in the activity of creation, and so creation – all matter that exists – must be accidental. It is just a kind of 'spin off' from God's intellectual self-reflection and is not God actually doing anything in addition to that, because 'in addition' would require more from God, who is perfect and so there is no 'more'. This divine being, then, is 'thought thinking thought' and, as He reflects upon his own goodness, beauty and perfection, is also 'love loving itself'. This process of thought and loving results in an emanation, or overflow, of goodness that leads to the material universe. As an analogy, the sun is a good example here for it is self-sufficient as a ball of energy but as a consequence of this energy we have light and life, although this consequence does not affect the sun in any way. Another helpful analogy is to imagine this emanation like ripples that emanate from a pebble thrown into a lake, and here we have a hierarchy of creation with the First Being at its centre and levels of imperfection emanating out; the further away from the centre, the less perfect this level is. Here, then, is the hierarchy:

- 'The First'. This is the Divine Being that contemplates itself and, as a result, this emanates a second Being.
- 'The Second'. Like the First, an immaterial substance, and which Alfarabi refers to as the First Intellect. The first ripple is also intellect, but differs from the First Being in that, whereas the latter contemplates itself, the former contemplates the First Being. This very act of contemplation produces the third being as well as the body and soul of what is called the 'First Heaven'.
- 'The Third'. This is the Second Intellect, and its contemplations produce the Fourth Being and more astral phenomena.
- And so on: each Being, through contemplation, producing astral phenomena such as the stars. The results of this hierarchy of intellects, each contemplating what comes before it, is the emanation of the heavens, the stars, the planets etc., until we come to:
- The Eleventh Being or the Tenth Intellect. This is also referred to as the Active Intellect because this is what actualizes the intellect of human beings, as well as giving material form to humans and what is referred to as the 'sublunary' sphere. This idea of the 'sublunary' goes back to Greek astronomy and is the region of space from the Earth to the Moon, consisting of the four basic elements (earth, air, fire and water).

It is an extremely complicated and confusing picture that this modest book cannot go into in any detail, and the modern reader may well be bewildered by the cosmology that emerges here. But a couple of points to keep in mind: not a single generation has gone by in human history when mankind has not attempted to explain the existence of the stars above us and why we are here, and although our scientific knowledge today may make this Neoplatonic picture of the cosmos seem like a fairy tale to us, it was nonetheless an attempt to answer the key questions of existence whilst avoiding some serious rational contradictions. Perhaps the most important point of this whole cosmological picture to take way with you is that, despite the human, pathetic physical body being considerably far away in nature from the Divine Beings – that 'pebble' that initiates emanation – the fact that human beings possess reason – intellect – means that they have the potential to 'tap into' this intelligible world. The importance of the human rational faculty is something that has been emphasized by so many philosophers, including Plato and Aristotle; in fact, it is perhaps best expressed by the French philosopher **René Descartes** (1596–1650), who sees reason as giving Man 'God's eyes' to see the world as it really is, despite the soul being 'trapped' within the confines of the physical body.

Inevitably this will raise concerns, which have already been touched upon, amongst traditional theologians who wish to emphasize revelation over reason. Another concern, however, is what exactly are we to make of Alfarabi's God? We have seen how Aristotle's God is 'Pure Actuality': as God is perfect, it cannot potentially be anything other than what it is. In fact, more accurately, God is unique in being both Actuality and Potentiality in one. Alfarabi replaces the terms 'actuality' and 'potentiality' with 'essence' and 'existence', and so instead of saying that an acorn has the potential to be an oak tree, Alfarabi would say that the 'essence' of an acorn is 'oak tree'. Likewise you and I both exist, but we also share an essence that is 'humanity'. This way, Alfarabi declares the presence of essences as universals, while also asserting the presence of individual existences: you and I are not illusions so far as Alfarabi is concerned. However, try as hard as we might, you and I can never share the essence of an oak tree! All this is very well, but how are we to come to grips with the idea that God is both essence *and* existence and they are the very same thing, given that Alfarabi wants to state that our essence is separate and different from our existence? Alfarabi's answer is quite a simple one: we cannot understand the nature of God because we are limited human beings with limited human intelligence, so no wonder we cannot grasp the nature of fundamental reality.

It is a way for Alfarabi to try to avoid the problems of the Quranic God creating the universe *ex nihilo* for, as we have said, philosophically (i.e. rationally) speaking, 'nothing' is an 'illegal concept'. As a result, we are presented with a very remote God who has really nothing to do with the world that we live in; all that is left is the Active Intellect which, at best, means we can share in God's nature only to the extent that reason is a universal phenomenon which we are all subject to. Whilst God is indirectly responsible for creation, in that 'He' is the source of emanation, He hardly seems a God worth worshipping. However, Alfarabi is not always consistent in his writing when referring to God, for in some cases he gives us the more traditional Quranic God, referring to Him as 'Lord of the Worlds' and 'God of the Easts and Wests', and he also occasionally utters prayers to God, which suggests that Alfarabi worshipped a God that would indeed respond to prayer.

Avicenna and the Necessary Being

Hopefully by now the reader will appreciate just how important Neoplatonism is in the development of Islamic philosophy. Despite its complexity and, at times, what seem to be bizarre elements to the modern mind, it is not a topic we can avoid, and hence my urging you to familiarize yourself with at least some of the basic tenets of Neoplatonism. Whilst Alfarabi has been credited as the philosopher who rediscovered Neoplatonism for Muslim thought, it was his successor Avicenna who was able to give Islamic Neoplatonism a more coherent and fluent account, which was much more amenable to his Muslim audience.

There is no doubting that Avicenna's contribution to philosophy and medicine has been immense. To this day, in Iran especially, his philosophy continues to be influential, while his research in medicine remained standard teaching until the seventeenth century, and so he is deserving of the title 'Prince of Physicians'. He was born in the small village of Afshanah near Bukhara in western Uzbekistan. His father was an officer in the nearby citadel of Bukhara. Should you ever get the opportunity to visit Bukhara today you would not be disappointed as its centre maintains its medieval features so that upon entering you could feel you were back in the time of Avicenna. Bukhara became an important cultural centre for the Abbasid Caliphate from the early eight century, and, by the time of Avicenna, it was one of the most important cities economically and culturally in the Islamic world, until it was sacked by the Mongols in 1220. As a young boy, Avicenna arrived in this city which, at that time, had become virtually independent of Abbasid authority, establishing its own Ismaili dynasty called the Samanid. Avicenna's father became initiated into the Ismaili sect, with Avicenna himself being introduced to its teachings. **Ismailism**, which at that time was the largest branch of Shia Islam, is significant for Avicenna's philosophical development as it is more esoteric and inclined towards the abstract than its more legalistic Arabic Sunni counterpart.

Avicenna was a precocious child, having memorized the Quran by the age of ten and already by that age familiar with many of the great works of Arabic literature. If we are to believe Avicenna's autobiography, he says that by the age of 14 he knew more than his teachers and by the age of 18 he had mastered a number of the sciences, including medicine, which he claimed he had found easy. His medical expertise was such that others felt willing to subject themselves to the young man's skills as a physician, including a Samanid prince whom he cured of an illness. The prince, out of gratitude, gave Avicenna free access to his considerable private library, allowing the youngster the opportunity to pursue his own independent studies in law, medicine and metaphysics. Perhaps Avicenna had a photographic memory as he claims to have read and understood the entire collection of works within 18 months. In the course of this he states that he gained a thorough grasp of Aristotle's *Metaphysics* – with the aid of a commentary by Alfarabi – and he wrote his own book on philosophy when he was just 21 years old, which, by all accounts, was not a bad effort for one so young. In fact, the autobiography was something of a rare genre at the time, certainly in the Islamic world, and we can be grateful for Avicenna's as it offers a rare insight into the mind of this young prodigy. This snippet gives you some idea of his mind at work:

> Whenever a perplexing problem confronted me or a middle term in a syllogism escaped me, I would repair to the mosque, there to pray and implore the All-Creator until the hidden was revealed and the difficult eased. Returning home I would at night set a lamp before me and engage in reading and writing. Whenever sleep or fatigue came near overcoming me, I would resort to wine and drink until my strength was fully recovered. Thereupon back to reading I would go. In case slumber did overtake me, I would go on in my sleep considering what I was considering before. In fact many a problem was thus solved. Thus I continued until I had mastered the totality of sciences. My comprehension of them then [at age 18] attained the limits of human possibility. All that I learned during that period is precisely what I know now.
>
> (Al-Qifti 1903: 415)

Essentially, then, Avicenna had learned all there was to know by the age of 18! However, Avicenna does admit that he read Aristotle's *Metaphysics* some 40 times in an effort to understand it, and it was not until he read it alongside Alfarabi's commentary that he was able to grasp its meaning fully, which says much for Alfarabi's achievement. Following on from this, it was philosophy that Avicenna became particularly attached to, especially Neoplatonism.

Avicenna was employed as a minister in the Samanid government. However, whereas the Samanids may be considered more liberal minded in terms of belief and, for that matter, lifestyle (note Avicenna's reference to wine-drinking in the above quote) their power was on the wane at this time, and in 999 Bukhara was conquered by a Turkish dynasty known as the Ghaznawids. This dynasty is a sharp contrast to the Samanids, the former being far more orthodox and ruthless, with little regard for philosophical reflection or learning of any kind. This was also not good news for Avicenna who, having now lost his royal patronage, lived a more precarious existence, as he found himself frequently having to pack his bags to flee to another city in the hope of evading Ghaznawid intolerance. His survival primarily rested on his abilities as a physician, curing various local rulers of whatever maladies they had. Earning a living by day as a court physician, he wrote his great works of philosophy by night. No longer having access to great libraries, he had to rely on his incredible memory for source material in his efforts to synthesize the works of classical Greek philosophy with Islamic thought. Avicenna spent the final 14 years of his life, however, in one place: as physician in the Buyid court in Hamadan (in what is now western Iran). The Buyid dynasty were Shia Persians who claimed descent from the pre-Islamic kings of Persia, and for many years they had virtually ruled Baghdad, with the caliphs as little more than symbolic puppets of their regime. While not always secure – he was occasionally imprisoned – Avicenna nonetheless achieved the rank of vizier, a ministerial position of considerable power. But, by some accounts, he was considered an intellectual snob and did not find it easy to win friends and influence people, preferring his own company and his books. It was perhaps his medical skills that prevented him from losing favour entirely or spending even more time in prison than he did.

Avicenna died at the age of only 57 in 1037 following an illness contracted 3 years earlier while on campaign with the ruler. Alas, not all of Avicenna's works have survived the various conflicts, and some were lost during Avicenna's lifetime as a result of the political upheavals. His corpus certainly equals that of Alkindi in terms of quantity, and more modern biographies catalogue over 270 works attributed to him, of which some 200 have survived. Three encyclopaedic works stand out: two in philosophy, entitled *Healing* and *Directives and Remarks*, and one in medicine, *Canon*. *Healing* is the longest work he wrote and, in fact, is probably the longest book of its kind written by one man, consisting of four major books in logic, physics, mathematics and metaphysics. His *Canon* records the accumulated contemporary learning on this topic and his own discoveries and experiences. Of immense range, for almost 700 years it remained the single most famous and influential book on medicine. His *Directives and Remarks* is his most personal work, in which he depicts the stages of enlightenment for the mystic.

Avicenna's keen speculation on philosophical matters inevitably roused the suspicions of the orthodox. As we have seen, Avicenna was particularly diligent when it came to Aristotle, especially what the ancient Greek philosopher had to say about the nature of being (ontology), and his remarks here are also reminiscent of Alfarabi:

> Every series arranged in the order of causes and effects – whether finite or infinite – if it includes only what is caused, clearly needs an external cause linked to it at one end of the series. It is equally clear that if the series does not include anything uncaused, this is the end of the series, its limit. Every series therefore ends at the Being, which is necessary by itself.
>
> (Avicenna 1958: 455)

This passage is interesting in that, although it does borrow heavily from Aristotle, it also reflects what is now referred to as the cosmological argument for the existence of God, or the argument from contingency, which students of philosophy of religion will no doubt be familiar with through, most notably, the Christian scholastic scholar St Thomas Aquinas (1225–74), although he lived over two hundred years after Avicenna. In particular, Avicenna focuses on 'contingency' and 'necessity', rather like Aquinas' 'Third Way' in his *Summa Theologica*.

Avicenna presents his argument in the following manner:

1. When we look at the world, we are aware that beings exist.
2. These beings must be either contingent (i.e. possible, or dependent upon something else for their existence or non-existence) or necessary (independent of anything else for their existence).
3. If it turns out that we can observe a being that is necessary, then that being must be God by definition (for God is not dependent upon anything else for its existence).
4. We can only recognize contingent beings in this world, but contingency cannot go on forever (i.e. there cannot be a series of causes).
5. Therefore there must be a Necessary Being which all things depend upon, and this we call God.

Now, this argument has been countered by a number of scholars since Avicenna's day, and this is perhaps not the place to consider them all. The reader is advised to pick up any good book on philosophy of religion, which will outline the problems with such an argument, not least of which is the requirement for a first cause at all, and even if a first cause is required we are still faced with the problem of why that should in any way resemble what religious believers call God. Nonetheless, the point to be made here is that much criticism of the cosmological argument is directed against Aquinas, while the contribution of Islamic philosophers is largely ignored or barely mentioned. Partly the aim of this whole book is an attempt to redress this imbalance to some extent, while also acknowledging the key importance of the Greeks ultimately here.

It will also be evident that Avicenna is reliant upon what was also to become known as the ontological argument, which, again, is something Aquinas (and Descartes) also relied upon, for to respond to the critics of the cosmological argument who state that there is no requirement for necessity (and therefore there is only a series of causes) is to ignore the logical problem encountered when denying necessity. Avicenna argued that this is simply not possible: the fact that you can conceive of a Necessary Being means that this Necessary Being *must* exist, because otherwise it would be contingent.

Once Avicenna has provided an argument for the existence of a Necessary Being there is, as noted, the other rather important consideration of what the nature of this Necessary Being *is*. Aside from the feature of necessity, Avicenna, like his predecessor Alfarabi, stresses the importance of God as One, or tawhid. This, again, makes perfect rational sense for Avicenna, given God's necessity, for if God was made of 'parts' – in the way that all other contingent things consist of a multiplicity of things (i.e. essence and existence, potentiality and actuality, as discussed above) – then God would also have to be contingent for these parts to come into and out of being. Oneness implies no-change, whereas multiplicity implies change. Therefore, God's essence is identical with His existence, free from matter, One, and simple in every way. As such God is beyond definition, for to define something is to give it a genus which God, being God, cannot have. 'God', then, is simply a name we give this entity. Consequently, it is difficult to say what God is, and it is much easier to assert what God is not: i.e. not physical, not in time or space and so on.

Although God can be known *via negativa*, Avicenna asserts some positives about God too, as these follow from what God is not. For example, because God is *not* material, he *is* also good. Why this should be the case is because Avicenna argued that evil is a privation, and the source of privation is matter. This needs unpacking a little: again, we must go back to Aristotle here, who stated that, when confronted by two contraries, one is negative in relation to the other. For example, darkness is an absence of light; poverty is an absence of wealth; ugliness is an absence of beauty; and, of course, evil is an absence of good. Aquinas was influenced by this idea, and in *Summa Theologica* he stated that evil isn't a 'thing' at all, but is, rather, an *absence* of goodness. Evil, for Aquinas, cannot possibly be a 'thing' because God creates all 'things', and God, being all-good, would not create evil things. Evil, therefore, is a privation of good (in Latin, *privatio boni*). This was something that Avicenna also picked up on from Aristotle. Matter, being imperfect, contains the possibility of evil, whereas the immaterial cannot. For Aquinas, incidentally, it was also a neat way of getting around the issue of the problem of evil because God, being pure goodness, does not, and can not, create evil. God only creates what is good. Therefore, Man's true nature is to be good. If Man does not live up to his nature then, in this sense, he or she is evil: *but he or she wasn't made 'evil'*.

What also follows from God's immateriality is that he possesses the positive features of 'simplicity' and 'pure intellect', which are also immaterial and hence not something separate from God; it makes no sense in fact to say 'God's intellect' for God *is* intellect. God is the highest (as in pure) beauty because there can be nothing more beautiful than God and so, in a Platonic sense, the more a person can apprehend beauty, the more one is in touch with God. As Avicenna himself puts it in his work *Deliverance*:

> Thus the Necessary Being, who is most beautiful, perfect, and best, who apprehends itself at this ultimate beauty and goodness and in the most complete manner of apprehension, and who apprehends the apprehender and the apprehended as one in reality is in essence and by its essence, the greatest lover and beloved and the greatest thing pleased and pleasurable.
>
> (Avicenna 1985: 282)

The connections with Alfarabi and Neoplatonism now become more obvious, for God's goodness and beauty inevitably overflows, or emanates, as a result of pure generosity. The hierarchical process that follows is not dissimilar to Alfarabi's concept of emanation described above, and it is not necessary to essentially repeat it here.

What can God know?

An important related philosophical question here that was to concern the learned for centuries to come is, What can God know?

It is, of course, assumed that God does in fact have knowledge, and this is usually based on the view of God as perfect; if God did not have knowledge, He would be imperfect, since it is better to know than not to know. The nature of God's omniscience is, taken literally, to mean 'all-knowing'. But what does this mean in terms of God? For example, if one were to say that Paul knows what the capital of France is, and knows how to bake a cake, and knows the time, and so on, we are, of course, not only talking about different kinds of knowledge – what in epistemological terms are referred to as 'knowing what', 'knowing how', 'knowing when' etc. – but also knowledge of particular things: places, times and so on. Now this is fine for contingent, embodied mortals like us, but presents problems for a necessary, immutable, immaterial being. As an example, if Paul were to say, 'I know it is four o'clock now in London and it is sunny,' then Paul is making reference to a specific time, place and situation, but how can a timeless, placeless God talk of 'now'? To say it is sunny in London now means that it will not be sunny in London at some other time, or to say that the prime minister is 45 years old means that he will not always be so. How can God know things that are subject to change, that are mutable, given that God is immutable? Can that which does not change know that which changes and not be changed itself in the process? Can a perfect being know imperfect things?

The simple response to this is, yes, why not? Why can't God know that for Paul, at a certain given time in a certain given place, it is sunny? In fact God's omniscience means that He can know all given times for given places for given situations for given people. This, surely, is what 'all-knowing' means. Needless to say, this is more complicated than the simple answer will allow, and, again, the reader is urged to read more on this from a good book on the nature of God, although, for now, just consider these related concerns: Can God also know all possibilities of things that turned out not to be the case? For example, the writer of this book could have decided not to write any more today, or today could have been hot instead of cold, or it could have snowed, or … you get the picture. Surely an omniscient God would know *all* possibilities.

Also, as noted above, there are different kinds of knowledge. For human beings, much of our knowledge (if not all of it) depends on being physical creatures. As Kant pointed out, what we know about the world is entirely dependent upon our human apparatus (our physical bodies or consciousness etc.). God, however, is immaterial and, therefore, has no 'apparatus' with which to acquire knowledge or, at best, does not have the same apparatus that humans have; presumably God would have consciousness, but He would not have a body with which He could make use of senses. However, it really makes no sense to say that God 'acquires' knowledge because then He moves from one state (not knowing) to another (knowing), which a perfect being cannot do. This has led many Islamic philosophers to conclude that God's knowledge is limited to abstract and necessary truths, but this was ammunition for Ghazzali's attack on the philosophers that God cannot be limited in what He can know, and surely God could know particulars. Avicenna stated that God does indeed know everything but 'in a universal way', which is somewhat ambiguous, but he also tends to be in agreement with Ghazzali that nothing escapes God's knowledge, even the smallest of things.

Averroes

Today, just outside the city walls of the Spanish city of Cordoba stands the statue of the great Averroes, for he is a Muslim philosopher born in Spain at the time when much of the country – the region known as Andalusia – was ruled by Muslims. In the twelfth century, this region of Spain was flourishing culturally and economically, and Cordoba stood at the apex of this boom. Apart from Averroes himself, Andalusia could at that time boast of the presence of such great Islamic polymaths as Avempace and his student Ibn Tufayl (1105–85). Averroes, in his quest for philosophical knowledge, would not have been short of resources. Cordoba's library contained some 400,000 books, which was a greater number than all the other libraries in the whole of Western Europe combined at that time. Its university had a reputation for being one of the finest in the world, and Averroes studied law and medicine there. Both his father and grandfather had served as jurists in the Maliki school of law, and Averroes also became a judge (*qadi*), serving initially in Cordoba before being appointed judge of Seville (then the capital of Andalusia) in 1169. Ten years later he returned to Cordoba as judge, only to be appointed a second time to Seville in 1179 and then, subsequently, returning to Cordoba three years later as its chief judge.

Aside from his legal work, Averroes was also a practising physician, and he followed on from Tufayl to become the new court physician to the Almohad Amir Abu Yaqub Yusuf (1135–84). It was Tufayl who recommended him to Yaqub, and Averroes himself reports of this first meeting:

> The first question addressed to me by the commander of the believers, after inquiring about my name, my father's name and my pedigree, was: 'What are the philosophers' views about heaven [the world], is it eternal or created?' So abashed and terrified did I feel that I began to offer excuses, even denying that I ever dealt with philosophy. I had no idea then what the sultan-caliph and ibn Tufayl had in mind for me …
>
> (al-Marrakushi 1881: 174, 175)

Averroes' concern is understandable, for to take a side on such doctrinal issues can lead to either royal patronage or banishment, depending upon which answer is given. Fortunately for Averroes, the amir seemed satisfied enough to appoint him as his new physician. This appointment was a valuable one for Averroes, as it not only provided him with relative financial security – for a time at least – but it also allowed him to pursue his philosophical interests in terms of research and writing. This pursuit was actively encouraged by the amir, who was keen especially for him to make Aristotle more intelligible, which would be no easy assignment for Averroes as he did not speak Greek himself and would therefore have to rely on translators or already available Arabic translations. However, this security was, unfortunately, not to last: after Yaqub's death in 1184, the succession of the new amir, Abu Yaqub al-Mansur (*c.* 1160–99), was to result in Averroes falling out of favour at the new court. Why this should be the case remains something of a mystery, but quite possibly it is a result of a doctrinal dispute or of pressure placed on the amir by the powerful orthodox religious scholars. Whatever the reason, at 68 years of age, Averroes was exiled to the small, largely Jewish town of Lucena to the south of Cordoba, and most of his books were burnt. This exile was brief, as he was asked to take up his post again two years later, but soon after returning to Cordoba, he fell sick and died in December 1198.

The tragedy that so many of Averroes' writings were burnt means that we no longer have access to much of his work and cannot even be sure how much survived. Nonetheless, what remains is some 50 or so books on philosophy, medicine and law. His medical work *Generalities in Medicine* is an encyclopaedia with sections on such topics as anatomy, physiology, disease and hygiene. It was translated into Latin (*Colliget*) but was soon supplanted by Avicenna's *Canon*. Averroes was, however, much better known as a philosopher than a physician. Despite the challenging task the amir had set him of making Aristotle more accessible to a largely uninitiated, Arabic-speaking audience, he managed to produce unmatched commentaries on Aristotle's known works for three different levels of reader: beginner, intermediate and advanced. For the advanced, he dissected Aristotle's works paragraph by paragraph, providing detailed commentaries, therefore adopting the science of **tafsir** (interpretation) that was well-known to Quranic scholars. Averroes also wrote a commentary on Plato's *Republic*. But it was Averroes' commentaries on Aristotle, especially, that led to recognition as one of the great Muslim philosophers. From the thirteenth century, his reputation was enhanced by those Jewish and Muslim scholars prepared to translate his works into Hebrew and Latin; and indeed 'Averrorism' – studying Aristotle through Averroes' commentaries – became an important discipline in universities. As a legal scholar, Averroes no doubt could boast fine religious credentials, yet he was often accused of being an infidel; after his death his books were regarded by many of the ulama with considerable suspicion and were banned or, as already stated, burnt.

Why was Averroes subject to such suspicion and attack? Largely, this was the result of most theologians' belief – as readers of this book will no doubt now be aware – that the practice of true philosophy was anathema to the Islamic sciences. In his study of philosophy, and his desire to publicize his findings, Averroes was confronted by the legacy of a figure that, at the time, overshadowed all other Muslim thinkers: Ghazzali. For example, Ghazzali states that philosophers are:

> … opposed to all Muslims in their affirming that men's bodies will not be assembled on the Last Day, but only disembodied spirits will be rewarded and punished, and the rewards and punishments will be spiritual, not corporal. They were indeed right in affirming the spiritual rewards and punishments, for these also are certain; but they falsely denied the corporal rewards and punishments and blasphemed the revealed Law in their stated views.
>
> (Ghazzali 1980: 76)

The soul and the after-life

Averroes' work *Long Commentary on the De Anima* is a prime example of how a great Muslim philosopher approaches the thought of a great Greek philosopher and attempts to reconcile the two seemingly opposite views on the nature of the soul. To understand what Averroes' views on the soul were, we must first consider what Aristotle had to say about this in his work that is usually given the Latin title *De Anima* (in Greek, 'soul' translates from *psuche*) or, in English, *On the Soul*. The term 'soul' can be somewhat misleading as for Aristotle the concept of the soul is much broader than one might associate with the more mysterious Christian or Islamic connotation. For Aristotle, all living things – from people, to animals, to trees and flowers – have 'souls' in that they are 'alive' or possess an 'animating force', and so the Latin term *anima* may seem more appropriate here. To 'be ensouled' is synonymous with to 'be alive'.

Aristotle's outlook on the world is teleological; that is to say, he saw the world, and all the things within it, as purpose driven. As all things are aiming towards something, the soul is that to which a living thing is aiming in the sense of 'being alive'. Without having purpose, things are, well, just 'things'. It is not sufficient to simply say that things are 'alive' by the simple definition that they are living things; for Aristotle it is much richer and more complex than that, and, indeed, the more complex the soul, the richer life is (or can be). The soul of a tree may well be nothing more than fulfilling its purpose of engaging in nutritive activity and having the necessary foliage, roots and so on in order to achieve this aim, but it is nonetheless end-directed and, if it is unable to fulfil this purpose, the tree is not fully a tree in the true sense of the word. Things become much more elaborate when relating this teleological view to human beings: if the highest and most important faculty of the human soul is reason, then a failure to act rationally means that a human has not reached his or her full potential. This means that the human is unhappy, unfulfilled, lacking **eudaimonia** (this Greek word is often translated as 'happiness', but 'fulfilment' might be a more suitable translation). And so, while in one way the tree and the human may seem radically far apart, in another way they are not at all, when seen from the point of view of Aristotle's appealing and holistic world of purpose.

Provided with this Aristotelian picture of the soul, the question that occupied Averroes was how the soul related to the body and whether it could survive bodily death. This was important, for the Quranic view of the soul requires a form of dualism: a non-physical soul that survives the death of the body. Muslim theologians subscribed to the Quranic view that the soul does depart from the body after death, but God will nonetheless reunite the souls with their bodies on the Day of Judgement, despite the fact that each and every 'atom' of each body has been scattered after the death of the individual. Does this Islamic view of the soul fit with the Aristotelian view? In some respects it does: like the Quranic account, Aristotle rejected the view that reality is entirely made up of material substance only. There is, therefore, more than the physical world that we see, touch, taste and feel. However, Aristotle – unlike his mentor Plato – does not subscribe to a form of dualism whereby a non-physical soul survives the body which, in the Islamic sense, will be resurrected come the Day of Judgement (in the Platonic sense it will be reincarnated, unless the soul is fully enlightened and can then reside within the realm of the Good).

Aristotle's concern with materialism is that it fails to provide sufficient explanation for why living things engage in purposeful activity. For the materialist, matter is just matter, it does not have end-direction. Connected with this are Aristotle's views on form and matter, which are complicated, but suffice to say here that he believed that matter on its own cannot take a 'form'. For example, when an animal (and a human) is dead then it no longer has the capacity to do the things that animals of its kind can do. A dead dog is actually no longer a dog at all, just a lump of matter. With the death of the material body comes the end of the soul's capacities. These 'capacities', however, are not parts of the soul, but are rather the materials the soul requires in order for the living thing to fulfil its purpose. The body and the soul are two separate elements, but are also one thing! The soul acts as the unifying force but it cannot be material because matter has parts and we would then have the same question of what, then, unifies the soul if it has parts? From this, Aristotle concludes that the soul must be different from matter.

But what then happens to the soul once the body dies and how does this fit in with the Quranic concept? In the Quran, it says the following: '[Prophet], they ask you about the Spirit ['*ruh*', which can translate as soul]. Say, "The Spirit is part of my Lord's domain. You have only been given a little knowledge"' (17:85). And so, from this short passage, discussions on what Islam has to say about the soul will be of limited use, given we can know very little. This, however, has not stopped theologians and philosophers from trying, and there are other passages that can help us:

> How can you ignore God, when you were lifeless and He gave you life, when He will cause you to die, then resurrect you to be returned to Him?
>
> (2:28)

Here, then, there are two deaths and two lives. And the following:

> Exalted is He who holds control in His hands; who has the power over all things; who created death and life to test you [people] and reveal which of you does best.
>
> (67:1,2)

When the soul is first created it lacks a physical body, and this is what is meant by '*ruh*' and by the first death. Then the soul is embodied and lives through a life in order to be 'tested' before, at the death of the body, returning to its disembodied state until the Day of Judgement when it will be returned to the body once more for eternal life.

When he reads Aristotle on the soul, Averroes would be only too aware of having to equate such statements as the following from Aristotle's *On the Soul* with the Islamic soul:

> If then we must say something in general about all types of soul, it would be the first actuality of a natural body with organs. We should not then inquire whether the soul and body are one thing, any more than whether the wax and its imprint are, or in general whether the matter of each thing is one with that of which it is matter. For although unity and being are spoken of in a number of ways, it is of the actuality that they are most properly said.
>
> (Aristotle 1987: 412a)

Put more simply, Aristotle here seems to be saying that it does not make sense to talk of the soul and matter as separate things, 'any more than whether the wax and its imprint are', or, perhaps more accurately, Aristotle is saying it makes no sense to even set out to determine whether one is separate from the other. In other words, to ask the question, Is the soul separate from the body? is to ask the wrong question. Aristotle would, it seems, talk in terms of potentiality and actuality, being aware himself of the problems with dualism. Yet, Aristotle also says the following:

> It is quite clear then that the soul is not separable from the body, *or that some parts of it are not* [my italics], if it is its nature to have parts. For with some of the parts of the soul the actuality is of bodily parts themselves. Not that there are not some parts that nothing prevents from being separable, through their not being the actualities of the body. But it remains unclear whether the soul is the actuality of a body in this way or rather it is as the sailor of a boat.
>
> (Aristotle 1987: 413a)

This is a very important quote, especially the reference to 'parts' of the soul here, because previously Aristotle had argued that the soul was simple: it does not have parts. This would follow from the fact that material things do have parts, whereas the soul is immaterial because it does *not* have parts. However, we may be generous with Aristotle and come back to the earlier quote where he says, 'If then we must say something in general about all types of soul', for he is portraying a certain reluctance to commit himself to what can really be said about the soul, and this is due to the fact that language always lets us down here. It is also reminiscent of the Quranic quote above, 'You have only been given a little knowledge.' There is so little we can really know about the soul, that we are confronted with the problem of being able to say much in any great depth. This is due to our preconception of the soul as a *thing*, whereas Aristotle insists that such a conception does not make any sense at all.

Averroes follows Aristotle closely by classifying the soul into faculties or powers, and also like Aristotle the faculties of the soul are hierarchical, with the higher faculty always presupposing the lower. To begin with, there is the vegetative – or nutritive – faculty, which is required for all life as this provides the power to acquire the essential nutrients for survival. Second, there is the perceptual – or sensitive – faculty, which is possessed by animals and humans, but not plant life. This is because the ability to perceive the world around us is not a requirement for plants to fulfil their purpose, but it is for higher life forms. Next, for Averroes, is the faculty of the imagination. Averroes defines the imagination as the faculty that is able to 'perceive' objects which are no longer actually present before the senses, and so this faculty cannot be the same thing as the sensitive faculty. In addition, the faculty of the imagination is able to conceive of things that do not exist (e.g. unicorns) and to compound things that are perceived by the senses separately (e.g. 'man' and 'horse' to 'man on horse'). The imagination, however, is not the same faculty as that of reason because whereas the former only relates to the particular and material, the latter relates to that which is universal and immaterial. Averroes sometimes refers to the imagination as the 'imaginative intellect' or the 'passable intellect', whilst reason is the material intellect which 'discerns universal intentions'. The imagination cannot exist independently of the material world, for these are the objects that cause the imagination to be (although a creature can, of course, have sense perception and no imagination).

And so, finally, we come to the faculty of reason, as already mentioned. It is the possession of a rational soul that distinguishes humans from other living things. At the practical level, reason works alongside the sensitive and imaginative faculties, which results in the ability to engage in such things as artistic skills, practical ethics, the forming of political systems and so on. However, what particularly gives reason its privileged status in the hierarchy is that the object of reason is that which is 'universal'. Reason is able to extract from the physical object itself and to form judgements about it. Reason can also work at the theoretical level, seemingly independent of the world of the senses and able to 'grasp' universals. This all sounds very Platonic in the way that Plato talks of grasping knowledge of the Forms. Averroes describes the universals as independent of the material, as simple, infinite and unchanging. They are therefore radically different from the material world, and do seem remarkably similar to Platonic Forms. There is, however, a subtle, though important, difference: Averroes is eager to stress that apprehension of these universals is achieved through stages, with perception coming first, then followed by imagination, which, in turn, allows one to grasp the universal. As Aristotle himself points out in *On The Soul* (1987: 32a) if a human is blind and has never perceived colour, then it is impossible to apprehend the universals associated with colour. This, in fact, is reminiscent of Hume, who, in his *Enquiries Concerning Human Understanding*, argues empirically that the mind cannot conjure up ideas that do not have their origins in impressions. However, he then provides his own exception to this rule: when presented with differing shades of blue, the mind is able to form an idea of a 'missing shade' without having previous experience of that particular shade. This certainly differs from Plato's epistemology whereby comprehension of the Forms involves a process of recollection and, in fact, the material world gets in the way of this apprehension, as opposed to being an essential stage towards it; although, of course, any student of Plato will tell you that it is not always clear (given, say, his Line Simile) whether that is how Plato himself understood it.

Despite the Aristotelian leanings of Averroes, the Muslim philosopher is nonetheless keen to agree with Ghazzali that the resurrection of the body is not open to question, regardless of what philosophical demonstrations are employed to show that this is not the case. Whilst Averroes defends the use of philosophy, he also believes that philosophical method would result in the same conclusion as methods employed by theologians. In *On the Harmony of Religion and Philosophy*, Averroes made a point of arguing that philosophy and religion are compatible. As he states:

> Philosophy is the friend and milk-sister of religion; thus injuries from people related to philosophy are the severest injuries [to religion] apart from the enmity, hatred and quarrels which such [injuries] stir up between the two, which are companions by nature and lovers by essence and instinct.
>
> (Averroes 1961: 70)

Given what Averroes says here about philosophy being the 'milk-sister of religion', it may seem surprising that theologians were none too happy with his writings. A similar fate, as mentioned already, fell to Averroes' predecessors Alfarabi and Avicenna. Alfarabi's philosophy is a mix of Plato and Aristotle, with the Platonic influence evident in his belief that the soul ultimately desires to be free from the material body and to join with the intelligible world. Alfarabi's link with Aristotle is in arguing that the soul can only achieve fulfilment, eudaimonia, by interaction with others (friendship) in the physical world, and to achieve that the soul needs to be housed within a physical body. Alfarabi, though prepared to accept the possibility of an after-life with the continued existence of the soul as a separate substance, is not prepared to countenance the possibility of the resurrection of the body, hence Ghazzali's ire. To a great extent, Avicenna follows in Alfarabi's footsteps and, if anything, the former is more mystical and Platonic when talking of the soul in relation to an abstract Active Intellect. Given these Aristotelian pictures of the survival of the soul – seemingly lacking any personality – that seem so different from the Quranic picture of bodily resurrection, it is hardly surprising that Averroes would be accused of being the enemy of Islam, with its portrayal of a very close, personal relationship between the believer and God that continues in the after-life. How Averroes deals with this seeming dichotomy between the philosophical picture of the soul and the Quranic picture presents us with an interesting portrayal of an individual who quite possibly struggled himself with the demands of the theological – he was a Muslim after all – and the rational requirements of the philosophers, especially with the great Aristotle looming over his shoulder.

The philosophy of language

How Averroes copes with this conflict between the philosopher on one shoulder and the theologian on the other can be better understood by considering what he has to say about scriptural interpretation, which he elaborates upon in the *Decisive Treatise*. Here we enter the realms of philosophy of language and, to understand Averroes' views, we must refer back briefly to Alfarabi once more, for, as we have already seen, he wrote extensively on the subject. Alfarabi was concerned about the relationship between philosophical logic and the grammar of ordinary language, given that the former is the tool of the philosophers and the latter is the tool of, amongst others, those who read and interpret texts such as the Quran. But what is important here and what has already been alluded to above is that, for Alfarabi, these were not separate realms – thus avoiding a possible perception of a conflict between them; logic was nothing more than an expression of universal truths that provides the ground rules for rational thought. Logic, therefore, does not 'belong' to the ancient Greek philosophers, but to anyone who believes in truth. Philosophical logic is nothing more than the expression of human reason, which, in turn, needs to be expressed through the medium of language. The relationship between logic and language, therefore, is that the latter particularizes the former. By particularizing that which is universal, the understanding of reason becomes heavily dependent upon how it is interpreted through the medium of the chosen language. Philosophers are duty-bound to not only seek after truth – which is what the tool of logic is there for – but also to communicate this truth to the non-philosopher through the arts of such things as rhetoric, poetry and dialectic. However, the problem with the 'arts' is that they particularize; they are more subjective and open to differing interpretations. In this respect, language is 'inferior' to logic, but necessary and important nonetheless. Here is the fascinating link that Alfarabi makes between the world of philosophy and the world of theology: the Prophet Muhammad – and, indeed all prophets – was first and foremost a *philosopher*. This, for Alfarabi, made perfect sense, for prophets had access to universal truths (logic) through revelations from God but were then also duty-bound to communicate these truths to others; in the same way Plato portrays Socrates (and his philosophers in his famous Cave Analogy in *Republic*) as required to tell others of the truth he has seen, regardless of the risk to his own life that may result from those who prefer to deny such truth.

Alfarabi was also influenced by the Neoplatonic views, and he equated God with the Active Intellect, a Perfect Being who, being all-good, 'emanates' this goodness which then results in creation, including that of human beings. As already explored (see above), human beings − though quite low down in the hierarchical process of emanation − nonetheless possess a 'spark' of the Divine within them because all human beings possess a soul which ultimately derives from the Active Intellect and strives to break away from the trappings of the physical world. Alfarabi adopted a somewhat elitist position, not unlike that of Plato, in believing that philosophy was the domain of the few who were burdened with the responsibility of communicating the truths of the world to the uninitiated as best they could through the inferior medium of language. Alfarabi, then, distinguished between the few who were capable of philosophy, and the majority who needed religion, for the latter lack the mental capacity needed to comprehend the inner meanings of revelation and, therefore, are blind to God's true commands.

Averroes, for his part, is largely sympathetic to Alfarabi's philosophical elitism, arguing that philosophical interpretation of the Quran is restricted to those 'well grounded in knowledge' (*al-rasikkhun fi al-'ilm*), whilst the majority of the non-philosophical believers are restricted in their understanding of the subtlety and ambiguity of the text, for any attempt by them to understand it could result in a dangerous misinterpretation of God's word. What, then, of those verses in the Quran that refer to the next life? Averroes discusses this in some depth in *The Book of the Exposition of the Methods of Proofs Regarding the Beliefs of the Religion*. Here Averroes states that whether or not a scholar of the Quran is a philosopher, all should accept literally the view that there is an after-life, although it is nonetheless incumbent upon scholars to debate the descriptions of this after-life:

> The resurrection is one of the things concerning whose existence [all] religions agree and for which there has been demonstrative proof among scholars. Religions have only differed on the nature of its existence, though, in reality they do not differ [so much] regarding the nature of its existence, [as they do] regarding the observable things [they have used] to symbolize this unseen state.
>
> (Averroes 1921: 118)

This is quite deliberately obscure by Averroes, and one wonders here over the extent to which he did entirely agree with the Quranic view of the bodily after-life or not, keeping in mind that it would have been a danger to his own life to outwardly 'come out' and declare any sentence of the Quran as a nonsense. So how are we to determine what Averroes does have to say about the after-life? In his *Incoherence*, he rejects Ghazzali's accusation that philosophers have denied bodily resurrection by noting that, in actual fact, past philosophers have simply avoided making any comment upon it at all! The reason for this, Averroes argues, is not because philosophers do not consider such a topic worthy of discussion, but the complete opposite: they have such a high regard for this doctrine that they consider it unworthy of them to attempt to engage in any analysis of it. In fact, Averroes states that all Muslim philosophers have such respect for religious belief, that they are not in any position to challenge the fact, given that so many religions seem to be in agreement in bodily resurrection. This response does seem to be fudging the issue, for it is quite possible to appreciate the value of religion, without agreeing to all its precepts, and in fact it does seem that Averroes is saying that philosophers should accept bodily resurrection because religion says so, which seems intellectually weak from a philosophical point of view, although it may well have pragmatic value. That is to say, because the Quran provides a description of the next life in strongly physical terms, this is a good reason to uphold it because it provides an important framework for moral virtue and, without such a framework, philosophers cannot flourish in society.

Such pragmatism from Averroes is disappointing, but understandable. We are, thankfully, not generally speaking so intellectually constrained as he would have been. Whilst we cannot be sure why Averroes was banished from Cordoba, the most likely explanation is that his philosophical investigations went against the increasingly fundamentalist religious climate of the time, and so we have to rely upon his surviving writings to read between the lines. Therefore, it seems that in his writings Averroes praises Ghazzali for condemning those philosophers who question the after-life and aligns himself with Ghazzali by stating that the soul is immortal and, upon resurrection, will be housed within a replica of the earthly body. However, a closer reading of the works of Averroes suggest that he was far more supportive of Aristotle's abstract universal soul than he was able to explicitly subscribe to.

Further reading

Aristotle (1987), *De Anima (On the Soul)*, trans. by Hugh Lawson-Tancred, London: Penguin.

Fakhry, M. (2001), *Averroes*, Oxford: Oneworld.

McGinnis, J. (2010), *Avicenna*, Great Medieval Thinkers, New York: Oxford University Press.

Netton, I.R. (1999), *Al-Farabi and His School*, Abingdon: Routledge.

Watt, W.M. (1963), *Muslim Intellectual: A Study of al-Ghazali*, Edinburgh: Edinburgh University Press.

5 Faith versus reason

Suhrawardi and Illuminationism (*Ishraq*)

Shahāb ad-Dīn' Yahya ibn Habash as-Suhrawardī (1154–91), or **Suhrawardi** for short, possesses the honourable title of *Shaykh al-Ishraq*, the 'Master of Illumination'. Suhrawardi is a well-known figure in the philosophical and mystical tradition, considered to be the founder of a school of philosophical thought known as the Illuminationist (*Ishraqi*) or, more traditionally and somewhat unhelpfully, 'Oriental'. Suhrawardi was a prolific writer who aimed to bring together Islamic thought with that of Platonic, Neoplatonic and Persian philosophy. What many readers of his work, of which a great deal has thankfully survived, find appealing is not just the content, but his sophisticated and poetic writing style, which, in Arabic anyway, allows the reader to engage personally with the material. This is helpful given the often abstract and complex nature of the topic of **Illuminationism** itself.

Suhrawardi wrote four major works of philosophy: *The Intimations*, *The Oppositions*, *The Paths and Heavens* and the *The Philosophy of Illumination*. Suhrawardi stated that these should be studied in the order they were written because they progress from a more discursive, empirical form of philosophy to the latter works that are more concerned with intuitive knowledge. By reading these works in this order, the reader engages in the same path of knowledge. Suhrawardi also wrote, in both Persian and Arabic, collections of symbolic narratives, short treatises and prayers and invocations.

At the time, however, many of his writings were regarded as heretical, and, as a result, he was executed at the age of 37. Exactly what led to his execution is unclear, although a fair amount about his life is better known. He was born in northwestern Iran (near Azerbaijan) in the town of Suhrawardi, hence his name. It is not, as the reader of this book may have observed, unusual for well-known figures to be named – usually given years after their death – after the place of their birth, which can sometimes be confusing if it is a place that has a habit of producing great figures. In fact there is also the founder of the Suhrawardiya Sufi order, Shihab al-Din 'Umar b. 'Abd Allah al-Suhrawardi (1144–1234), and also an acknowledged authority on hadith, Abu Najb Suhrawardi (d. 1168). As a result, 'our' Suhrawardi is also known as Suhrawardi Maqtul: 'the executed'!

As a very young man he travelled, in a quest for knowledge, amongst the regions of the ruling Seljuk dynasty of the time. In the city of Maraghah in Azerbaijan he studied under the great mystic Majd al-Din al-Jili, who was also the teacher of another great philosopher we have come across in this book, Alrazi (see Chapter 3). Suhrawardi travelled much further afield, to southwest Anatolia (today, mostly Turkey) where he was fortunate to receive the royal patronage of several of the Seljuk princes and rulers. In 1183 he moved once more, this time to Aleppo in Syria. He was able to indulge in his writing and research thanks to further royal attention, this time from Prince al-Malik al-Zahir Ghazi, whom he tutored. This patronage was, however, to prove his downfall, and we are presented with a familiar story here (look back, for example, to Chapter 3 and the problems for Alkindi and Alrazi) of jealousy amongst the courtly entourage and annoyance from the traditional ulama. By all accounts, Suhrawardi presented an interesting figure in court, adopting the Sufi attire of a simple woollen cloak called a *khirqa*. He was, however, regarded as self-effacing, preferring when possible to engage in such ascetic practices as solitary retreat, meditation and strict fasting. Nonetheless, he was a fearsome opponent when it came to philosophical and theological debate. Prince Ghazi was very fond of him, but it seems that he also relented to Suhrawardi's execution as a result of pressure from his opponents, who would regularly write to the prince's father complaining that Suhrawardi was a disruptive and corrupting influence on the prince and, by extension, on the court and the region. The prince's decision was also no doubt affected by his father telling him that he should accede to these requests. The prince's father was not a man one would want to cross for he was the renowned Seljuk sultan Ayyubid Salah al-Din, better known in the West as Saladin, the great opponent of England's King Richard 'the Lionheart' in the battles of the Crusades.

It was Suhrawardi who established the ideas, the language and the methodology of what is called the Illuminationist school, which, in turn, became a highly influential school of thought upon Islamic philosophy, mysticism and, to some extent, even politics. However, as it has already been hinted, Illuminationist philosophy – despite the aid of Suhrawardi's writing prowess – is not the easiest of schools of thought to get to grips with, and it is made more difficult if the reader is unfamiliar with the philosophical tradition in which it belongs, notably Greek and Persian thought, and also the work of Avicenna (see Chapter 4). The reader, at this point, is advised to go over Chapters 3 and 4 once more before going on.

Like any '-ism' the term 'Illuminationism' refers to a collection of different ideas within a philosophical system, but nonetheless sharing certain features that allow it to come under an umbrella title. The finer details of what actually qualifies as Illuminationist are disputed, not least by Suhrawardi himself, who argued that – although he was influenced by the thought of his predecessor Avicenna – he was not an Illuminationist but a 'peripatetic' (in Arabic, *mash-sha'i*), which is really another word for a Neoplatonist. Curiously, Avicenna himself did not wish to be referred to as peripatetic but an Illuminationist! We need not burden ourselves here with such intricacies and, while it is a multi-faceted discipline, its relevance for this chapter is the impact it has had on epistemology (theory of knowledge).

If we go back, very briefly, to Neoplatonist thought and consider this in relation to epistemology and that key philosophical question, 'What can we know?' (and by 'know' we mean genuine knowledge, truth), the answer would at first seem to be 'not a great deal' from a Neoplatonic perspective, because in the hierarchy of emanation – the world of matter – mankind seems to be as far removed from the One, or from God, or from 'the Good', as it is possible to be. However, recall that the Neoplatonists believed that mankind was possessed by a soul and so is not *purely* matter: the body is tied to matter and all its negatives such as plurality, evil and so on, but the human also has a soul which is a 'spark' of the One's 'light'. The use of 'light' and 'dark' with reference to knowledge is not an uncommon one; think of Plato's own analogy in *Republic* of the sun to represent the Good, for example, for the sun is both light in itself but it also allows us to see what is in front of us and so avoid being deceived. Darkness tends to represent ignorance and evil, whilst light represents what is true and good. We can, therefore, see why the term 'Illuminationist' is appropriate here, and why Suhrawardi refers to the 'One' at the top of the tree and emanator as 'Light of Lights'.

Suhrawardi's view of the soul is that, in a very Platonic sense, its natural home is the immaterial world of pure light and that, when the individual soul enters the material body, it is divided into two parts: one part remaining in the immaterial world and the other trapped within the physical body, yearning to become whole once more. It is the function of the human to engage in the practice of purifying this half of the soul so that it can return to its other half. This quest to purify the soul is essentially the path of the philosopher, and results in self-awareness. This requires physical practices such as fasting and retreating from the distractions of the world, but these are all tools towards the mental awareness of objective truth. The peripatetic view of knowledge is that it is 'acquired' (*al-'ilm al-husuli*); that is, you gain knowledge through empirical experimentation, reading books and so on, whereas the Illuminationist view is that it is far more intuitive, that it is knowledge 'by presence' (*al-'ilm al-huduri al-ishraqi*). For Suhrawardi, the acquisition of knowledge is very much a subjective experience, which includes dreams, visions, 'flashes' of illumination and even out-of-body experiences. This raises questions concerning what constitutes knowledge, for in the more 'empirical' world of the twenty-first century, Suhrawardi's emphasis on these forms of intuitive knowledge would not be regarded as knowledge at all because it is simply *too* subjective. However, for Suhrawardi, the form of knowledge 'by presence' is higher than the peripatetic 'acquired' knowledge because the former consists of the most fundamental kind of knowledge, that of self-awareness. He would dimiss the criticism that because this form of knowledge is acquired subjectively, then it is not possible to know that it is genuine knowledge (i.e. access to objective reality) by stating that the subject knows *intuitively* that it is genuine knowledge.

Through ascetic practices the subject will, in time, receive personal revelations and visions, or what Suhrawardi calls a portion of the 'light of God' (*al-bariq al-ilahi*). This may seem a way of avoiding the elitism of acquired knowledge, for presumably we are all capable of obtaining such experiences. However, this is not quite the case, and comparison between the 'acquired' empirical approach to knowledge and the 'by presence' intuitive approach is stronger here. To illustrate: provided we have all our senses, then all human beings are capable of having empirical experiences: we are all confronted by 'sense data' which, on the whole, we all share in common, e.g. if there is a blue car that drives by me, then anyone who is at that point will see the same blue car that I do. Therefore, we all have a shared empirical experience. But the next stage is what is done with that empirical experience. In the case of the blue car, it is such a mundane everyday experience that it is promptly dismissed, but there are many other experiences that are subject to further study. For example, we may study newly discovered planets circling a distant star through a tele-scope but not simply dismiss these as 'mundane': the desire for humans to know more leads to us engaging in reasoning to find out more about these observations, and this is where the science of astronomy comes in. Similarly, the intuitive approach requires subsequent discursive analysis as a result of the visionary experience, and this requires the skills of the 'science' of philosophy. Whereas the empirical is shared 'sense-data' as the foundation for study, the acquired is subjective revelation – which differs from one person to the next – as its foundation for the science of illumination. Whilst these visions will differ from one subject to the next, for some may see visions of angels, or perhaps a historical figure – Suhrawardi himself often had visions of Aristotle – the end result, as in the knowledge acquired, will be the same for all.

Suhrawardi does raise interesting questions concerning what constitutes knowledge that continue to preoccupy us today. We can see echoes of this debate, for example, in responses to Richard Dawkins' view that only science (and what constitutes 'science') gives us knowledge from, for example, some theistic philosophers who argue for the importance of 'personal explanation'. Although the origins of the debate go back to Plato and Aristotle in philoso-phy, Suhrawardi also pre-dates the writings of early 'existentialists' (using this term loosely here) such as Kierkegaard and Nietzsche in recognizing the importance of myth, dreams and fantasy in providing us with knowledge of the world that is just as valuable as that provided by scientific views. Illuminationist philosophy continues to be a dominant school of thought in Shia philosophy and, in actual fact, today many philosophers in Iran are often pigeonholed as being either peripatetic or Illuminationist rather like philosophers in the West have often been labelled as rationalists or empiricists.

Mulla Sadra

One philosopher greatly influenced by Suhrawardi was Muhammad ibn Ibrahim al-Qawami al-Shirazi (*c.* 1572–1640), better known as '**Mulla Sadra**'.

Like Suhrawardi, he was named after his place of birth, Shiraz in southern Persia. He came from a wealthy family as his father, a well-known scholar of the time himself, Ibrahim Shirazi, was a minister for the royal court of the Shia Safavid dynasty. Sadra, after completing his elementary studies in Shiraz, continued his education in the capital city of the Safavid dynasty, Isfahan. At the time, Isfahan was a very new capital indeed, only achieving that status in 1598 when the Shah, Abbas the Great, moved it from Qazvin because it was more central. As a result, Isfahan became the cultural centre of Persia and maintained this until it was sacked by Afghan invaders in 1722. Here, Sadra had the opportunity to be tutored by some of the greatest thinkers of that time and place, including Astarabadi (d. *c.* 1631), better known as Mir Damad, who was a Neoplatonist philosopher and regarded as the founder of the School of Isfahan. Mir Damad himself sang the praises of Sadra for his intellectual prowess, and within a few years Sadra had mastered the Islamic sciences and, indeed, had surpassed many of his teachers in expertise. He became expert in what are regarded as the two branches of Shia learning: the transmitted and the intellectual. The 'transmitted sciences' (*al-'ulum al-naqliyyah*) relate to jurisprudence, Quranic interpretation and hadith scholarship. The 'intellectual sciences' (*al-'ulum al-aqliyyah*) include philosophy and mysticism.

After Sadra had completed his formal studies he embraced Suhrawardi's idea that the acquisition of knowledge requires contemplation and asceticism by leaving the city of Isfahan and finding seclusion in a small village called Kahak, which is near the holy city of Qom. Despite this, his intellectual reputation meant he frequently had to decline offers to reside in the royal court. He avoided the trappings of wealth and increased status by preferring, in later life, to return to his hometown of Shiraz to teach at a religious school. Throughout his life he led a humble and pious existence and it is said that he made the pilgrimage to Mecca on foot seven times during his life: a distance of some 1400 miles. He died in Basra while returning from his seventh pilgrimage.

While he may well have shunned the limelight of the royal court, this did not prevent him from being a prolific writer, with over 50 books attributed to him. He wrote commentaries on the works of Suhrawardi, of course, and also of Avicenna, as well as original works on various theological and philosophical topics. His major works are *Apprehensions*, *Breaking the Idols of Paganism* and *Transcendental Wisdom* (better known as *The Four Intellectual Journeys*).

His *Four Journeys* is especially interesting in terms of philosophy as here he expresses a concern that philosophy as a discipline is often unfairly neglected, usually in favour of theology and law, and he also presents a case for the beneficial compatibility of philosophy with religion. Sadra argues that philosophy and religion present the same truth, which was initially revealed to the first man, Adam, and has been transmitted through time to the prophets of all religions, as well as philosophers and mystics of the past and present. Whilst this attempt to level the playing field to some extent in terms of who has access to truth may be a worthy one, it was also dangerous as it offended many orthodox Muslims, who accused Sadra of blasphemy and atheism. By not distinguishing between the knowledge acquired by the philosophers and that of the prophets, which would include Muhammad, Sadra essentially put philosophers such as Empedocles, Pythagoras, Socrates, Plato, Aristotle and Plotinus on the same level epistemologically as the prophets. They are all, in his words, 'pillars of wisdom' who have received the 'light of wisdom' from the 'beacon of prophethood'. Consequently, prophets and philosophers, Sadra argues, share the same views on such topics as the unity of God (tawhid), the creation of the world and resurrection, despite the fact, as this book demonstrates, that this does not seem to be the case in reality!

Sadra's epistemology also raises questions concerning how truth is to be accessed. For the theologian, truth lies with God, who reveals this through His prophets. Given the almost universally accepted view amongst Muslims that Muhammad is the final prophet, then how are believers to acquire any new knowledge? The traditional view is that the Quran ultimately provides all the knowledge we should need and that the task of Muslims is to strive to interpret this knowledge. Whilst something of a generalization, this view is more prevalent amongst Sunni Muslims, but less so for Sufi and for Shia Islam. Sadra accepts that the Prophetic Stage of history has indeed come to an end with the death of Muhammad. There are to be no more prophets. What Sadra, being Shia himself, does state is that the end of the Prophetic Stage is followed by the Imamate Stage: the succession of spiritual leadership by the twelve Shia Imams. Muslims are still today in this Imamate Stage, for the twelfth Imam, the '**Mahdi**', is in temporary occultation (*ghayba*). Whilst the Imams do not have the status of prophets they are what Sadra calls 'executors' because they execute the truth that is revealed by the prophets. In the same way that prophecy goes back to the first man, Adam, the first executor was Seth, the third son of Adam and Eve:

> Know that philosophy first issued from Adam, the chosen one of God and from his progeny Seth and Hermes and from Noah because the world can never be free of a person who establishes knowledge of the unity of God and of the return [to God]. The great Hermes disseminated it [philosophy] in the climes and in the countries and explained it and gave benefit of it to the people. He is the father of philosophers and the most learned of the knowledgeable ... As for Rome and Greece, philosophy is not ancient in those places as their original sciences were rhetoric, epistolatory and poetry ... until Abraham became a prophet and he taught them the science of divine unity. It is mentioned in history that the first to philosophise from among them [the Greeks] was Thales of Miletus and he named it philosophy. He first philosophised in Egypt and then proceeded to Miletus when he was an old man and disseminated his philosophy. After him came Anaxagoras and Anaximenes of Miletus. After them emerged Empedocles, Pythagoras, Socrates and Plato.
>
> (Sadra 1999: 153–54)

However, as the Twelfth Imam is effectively 'hidden' and, therefore, unable to act as 'executor', such access to knowledge is available to Muslim philosophers and Sufis. This is a little puzzling, however, as it is not at all clear who has acquired 'prophetic' knowledge at any one time and whether it is available to more than one person at the same time.

Like Suhrawardi, Sadra places great emphasis on intuitive knowledge and claims to have himself had visions in which he experiences a single Reality (*wujud*). This Reality, which is the foundation for the multiplicity of the objects we all experience on an everyday level, can only be experienced through ascetic practices and intensive mental preparation. The Illuminationist theme is promoted with Sadra's analogy of Reality as the sun, with the manifestations of many existent things as the rays of the sun. This also bears a similarity with the Neoplatonic idea of the rays of the sun as emanations of the Active Intellect. Reality itself is God, and the existing things are emanations of God. Hence there are degrees of being or 'gradation of being' (*tashkik al-wujud*) from the simplest of molecules to God. Because Sadra was so influenced by Suhrawardi, it is sometimes difficult to distinguish their philosophies, but it is this notion of 'Being' where they differ. Whereas for Suhrawardi, the act of intuition results in determining reality, or the 'essence' of things, for Sadra, the intuitive process results in the revealing of 'Being'. The distinction is subtle, but important. For Sadra, Being and essence are intertwined and so when Being is revealed, this then makes knowledge of the essence of things possible and this, in turn, makes Being comprehensible.

Sadra elaborates on the process of acquiring knowledge in some considerable detail as a series of stages, starting with perception of the external world, i.e. sense experience, as the bottom rung of the epistemological ladder; it resembles the German philosopher **Hegel's** (1770–1831) hierarchy of knowledge in his *Phenomenology of Mind* to some extent, although the difference is that Hegel stops at rational knowledge, for the power of reason is the home of absolute knowledge and gives the knower an understanding of the world. Sadra, however, goes one step further and is more 'mystical' than Hegel by arguing that acquiring Reality does not require rational discourse, but a power that transcends reason, which is when the soul unites with Being, or the Active Intellect. In Platonic terms – with reference to Plato's Cave Analogy in *Republic* – it represents that stage when the freed prisoner of the cave sees the light of the sun. In the *Four Journeys* it is the stage of the third journey and, like the prisoner who must return to the cave to teach the others what he now knows, Sadra's philosopher must do the same in the fourth journey.

The fourth part of Sadra's *Four Journeys* focuses on resurrection and eschatology, and unfortunately this book does not allow for a full and proper exposition of his views here. Briefly, Sadra provides an account of the spiritual path of the soul through its four journeys as the individual engages in ascetic and spiritual practices in the quest for knowledge: first, the individual soul becomes detached from the physical world and seeks extinction in the divine; second, the soul reaches the state of sainthood in which the individual can now see, hear and act through God; the third journey results in the extinction of the self entirely; finally, the saint returns to the world in order to fulfil the spiritual and philosophical duty to guide others along the spiritual path. As a slight aside, but interesting nonetheless, is Sadra's view of the path of the soul upon the death of the body, for the soul is not entirely disembodied but possesses a body which is 'woven' by the actions that the person engaged in during their earthly life and so, if someone has led a particularly evil life, they will end up in hell, weighed down by bodily sins. Sadra's philosophy is a fascinating study, and there is still much to be explored. Thankfully, more recent thinkers such as Henry Corbin, James Morris, Seyyed Hossein Nasr and Fazlur Rahman have been devoting their energies to producing important works on the philosopher.

Incidentally, for Sadra, the Quran – as it is the word of God – is also Being itself, and so part of Sadra's own philosophical pursuit is to study and write commentaries on the Quran. He was opposed to only a literal, or 'outer', interpretation of the text, instead emphasizing its inner meaning, and this is where Sufism can particularly contribute while, at the same time, stressing that one should not ignore the literal meaning altogether; rather a balance between the two is preferred.

Soroush

The Iranian philosopher Abd al-Karim **Soroush** (born 1945) is an important thinker on the topic of religious knowledge and how this relates to reason. His best-known work, *The Hermeneutical Expansion and Contraction of the Theory of Shari'a*, is particularly concerned with epistemology and the sociology of knowledge. Soroush has a strong familiarity with Western philosophical ideas, which he synthesizes with his in-depth knowledge of the traditional Islamic sciences, as well as an awareness of more contemporary trends in Islamic intellectual thought, a man very much in touch with the Islamic *zeitgeist*. In his work on hermeneutics he raises the issue of the role of religion in the modern world, and he argues that it is quite possible for Islamic culture and values to survive whilst a society is modernized and secularized; the two need not conflict with one another. It is these arguments for a synthesis of religious knowledge and authority with that of secular and political liberalism that has resulted in Soroush being labelled the 'Martin Luther of Islam' (although this is a label also given more recently to Tariq Ramadan, see Chapter 6).

Soroush was born in Tehran and he attended the Alavi High School, which was sufficiently liberal to allow him to have religion and science as part of its curriculum. He went on to study pharmacy at university in Tehran and, after graduation, he spent his two years 'military' service as director of the Laboratory for Food Products, Toiletries and Sanitary Materials. He left Iran to continue his studies in England in the mid to late 1970s. During this time abroad, events in Iran were to take a severe turn in its history: when Soroush left for England, Iran was a prosperous, pro-Western democratic state ruled by an

Oxford-educated Shah. However, when Soroush returned to Iran in 1979, it had undergone a revolution and was now an anti-Western, impoverished theocracy ruled by an Ayatollah and the Shia Islamic clergy. This Ayatollah's name was **Khomeini**, and more will be said about this charismatic individual in Chapter 6, for his philosophical background and his rise to effective ruler of a state raises interesting issues, especially in the field of political philosophy. Despite the growth in prosperity in Iran during the early 1970s, there were many anti-government demonstrations, especially amongst the intellectual elite, young students and the poorer classes outside of the more prosperous cities. The Shah responded to this with increased oppression and made use of technology and weapons provided by the West to impose his rule, which resulted in greater anti-Western feeling. As a result, riots broke out in many Iranian cities, led by the Shia clergy who were seen as liberators. This is what became the Iranian Cultural Revolution. The principal ideologue, Khomeini, directed the demonstrations from his refuge in Paris. By late autumn of 1978 Iran was virtually in a state of civil war and, in January of 1979, the Shah fled abroad. Soon after that Khomeini returned to Iran as their new hero and ruler.

Soroush, while residing in England during these tumultuous times, nonetheless kept an eye on events and he became active amongst Muslim groups in London, whilst also continuing his studies, first acquiring an MSc in analytical chemistry at the University of London and then researching the field of history and the philosophy of science at Chelsea College. Outside of his formal studies, he developed an interest in significant Iranian thinkers, notably Ali Shariati (see Chapter 6), and took to giving public lectures, some of which were published in his first work *Dialectical Antagonism*, which was a criticism of Iranian leftist and Marxist movements. He then wrote *The Restless Nature of the World*, which looked at the foundations of Islamic philosophy. Both of these works were published in Tehran and, consequently, upon his return to Iran, his reputation preceded him. He was seen as an ideological ally by Khomeini, to the extent that the latter was personally involved in the appointment of Soroush to the Advisory Council of the Cultural Revolution. In addition, Soroush became director of the Islamic Culture Group at Tehran's Teacher Training College. Soroush's task as a member of the Advisory Council, together with six other members, was to completely restructure the university syllabi so that all knowledge was 'Islamicized'. This, in practice, resulted in the expulsion of a number of academics and students from these universities who did not fit with the new ideology, and also a number of scholars were arrested, imprisoned and, indeed, executed.

Khomeini's enthusiasm for Soroush may have been misguided, however, especially as the new Iranian Republic became more oppressive. Soroush left his post on the Advisory Council after four years, citing 'professional differences', and in 1983 he became a member of the research staff for the Institute for Cultural Research and Studies until 1997. During the 1990s, Soroush became increasingly critical of the Iranian rulers and argued for religious pluralism and tolerance and the use of hermeneutics (see below and Chapter 9). He voiced his views through the monthly magazine *Kiyan*, which he co-founded. As a result, the Islamic Republic forced the magazine to close down in 1998. As Soroush himself became the subject of state harassment and censorship, he has moved his activities abroad since 2000, as a visiting scholar in Harvard University teaching Rumi poetry, philosophy, Islam and democracy, Quranic studies and philosophy of Islamic law. He is also a scholar in residence at Yale University, and he taught Islamic political philosophy at Princeton. This admirable track record of scholarship highlights his importance for Islamic philosophy today. A key theme throughout much of his work is the emphasis on the coherence of Islamic knowledge with that of 'secular' thought, with the latter understood as what is regarded as rational and scientific, rather than 'anti-religion'. In this sense, it is not the case of religious versus secular, because Soroush argues that Islam is neither irrational nor non-scientific, for the developments in science and knowledge do not necessarily come at the expense of religion, but rather they work together mutually in helping us to understand religion and its proper place in society.

Soroush's emphasis on the tools of hermeneutics is a growing field amongst Islamic scholars today, perhaps most notably promulgated by the controversial figure of Nasr Hamid Abu **Zayd,** who was born 1943 in Tantra, Egypt. It is worth devoting a little space to Zayd here before returning to Soroush's views. Zayd studied and lectured in Islamic studies at the University of Cairo. However, in 1995, the tenure committee refused him tenure as a result of an unfavourable report. This raised some eyebrows considering the scholarly level of his work and his case was brought to the attention of the Egyptian press. Subsequently the Egyptian Appellate Court also ruled in favour of a suit brought against Zayd by an Islamist lawyer. This suit required that Zayd be forcibly divorced from his wife on the grounds that he is an apostate. It was this particular case that attracted the foreign media, and he now lectures at the University of Leiden in The Netherlands. The case of Zayd is relevant here because of what his works represent, for he is a strong proponent of the use of the tools of hermeneutics, particularly in relations to Quranic tafsir ('interpretation'). The case of Zayd also raises an important question: just how far can textual analysis go before the text ceases to have any objective value at all? This was a concern of the French philosopher Paul **Ricoeur** (1913–2005) in relation to Hans-Georg Gadamer's hermeneutic in that, for Ricoeur, it offers no methodology for gaining real meaning and becomes too subjective (see Chapter 9).

Not surprisingly, Soroush's views on the use of hermeneutics raises similar concerns to those of Zayd and proved too contentious for the Iranian clergy. Like Zayd, Soroush argues that while the Quran, as the word of God, is pure, absolute and, therefore, unchanging, it is also important to take into account that the receivers of revelation are tied to a particular time and place that is inevitably subject to change, evolution and a particular perspective on the world. Those who receive revelation must interpret God's word so that they can understand it, and this inevitably results in a particular, rather than a universal, understanding of revelation. Whilst the word of God does not change, the *interpretation* of it does. Therefore, no interpretation is fixed and unchanging and no one culture, group, time period or individual has a monopoly on what is the right or wrong interpretation of the sacred sources. It logically follows that, while Soroush accepts the importance of the Islamic scholars – the clergy included – in their struggle to understand the word of God, it does not follow from this that we should accept their interpretation. This view is perhaps even more contentious amongst the Shia clergy than the Sunni, because religious knowledge is considerably more hierarchical in the former than the latter, which has led some to compare Shia Islam to Catholicism in this respect. In Shia Islam especially, much theological scholarship argues for religious knowledge as 'inherited' and privy to the elite clergy, whereas Soroush is presenting a much more democratic rendering, which would amount to an act of heresy for many of the ruling religious elite.

Soroush, then, considered religious knowledge to be effectively no different from other forms of knowledge in the sense that it is an evolving phenomenon that operates within certain specified parameters that qualifies it as 'religious' as opposed to, say, scientific or historical. In fact, these parameters are not exclusive, but overlap, and to some degree it makes little sense to talk of knowledge as divided into religious and scientific, for one form of knowledge affects another. This does not result in relativism for Soroush in terms of knowledge, for there are unchangeable truths – the actual word of God – which religion can reveal, but non-religious scientific knowledge can assist in revealing these truths rather than undermining them.

Soroush, however, has succeeded in offending the Shia clergy further by questioning the legitimacy of the contentious concept **vilayat-i faqih** ('guardianship by the clergy'), which was the central teaching of Khomeini's political philosophy. This philosophy will be considered in more detail in Chapter 6, but, briefly for the moment, Khomeini argued that the clergy have a religious duty to rule directly and not simply advise the government or, for that matter, stay out of political affairs altogether, as some Ayatollahs would contend. This view is contentious because it has little Quranic support, and Soroush questioned that Ayatollahs, being merely human, could possibly claim to possess a monopoly on religious knowledge. For Soroush, the knowledge that even the clergy possessed was human and, as such, fallible. Whilst this democratic approach to religious knowledge encourages people to search for knowledge themselves rather than to imitate or obey the rulings of religious clergy, this did not, inevitably, find favour with the clergy themselves.

Sharia, for Soroush, was subject to 'expansion and contraction', and by that he meant that it was not an infallible and static thing, but subject to a much broader framework of knowledge *per se*, which included science, mathematics, medicine, philosophy and so on. If it were to be contained within too narrow a framework, then its potential for true understanding and flexibility would be severely limited. Soroush presents a theory of knowledge under three general principles: first, the principle of coherence and correspondence (any understanding of religion bears on the body of human knowledge and tries to be in coherence with the latter); second, the principle of interpretation (a contraction or expansion in the system of human knowledge may penetrate the domain of our understanding of religion); and finally, the principle of evolution (the system of human knowledge is subject to expansion and contraction). In his work *Let us Learn from History*, Soroush casts an empirical eye on history to demonstrate that mankind is, in a very Hobbesian sense, weak and inclined to commit acts of evil, rather than adopting the more Rousseauian depiction of Man as innately good. Soroush has not shied away from criticizing many of the Shia clergy, accusing them of sacrificing the basic tenets of Islam for the sake of their own selfish gains. He has championed the cause of democracy because he believes it is the best system for Islam to thrive. People must be free to believe or not, and Islam, or any religion, cannot be imposed upon a people from above, which is what many Shia clergy try to do. Soroush has stressed that the clergy have no a priori right to rule, and that the people should choose rulers. To an extent, some of the clergy would not disagree with Soroush on some points, in particular that they should steer clear from political rule because of its corrupting influence, whereas other members of the clergy would dispute this, arguing that the clergy, because of their knowledge of what is good, would do nothing other than good and would be resistant to the corrupting powers of absolute rule.

Rumi

Soroush is a scholar of Rumi, and the former's views on religious knowledge makes this attachment to the Sufi mystic quite understandable. Here we need to consider another kind of knowledge or, rather, another way of accessing knowledge. In considering the Illuminationists we have, to some degree, seen the importance of knowledge as 'intuitive' and this is very much within the Sufi mystical tradition, but no account of a Sufi epistemology could leave out some reference to probably the greatest Sufi mystic of them all, Jalāl ad-Dīn Muhammad Balkhī, better known as **Rumi** (1207–73). Rumi is also particularly relevant here as someone who began as a *mufti* (a legal functionary) and hence is considered something of an expert in religious knowledge, as well as a poet and mystic and, therefore, an exponent of what is often referred to as esoteric knowledge.

Rumi was born at Balkh in the northern Persian province of Khorasan. This was, at that time, a flourishing city that, it is said, contained some 40 mosques, which is an indication of its size and religious activity. Rumi's family had lived in Balkh for several generations and their noble lineage was highly respected. In fact, they claimed descent from Arabic, rather than Persian, stock originally to the extent of family connections with the first rightly-guided caliph, Abu Bakr. Balkh, however, was invaded by Mongols and so, when he was just 12 years of age, Rumi and his family fled the city. There is an apocryphal story that while in Damascus in 1221, Rumi was seen walking behind his father by the great philosopher and mystic Ibn **Arabi** (1165–1240, see below), who then exclaimed, 'Praise be to God, an ocean is following a lake!' Though apocryphal, the story still has a message regarding the importance of Rumi for many philosophers and mystics alike. The family travelled to Baghdad, to Mecca and to Damascus before finally settling in Konya, which at that time was the capital of the Western Seljuk dynasty. At this time, Konya experienced relative peace and security, and it became a haven for many great thinkers, mystics and artists who were fleeing from the invading Mongols. Because of Konya's Byzantine past, the Turks often proudly referred to this city as Rum ('Rome'), and it was for this reason Jalal al-Din came to be known as ar-Rumi, 'the man of Rome'.

Rumi's father died in 1230 and, not long after his death, Rumi became attached to a former pupil of his father's, Burhanu al-Din Muhaqqiq of Tirmidh, who became Rumi's *Pir* (spiritual master). In time, his Pir guided Rumi through all the spiritual stages of Sufism and Rumi became a Pir himself, attracting disciples of his own, including the Seljuk sultan. Rumi was referred to by his disciples as 'Maulana' ('Our Master') or, in Turkish, 'Mevlevi'. In time, 'Mevlevi' was to become the name given to a well-known Sufi order, which exists to this day.

At the age of 39, a life-changing event occurred in Rumi's life with the arrival in the city of a mysterious, wandering mystic called Shams al-Din of Tabrizi, who, for Rumi, embodied what is called the 'Perfect Man'. In the case of the Sufi path an important part of the quest for knowledge is via this notion of the Perfect Man (*al-insan al-kamil*). This complex notion is explored in more detail in relation to the philosopher Ibn Arabi below. In brief here, many Sufis consider the Perfect Man as the living manifestation of God. In this respect, the status of Man is given considerable regard in that humanity can, in its highest (i.e. perfect) examples, embody the perfections of the universe, including that of God. In the Sufi quest for knowledge, associating with the Perfect Man is equivalent to being associated with God, to be under the 'divine light' of God. The Sufi path involves striving towards the highest perfection so that one can achieve one's own creaturely uniqueness in relation to the Divine, like looking into a mirror only to see God's attributes in your reflection. The theme of the Perfect Man recurs throughout Rumi's poetical works.

Keeping this important quest in mind, therefore, it should not be too surprising that Rumi and Shams became inseparable. This resulted in jealousy from Rumi's disciples, and in 1247 Shams 'disappeared'. What happened to Shams is not known, though suggestions have been made that Rumi's disciples had something to do with this. Rumi's son, Baha al-Din Muhammad-i Walad (or 'Çelebi', meaning 'fully initiated'), wrote his own poem describing how this loss affected Rumi:

> Never for a moment did he cease from listening to music (*sama'*), and dancing;
> Never did he rest by day or night.
> He had been a mufti: he became a poet;

He had been an ascetic: he became intoxicated by Love.
'Twas not the wine of the grape: the illumined soul drinks only the wine
   of light.

(Nicholson 1998: 22)

It is worthwhile considering this poem and what it reveals in terms of
Rumi's quest. First, here we have references to listening to music and to dancing. The Mevlevi Order, which was first institutionalized by Rumi's son, is
most famous in the world today for its religious dance, the **sama**, to the plain-
tive accompaniment of the reed-flute (*nay*). These dancing disciples are
referred to as the 'Whirling Dervishes' because this form of meditation involves
whirling, which represents a mystical journey of Man's ascent towards the
Perfect Man.

This kind of quest for religious knowledge is radically different from the
austere legalistic sharia-imbued quest of the theologians, or even the abstract
theorizing of many of the philosophers, yet for many Sufis it is another way
towards knowledge of God and, therefore, of Truth.

In Çelebi's poem, reference is also made to Rumi developing from being a
mufti to a poet, and it is his great works of poetry that have continued to
delight audiences to this day. He wrote *Poems of Shams of Tabriz* (*Diwan-i
Shams-i Tabriz*, usually referred to simply as the *Diwan*), which is a voluminous
work dedicated to the memory of Shams, although his greatest work is the
Mathnawi (*Spiritual Couplets*), which is a huge work consisting of 25,000
rhyming couplets. It opens with the following well-known lines:

Hearken to this Reed forlorn, breathing even since 'twas torn
From its rushy bed, a strain of impassioned love and pain.

The secret of my song, though near, none can see and none can hear.
Oh, for a friend we know the sign and mingle all his soul with mine!

'Tis the flame of Love that fired me, 'tis the wine of Love inspired me.
Wouldst thou learn how lovers bleed, hearken, hearken to the Reed.

(Nicholson 1998: 31)

Mention has already been made of the use of the Persian reed-flute as an
accompaniment to the sama. Symbolically, the devotee of God is like a reed-
flute, which only becomes a living instrument when it is torn from the earth.
The reed-flute represents the soul that, in its music, is remembering its union
with the Divine and a longing for a return to this Oneness once more. Here
the reader can perhaps identify with the Platonic and Neoplatonic quest for a
return to the 'Good' and the 'Active Intellect'. For Rumi, divine guidance can
come from many sources, whether it be from the works of a philosopher or
from the Quran, although he was less enthused by the practices of the traditional
ulama, as the following poem portrays:

Learn from thy Father! He, not falsely proud,
With tears of sorrow all his sin avowed.
Wilt thou, then, still pretend to be unfree
And clamber up Predestination's tree? –
Like Iblis [Satan] and his progeny abhorred,
In argument and battle with their Lord.
The blest initiates know: what need to prove?
From Satan logic, but from Adam love.

(Nicholson 1998: 165)

The 'Father' in the poem above is Adam who, according to the Quran, repented his sin and wept bitterly. This lack of pride is contrasted with the ulama, who devote their energies to discussing issues of predestination and free will (e.g. did Adam sin of his own free will or is God to blame?) while missing the point that what really matters is a simple love of God, which Adam fully understood.

The *Mathnawi* has often been referred to as 'the Quran in Persian' and many see Rumi's work as complementary to the Quran as a source of guidance as well as inspiration, although the work itself goes far beyond the scriptural text and combines traditional folklore with philosophical, Biblical and mystical thought. Not long after Rumi's death, thanks mainly to his son, the *Mathnawi* became known all over the Persian world, and the Mevlevi Order received patronage from the Ottoman Court. Today there are many Mevlevi 'lodges' (a place for spiritual retreat), not only in Turkey, but also in Egypt and Syria. Rumi's works have influenced many poets and they have been translated into most of the world's languages, with the English interpretations of Rumi's poetry by Coleman Barks (Barks doesn't speak or read Persian, so his poems are essentially 'paraphrases' of other English translations of Rumi, although he collaborates with Persian linguists) selling over half a million copies worldwide. The Mevlevi Order has influenced the Chishti Sufi Order in India, where the *Mathnawi* is widely read, and his universal outlook influenced the more pluralistic of Mogul emperors such as Akbar.

Ibn Arabi and the Perfect Man

In terms of Sufi philosophy, Rumi represents the more ecstatic and poetical tendency, whereas a more theoretical and speculative expression can also be found. The concept of the Perfect Man is particularly associated with the philosopher Ibn Arabi (1165–1240, henceforth referred to as Arabi). He was referred to by the Sufis as *Shaykh al-Akbar* ('The Greatest Master') and also as *Muhyi al-Din* ('Renewer of Religion'). In the words of James Morris,

Paraphrasing Whitehead's famous remark about Plato – and with something of the same degree of imagination – one could say that the history of Islamic thought subsequent to Ibn Arabi (at least down to the 18th century and the radically new encounter with the modern West) might largely be construed as a series of footnotes to his work.

(Morris 1986: 540)

'Abū 'Abdillāh Muḥammad ibn 'Alī ibn Muḥammad ibn 'Arabī, to give him his full name, was born in 1165 in Murcia, Valencia (south-eastern Spain); and he is not only a philosopher and mystic, but he also wrote commentaries on the Quran and hadith and even some poetry, though perhaps not quite of the standard of Rumi. Like that other great Andalusian philosopher Averroes (see Chapter 4), Arabi was able to experience an environment rich in varied cultures and religious traditions that, on the whole, allowed for the exchange of theological, scientific and philosophical ideas.

Arabi claims to have received a vision of Moses, Jesus and Muhammad, urging him to leave aside his studies of the religious sciences and to pursue the spiritual path. As a result of this, he went searching for spiritual knowledge and travelled to Seville and Ceuta in Spain, then further afield to Mecca, Jerusalem and Baghdad. He studied under many mystics and philosophers, including several women, who were especially inspirational to him. While in Spain, he encountered two old women mystics, Shams of Marchena and Fatimah bint ibn al-Muthanna of Cordoba, and of the latter, Arabi says,

> She lived in Seville. When I met her, she was in her nineties. Looking at her in a purely superficial way, one might have thought that she was a simpleton, to which she would have replied that he who knows not his Lord is the real simpleton. She used to say 'Of those who come to see me, I admire none more than Ibn Arabi.' When asked the reason for this, she replied 'The rest of you come with part of yourselves, leaving the other part of you occupied with your other concerns, while Ibn Arabi is a consolation to me, for he comes with all of himself. When he rises up, it is with all of himself, and when he sits it is with his whole self, leaving nothing of himself elsewhere. This is how it should be on the Way.'
>
> (Austin 1977: 143)

For some 30 years, Arabi travelled and studied. While in Mecca he received what he referred to as a 'divine commandment' to begin what was to become his monumental work on mystical doctrine, the *Meccan Revelations*, which was to take him the next 30 years to complete. He finally settled in Damascus in Syria, where he devoted his time to teaching and writing. His *Meccan Revelations* is a massive work that he did not complete until 1231; in modern editions, it consists of some 37 volumes of 500 pages each. Given that Arabi is also credited with about 300 other works (of which around one half survive) we can see here a very prolific individual. The *Meccan Revelations* is divided into 560 chapters and covers virtually all aspects of spiritual life, including the life and practice of the Prophet Muhammad, a spiritual exegesis of the Quran and the hadith and other topics including love, worship, law, cosmology, epistemology and politics. Curiously, Arabi makes little mention of other philosophers in the tradition and he claims that his philosophical views derive from flashes of inspiration that would overwhelm him so much he was compelled to put pen to paper. These moments of 'inspiration' are perhaps more fittingly described as mystical revelations, hence the title of his book. He describes the experiences as his 'unveiling' (*kashf*) and 'opening' (*fath*) and he would write at the command of God. Nonetheless, the terminology that Arabi adopts in his writings displays a strong familiarity with the philosophical and mystical tradition preceding him. Apparently he received another great work, the *Bezels of Wisdom*, in its entirety in a dream. This work is an extended meditation on the mystical significance of the major prophets that feature in the Quran and has been a significant influence on figures within Sufism, not least Rumi. It is even said to have reached the Italian poet and thinker Dante Alighieri (d. 1321). Professor Ralph Austin described Arabi's far-reaching influence in the following way:

> Ibn Arabi gave expression to the teachings and insights of the generations of Sufis who preceded him, recording for the first time, systematically and in detail, the vast fund of Sufi experience and oral tradition, by drawing on a treasury of technical terms and symbols greatly enriched by centuries of intercourse between the Muslim and Neo-Hellenistic worlds ... all who came after him received it through the filter of his synthetic expression.
>
> (Austin 1977: 48)

The above quote stresses the importance of making that perennial link between Islam and the 'neo-Hellenistic worlds' that has been such a characteristic feature of Islamic philosophy in its history. The links between mysticism and the more traditional approaches to Islamic thought are also important, for whilst Arabi talks of 'unveiling', dreams, visions and so on, in his acquisition of knowledge, he certainly does not neglect the importance of reason and serious study. In actual fact, Arabi asserts that reason is necessary in the acquisition of the true knowledge of the world. He regards humans as unique amongst all of God's creations because mankind was created in the image of God, with 'image' being synonymous with God's attributes, such as Mercy (*Rahmah*), Wrath (*Ghadab*), Justice (*'Adl*), Beauty (*Jamal*), Majesty (*Jalal*) and so on. Whereas angels, being spiritual and not material, are able to know God from a spiritual aspect, human beings are able to know God as both a spiritual Being, which he states is pure Reality, and the material manifestation of Reality, which is His creation. In fact, mankind itself is the highest physical manifestation of Reality, whilst also containing the potential for spiritual knowledge of God. This high status assigned to Man is represented first by God's creation of Adam and is identified with the Perfect Man. The Perfect Man, therefore, is actually the physical manifestation of God and embodies all the perfections of the universe, including those of the Divine. Mankind's teleology, his purpose, is to strive towards the highest perfection, to achieve the highest stage in the mystical path possible, the 'station of no station' (*maqam la maqam*) when he becomes the

'Verifier' (*muhaqqiq*) or 'the possessor of two eyes' (*dhu'l-'aynayn*). With one eye the Perfect Man can perceive his own creaturely uniqueness, whilst with the other he see his identity with God. These reference to the 'two eyes' recognizes a duality which also seems to suggest – from a more rational, logical perspective – irreconcilable dualities: the Perfect Man is near to God and far away from Him at the same time, but this is only if one is only prepared to be rational and logical about such things. To identify with God is to go beyond the rational, for God's essence is both unity and multiplicity, both necessity and contingency. By referring to God as possessing attributes, Arabi raises the philosophical dilemma of a God that is one and unchanging having parts in this way, but for Arabi there is no conflict with proposing God as having multiplicity. God is both the Creator and the *created*, the latter in the sense that God is the totality of all things, which must include those things that God also created.

Whilst all of creation partakes of God's nature, Arabi does not stray so far from traditional Islamic beliefs by arguing for a form of pantheism, although it may seem that way. Arabi's doctrine of the 'unity of being' (*wahda al-wujud*) makes a distinction between, on the one hand, God, the Absolute One, immutable and indefinable Truth (*Haqq*) and, on the other hand, God's creation (*khalq*) or what he refers to as *zuhur* ('self-manifestation'), which is mutable and in constant renewal. What unifies these seemingly distinctive things – God and His creation – is what Arabi calls the 'breath of the merciful' (*nafas al-rahman*), which flows through all things, giving it existence as a mother gives existence to her children.

The more rationally minded readers may be troubled by this attempt to reconcile these dualities but, for Arabi, that is the key problem with reason: it is so insistent on categorizing things into one thing or another and, as a result, fails to recognize the unity of all things. Arabi appreciates the importance of reason as it enables us to comprehend distinctions and differentiation and even to think more abstractly, but it nonetheless has its limitations: the rational mind is constituted to dissect Reality and reduces unity to parts. What is also required is the quality that, Arabi argues, the rational philosophers and theologians lack, but the Sufi possess, and that is imagination (*khayal*), which allows one to perceive God's presence in all things. Rational reflection alone, though important, is insufficient to grasp God's essence; rather it is the 'Verifiers' who are able to bridge the gap and see with both eyes God's presence for they have established an inner harmony between reason and imagination. The importance of Sufi ascetic practices in developing the ability to 'imagine' in this way, therefore, is vital for true philosophical comprehension of Reality. There is, therefore, a false distinction between philosophy (and, indeed, theology) and mysticism and those who believe otherwise deceive themselves into believing they can apprehend Truth.

It is this subscription to a more holistic view of Truth that has resulted in a number of individuals emerging since the time of Arabi who declare themselves to be 'Verifiers' and deliberately distance themselves from Islamic philosophers and theologians. Arabi's writings can be a struggle to understand, even for the best scholars, and it has been pointed out that there is still a long way to go:

> The real philosophic and theological unity and diversity of these writers have not begun to be explored in modern research ... none of the writers are mere 'commentators' of Ibn Arabi ... as with 'Aristotelianism' or 'Platonism' in Western thought, Ibn Arabi's writings were only the starting point for the most diverse developments, in which reference to subsequent inter-preters quickly became at least as important as the study of the Shaykh himself.
>
> (Morris 1986: 541–42)

For example, Arabi's most important disciple and the figure through which Arabi's own works became known was Sadr al-Din Qunawi (d. 1273), who has been so influential that many of those who have studied Arabi have done it through the teachings of Qunawi. As a result, as the above quote states, stu-dents are not receiving a mere 'commentary' on Arabi, but a particular inter-pretation. One key difference between Arabi and Qunawi is that whereas the former comes across as more mystical, with the emphasis on Sufi practices, Qunawi is more philosophically systematic in his discourse. Whilst Arabi is more philosophically rigorous than Rumi, for example, Qunawi and his direct followers helped to give Arabi's ideas even greater structure and philosophical coherence, despite the tendency within much of mystical Islam to resist such systematic philosophical exposition. We should not, however, accuse Qunawi of diverting attention away from Arabi's teachings, given how close he was to his mentor; Qunawi aims to make Arabi's teachings more responsive to the questions of his contemporary audience, who wanted to know more about what Arabi meant.

Muhammad Iqbal

Another important exponent of the concept of *insan al-kamil*, the Perfect Man, is the Indian scholar and poet Muhammad **Iqbal** (1873–1938). Iqbal's thought has been described as 'an integrated concept of the Self, fusing together the Sufi's passion for union with God, the idea of dynamism expounded by Bergson, the groping for self-assertion which was the philosophy of Nietzsche, and the Sharia of Islam' (Mujeeb 1967: 454). Iqbal is an example of a Muslim thinker who crosses the divide between East and West, as much as one can speak of a 'divide' at all. He received a classical, Western education as a boy at the Scotch Mission College in Sialkot (in the Punjab province of what is now Pakistan, but was part of India at that time). In 1905, Iqbal travelled to Europe and studied at Cambridge with R.A. Nicholson (1868–1945) – the noted Sufi scholar – and the neo-Hegelian John McTaggart (1866–1925). He then continued his studies in Heidelberg and Munich, and obtained his doc-torate for a thesis entitled *The Development of Metaphysics in Persia*. Hence we have a combination of studies of Islamic and Western thought: the Quran, hadith and Muslim thinkers like Ibn Taymiyya, Wali Allah and Rumi, and Western philosophers such as Hegel, Bergson and Nietzsche.

In the way that many of his Muslim predecessors had looked to ancient Greek and Persian philosophers, Iqbal made use of his studies of Western philosophy, especially the German philosopher Friedrich **Nietzsche** (1844–1900), to inform his understanding of Islam; almost all of Iqbal's most significant works were written after his return from Europe, and certainly a Nietzschean influence can be detected, especially in his poem *Secrets of the Self*, which he first published in 1915. For Iqbal, the Perfect Man of Islam is indeed the Prophet Muhammad, but also possesses the characteristics of Nietzsche's Übermensch, or 'Superman', as seen especially in the Prophet Zarathustra of Nietzsche's work *Thus Spoke Zarathustra*. For this reason, Iqbal has often been associated with an early form of existentialism, although it is difficult to say to what extent Islam can be 'existentialist' in the way it is understood in the Sartrean sense (i.e. the existential writings of Jean-Paul **Sartre**, 1905–80). Like Nietzsche's Zarathustra, Iqbal sees Muhammad as the archetype for a politics of redemption: one who founded a new metaphysics of morals that consisted of courage and honesty; one who cast aside the false idols. Iqbal sees the Prophet Muhammad as confronting the human predicament of the time, a time of *jahiliyya* ('ignorance': see Chapter 8 for an elaboration of this concept), in the same way that Zarathustra was confronted by the death of God and the consequent failure to have a belief in any moral values to replace divine guidance. At the time Iqbal was writing many of his contemporaries also believed that the Islamic world was returning to a state of jahiliyya, and there was concern for the very survival of Islam in India especially. One commentator on Iqbal, Subhash Kashyap, states: 'Iqbal is a Nietzschean in being a determined enemy of conventional values' (Kashyap 1955: 175). In his poem *Secrets of the Self*, the 'self', the self-creative ego, smells suicide in conventionalism and this life, one of decadence and traditionalism, and regards this as the same as no life at all. The role of the prophets, whether it is Zarathustra or Muhammad, is to be the destroyer of conventional values and to create new values.

Man is the highest of all created things, and it is his duty to say yes to life. In the same way Nietzsche, in *Thus Spoke Zarathustra*, writes of the 'three metamorphoses of the spirit', Iqbal talks of the three stages in the development of the self. Zarathustra gives a speech in which he talks of the three metamorphoses that the spirit of Man must go through, represented by first the camel, second the lion and third the child; and this matches Iqbal's three stages of obedience to the law, self-control and vicegerency of God. For Zarathustra, the camel represents obedience and domesticity, but it is also heroic because it takes on the responsibility of obedience and is able to carry this burden to get to the next stage in the path. Likewise, Iqbal argues that it is important to be obedient towards the will of God. To become the Übermensch you must revere the Übermensch. Thus, to become the Perfect Muslim you must revere the Perfect Muslim.

After a period of carrying the load of commandments and obligations, Man – for Nietzsche – passes from the camel to the lion stage: the stage of self-determination and control. For Iqbal, this quality is required in order to resist the temptations that the Western, modernist world has to offer, because they are brief delights and, ultimately, they undermine the spirit. The third transformation for Nietzsche is to the child:

> The child is innocence and forgetfulness, a new beginning, a sport, a self-propelling wheel, a first motion, a sacred Yes. Yes, a sacred Yes is needed, my brothers, for the sport of creation: the spirit now wills its own will, the spirit sundered from the world now wins its own world.
>
> (Nietzsche 1969: 55)

The child is yes-saying and is at the beginning of what will become the Übermensch. For Iqbal, this yes-sayer is the Divine Vicegerent: the lords of creation. Iqbal's Vicegerent is his Perfect Muslim, of which the finest example is the Prophet Muhammad:

> Muhammad is the preface to the book of the universe:
> All the worlds are slaves and he is the Master.
>
> (Iqbal 1920: 12)

On a number of occasions in the notes from the composition of *Thus Spoke Zarathustra*, Nietzsche portrays his Persian prophet as a lawgiver (*Gesetzgeber*), ranking him alongside Buddha, Moses, Jesus and Muhammad. As Nietzsche looked to Zarathustra as a response to the perceived decadence of moral malaise, Iqbal looked to the example of the Prophet Muhammad. For Nietzsche, however, the Übermensch is a potential for the future of mankind, and he rejects the transcendental. But Iqbal argues that Muhammad talks of the divine within the human, and so Man is capable of transcending his baser self and taking part in the divine. In this respect, the separation between the divine and human can be linked. In both the Übermensch and the Perfect Man, therefore, the emphasis is on Man: not to rely upon external salvation, but to look within oneself to be self-disciplined in overcoming animal-like inclinations and to strive for the divine spirit within us. It is to take risks and to put one's own life in danger for the sake of principle and truth. Muhammad represents a man – and he was 'only' a man – who, despite doubts as to his own purpose, puts aside the security of a successful business and a loving wife, as well as endangering his respected status in society. He becomes an outcast, mocked by many, and even believes himself to have gone mad. All signs of the Übermensch will appear as signs of illness or madness to the human herd: 'Everyone wants the same thing, everyone is the same: whoever thinks otherwise goes voluntarily into the madhouse' (Nietzsche 1969: 46).

Iqbal emphasized the importance of the unity of God, of tawhid, which, in his work *The Reconstruction of Religious Thought in Islam*, he regarded as 'the soul and body of our Community'. As Iqbal goes on to say: 'humanity needs three things today, spiritual interpretation of the universe, spiritual emancipation of the individual, and basic principles of a universal import directing the evolution of human society on a spiritual basis'. Iqbal described the self, or *khudi*, in the following way:

> Metaphysically the word khudi (self-hood) is used in the sense of that indescribable feeling of 'I' which forms the basis of the uniqueness of each individual. Ethically the word khudi means (as used by me) self-reliance, self-respect, self-confidence, self-preservation, self-assertion when such a thing is necessary, in the interest of life and power to stick to the cause of truth, justice, duty etc. even in the face of death. Such behaviour is moral in my opinion because it helps in the integration of the forces of the Ego, thus hardening it, as against the forces of disintegration and dissolution, practically the metaphysical ego is the bearer of two main rights that is the right to life and freedom as determined by Divine Law.
>
> (Vahid 1964: 80)

This understanding of khudi, of the 'self', can be seen in an existential sense as it raises a concern that frequently crops up in existential ethics: How can one be an 'individual' and determine one's own destiny (i.e. be free, or 'authentic') and yet still know what is morally right or wrong? This is a concern that goes back to Kierkegaard and whether Abraham, by obeying the command of God to sacrifice his only son, is also asserting his 'self' at the expense of morality. For Iqbal, the khudi, or 'self', is expressed in both an existential sense of emerging and evolving, but also in a communal sense of being part of the group consciousness of the umma. The agent's freedom is expressed through the communal, but he also wants to stress that the moral conclusions the individual draws are universal in nature.

Whilst there is the individual self, there is also the ultimate self, which is God. God is both transcendent, but also, in another sense, immanent, as He is intimately connected with human beings through His creative power. Iqbal's God is more akin to the Sufi conception of the divine as more close and personal than the more 'classical', traditional understanding allows. Iqbal writes of the self, or the ego, as something that evolves:

> Indeed the evolution of life shows that, though in the beginning the mental is dominated by the physical, the mental as it grows in power, tends to dominate the physical and may eventually rise to a position of complete independence ...
>
> (Iqbal 1989: 85)

This seems dualistic: the self as non-physical consciousness that can exist independently of the physical body, with God as the supreme consciousness. Therefore, as the individual human consciousness evolves and grows, it gets closer to the supreme consciousness that is God. The human ego evolves gradually from the position of possessing hardly any freedom at all, subject to the laws of nature of human appetites, to a more spiritual state of independence and dynamism: 'The "unceasing reward" of man consists in his gradual growth in self-possession, in uniqueness, and intensity of his activity as an ego' (Iqbal 1989: 94).

The paradigm for the Perfect Man is the Prophet Muhammad as the creator of new values. The purpose of human life on earth is the creation of self-creative egos, the men with khudi: the lords of creation. In an Aristotelian sense, Man has purpose, a goal, unlike the existential being that creates his or her own purpose. The 'goal' is 'life's caravan'. However, there is an 'existential' element to this: while some Islamic thinkers may agree with Iqbal that Man has purpose, but would question a human being's ability to behave responsibly unless they were closely guided by God's law, Iqbal has considerably more trust in the individual human to determine his or her own fate, and credits human beings with greater freedom to overcome animal instincts and the demands of the physical.

Whilst dualistic in terms of emphasizing a self, or consciousness, that is 'independent' of the physical, Iqbal is not Cartesian. For Descartes, the physical world is subject to strict mathematical laws that can be controlled by Man; the world is essentially there to be appropriated by Man, a 'utility' to be used for the service of mankind, for mankind are able to make themselves the masters and possessors of nature. Iqbal, however, follows Nietzsche by going *beyond* the dualism of 'physical' and 'non-physical'. Iqbal's existential philosophy, alternatively, allows the human body much greater freedom to escape from the limitations of scientific determinism. The concept of tawhid contains within it a unity of body and soul, spirit and matter, the individual and the communal. He regarded tawhid as the essential principle that brings the Islamic community together. God is one, and the doctrine of tawhid extends to all of creation. The world in which we are living is His creation: 'He created for you all that the earth contains; then, ascending to the sky, He fashioned it into seven heavens. He has knowledge of all things' (Quran: 2:29) Therefore, God's will is to be realized in every area of life:

> Christianity is essentially a mystery which veils the Divine from man … In Islam, however, it is man who is veiled from God … Islam is thus essentially a way of knowledge; it is a way of gnosis (*ma'rifah*) … Islam leads to that essential knowledge which integrates our being, which makes us know what we are and be what we know or in other words integrates knowledge and being in the ultimate unitive vision of reality.
>
> (Nasr 2001: 21, 22)

The above quote is from *Ideals and Realities of Islam* by Sayyed Hossein **Nasr** (born 1933), who is a prominent Persian Islamic philosopher; he is an example of combining rigorous philosophical method with Sufi mysticism. Man, Nasr argues, is a 'theomorphic being'; that is, he is endowed with the intelligence (*al-'aql*) which can lead him to the Truth, to knowledge of Allah and to unity (tawhid). This concept of a 'theomorphic being' owes much to Ibn Arabi's concept of the Perfect Man:

> Man needs revelation because although a theomorphic being he is by nature negligent and forgetful; he is by nature imperfect. Therefore, he needs to be reminded ... Man cannot alone uplift himself spiritually ... Intelligence does lead to God but provided it is wholesome and healthy (*salim*), and it is precisely revelation, this objective manifestation of the Intellect, that guarantees this wholesomeness and permits the intelligence to function correctly and not be impeded by the passions.
>
> (Nasr 2001: 22, 23)

Man possesses the ability to reason and needs to exercise this ability in order to gain access to the truth. This appears Platonic, or Cartesian, but raises the recurring question in this book of why one should then *need* revelation. Nasr above states that this is because reason alone cannot be relied upon, hence the emphasis on revealed doctrine, on 'this objective manifestation of the Intellect'. Reason can be viewed as a tool, a tool to understanding that which has already been revealed.

Tawhid is not only a metaphysical assertion about the nature of the Absolute; it is also a method of integrating the seemingly disparate parts of creation into a wholeness. It is the belief that Islam has been revealed in its complete and perfect form and that, therefore, the faithful should follow what is contained within the revealed text. The Quran is the instrument by which Man can discriminate between the Absolute and the relative, good and evil, truth and falsehood – and it is '*umm al-kitab*' – the 'mother of books', the prototype of all knowledge.

Further reading

Aminrazavi, M.A.R. (1996), *Suhrawardi and the School of Illumination*, Routledge Sufi Series, Abingdon: Routledge.

Barks, C. (2007), *Rumi: Bridge to the Soul*, London: HarperCollins.

Chittick, W.C. (1989), *The Sufi Path of Knowledge: Ibn Al-Arabi's Metaphysics of Imagination*, Albany: State University of New York Press.

Iqbal, M. (1989), *The Reconstruction of Religious Thought in Islam*, Lahore: Iqbal Academy.

Meisami, S. (2013), *Mulla Sadra*, Makers of the Muslim World, Oxford: Oneworld.

Nasr, S.H. (2001), *Ideals and Realities of Islam*, Cambridge: The Islamic Texts Society.

Nicholson, R.A. (1998), *Rumi: Poet and Mystic*, Oxford: Oneworld.

Rumi (2004), *Selected Poems*, Penguin Classics, trans. by Coleman Barks, London: Penguin.

Soroush, A. (2002), *Reason, Freedom, and Democracy in Islam: Essential Writings of Abdolkarim Soroush*, New York: Oxford University Press.

6 Islam and the state

Since the time of ancient Greek philosophy, the question of how important it is to uphold what are perceived as 'higher' values – whether they are moral, epistemological or even cultural – has come into conflict with what is regarded as the values of the majority. In the political arena, this may be regarded as a conflict between the belief in a meritocracy – rule by a select group of people who adhere to these higher values and impose them upon the mass of the population – and a democracy – rule by the masses which then results in society adopting whatever the values of the majority happen to be.

This kind of duality has also been expressed in Islamic political philosophy, with a particular concern that the values of the majority may act as a threat to the perceived higher values of religion. This battle between the mundane and the spiritual can also be detected in Western philosophy. Take, for example, the ancient Greek philosopher Plato and the German philosopher and philologist Friedrich Nietzsche. While both are, of course, diverse in their philosophies in many respects, it is possible to identify some common themes: they were both suspicious of democracy, and they were both proponents of forms of political and spiritual elitism. Plato, although in many ways a rationalist, can come across as somewhat mystical when talking of his Philosopher-Kings. Likewise, Nietzsche, though labelled as an atheist by many, frequently refers to his Übermensch as 'Noble Spirits' who are in touch with their souls, their 'spiritual sides', and are not the atheistic or nihilistic figures that are supposed by some commentators. Granted, how the term 'spiritual' would be interpreted by these philosophers would differ considerably, as would their understanding of democracy, given the political climates of fifth-century Athens – where democracy was of a very limited kind – and Nietzsche's nineteenth-century Europe, which was mostly aristocratic still. As we have seen in this book, the works of Plato and other ancient Greek philosophers have proven to be of immense importance in the development of Islamic philosophy, which, at times, has resulted in a rather uncomfortable relationship between faith and reason. As has also been evident, Nietzsche's conception of the Übermensch has also had its appeal for certain Muslim philosophers, most notably Muhammad Iqbal (see Chapter 5). Today, democracy is generally regarded as the best form of government, certainly by those who live in a democratic society, but it has not only had its critics amongst the ancient Greeks and the nineteenth-century Europeans, for we can bring this issue to more modern understandings of Western democracy and its critics by focusing on one Islamic political philosopher by the name of Mawdudi.

Mawdudi

Sheikh Sayyid Mawlana Abu'l-A'la **Mawdudi** (1903–79) was born on 25 September 1903 in the city of Aurangabad in Maharashtra state, India. These are mostly honorific titles, not names, an indication of how much regard Mawdudi is held in. Certainly, then, when the works of Mawdudi are cited they are given great respect and authority by millions of Muslims to this present day. Mawdudi wrote over 120 books and pamphlets on many subjects covering ethics, politics, religion of course, slavery, human rights, sharia, the Prophet Muhammad, sociology, literature and commentaries on the Quran to name but a few. Many of these writings are undoubtedly intelligent, persuasive and insightful. As Malise Ruthven notes:

> In his [Mawdudi's] hands 'Islam' becomes much more than a succession of hair-splitting legal judgements emanating from an archaic social system. It is a full-blown 'ideology' offering answers to every human and social problem. It is mainly for this reason that, despite its rigidity, Mawdudi is widely admired by Muslim radicals from Egypt to Malaysia … Along with Sayyid Qutb, he is the most widely read theoretician among young Sunni activists.
>
> (Ruthven 2000: 328)

Mawdudi and his father were brought up during the time of British colonial rule, which coincided with a decline in Muslim rule and an increase in power for the majority Hindu population. In addressing this decline in Muslim power Mawdudi looked to Islamic tradition for answers, although, at the same time, he can be described as a modern thinker, not merely burying his head in that tradition. Importantly, he did not see modernity as a final nail in the coffin for Islam, but rather saw modernity – at least certain aspects of it – as an opportunity to revitalize Islam. Mawdudi was concerned with how to be a Muslim in the modern age and he devoted his life to communicating what he considered to be the best way to be a Muslim. In that sense his message is strongly ethical in the Greek philosophical sense of the term: What does it mean to be good?

Mainly self-educated, he became a successful journalist and activist. He was an early supporter of the Khalifat Movement, which aimed to restore the central political institutions (including the return of a caliph as ruler) of the Muslim world after Turkey abolished them in 1924. By 1938 he was committed to the idea of a separate state for India's Muslims and, in 1941, he established the party *Jamaat-i-Islami* ('Islamic Party'), with himself as its leader, which exists to this day. With Mawdudi's writings and activity, we have a perfect example of an important tension that exists in modern Islamic political philosophy: the tension between a vision of an Islamic state that is ruled by God, by objective truth if you like, and the modern belief that the rule of the people, of democracy, is actually the way forward. This raises a number of important philosophical questions: How can you be a good Muslim in a democratic state? Is Islam compatible with democracy? To what extent can secular and spiritual power be separated in an Islamic state and still be considered 'Islamic'?

Mawdudi's treatment of democracy is a complex one and needs to be seen in the light of how he encountered it, for at the time Muslims saw Indian nationalism as a threat to the very survival of Islam in India and believed that democratization would result in Hindu supremacy. For that reason, Mawdudi was highly suspicious of democracy whilst, at the same time, aware that it had positive features too. Ultimately, rather like Plato, who saw his ideal state as a pattern in the heavens that should be imitated but may never be attained, or Nietzsche, whose Übermensch are an ideal to strive for, it has been argued that Mawdudi conceived of the Islamic state in ahistorical terms as an ideal type rather than intending to present a detailed account of what this state would actually be like. Nonetheless, as he did engage in the day-to-day political machine of his time, what we do have as a result are his writings that do go into the idea of an Islamic state in quite some detail.

On the 16 March 1948, Mawdudi gave a talk on Radio Pakistan entitled *The Spiritual Path of Islam*. Here is the opening:

> The idea which has influenced most the climate of philosophical and religious thought is that body and soul are mutually antagonistic, and can develop only at each other's expense. For the soul, the body is a prison and the activities of daily life are the shackles which keep it in bondage and arrest its growth. This has inevitably led to the universe being divided into the spiritual and the secular.
>
> Those who chose the secular path were convinced that they could not meet the demands of spirituality, and thus they led highly material and hedonistic lives. All spheres of worldly activity, whether social, political, economic or cultural, were deprived of the light of spirituality; injustice and tyranny were the result.
>
> Conversely, those who wanted to tread the path of spiritual excellence came to see themselves as 'noble outcasts' from the world. They believed that it was impossible for spiritual growth to be compatible with a 'normal' life. In their view physical self-denial and mortification of the flesh were necessary for the development and perfection of the spirit. They invented spiritual exercises and ascetic practices which killed physical desires and dulled the body's senses. They regarded forests, mountains and other solitary places as ideal for spiritual development because the hustle and bustle of life would not interfere with their meditations. They could not

conceive of spiritual development except through withdrawal from the world.

(Mawdudi, on Radio Pakistan entitled
'The Spiritual Path of Islam', 16 March 1948)

This has been quoted at some length because it not only represents the view that Mawdudi maintained throughout his life, but is also considered to be the view of so many Muslims: it is not only possible to be spiritual – i.e. to be a good Muslim – whilst engaging in the world, but it is also *obligatory* to do so. The challenge for Mawdudi was to devise a theory of the state that would encompass an Islamic framework in line with his view – and the view of the majority of Muslims – that there should be no separation between religion and state, and so the religious path is predicated upon social action. A Muslim does not leave his or her religion at home when walking out of the door, but every aspect of life should be regarded as an aspect of Islamic worship. There cannot be more than one authority: there is not a private life and a public life, there is simply an integrated spiritual path that encompasses all aspects of life. The first, and most important, step in this path is, naturally, obedience to God. As Mawdudi says in *First Principles of the Islamic State*:

> It [the Quran] is the first and primary source [of the Islamic constitution], containing as it does all the fundamental directions and instructions from God Himself. The directions and instructions cover the entire gamut of man's existence. Herein are to be found not only directives relating to individual conduct but also principles regulating all the aspects of the social and cultural life of man. It has also been clearly shown therein as to why should Muslims endeavour to create and establish a State of their own.
>
> (Mawdudi 1967: 5)

There is a simple logic here: if being a good Muslim encompasses all aspects of life, then the state and society as a whole must function according to God's laws. This, it may seem, is tantamount to a theocracy, for surely a democracy would allow for a plurality of views that would inevitably conflict with the principles set out in the Quran. However, Mawdudi seems to not be advocating a theocracy at all:

> Islamic theocracy is not controlled by a special religious group of people but by ordinary Muslims. They run it according to the Qur'an and Sunna. And if I am allowed to coin a new word, I would call it 'theo-democracy'. It would grant limited popular sovereignty to Muslims under the paramount sovereignty of God. In this [state], the executive and the legislature would be formed in consultation with the Muslims. Only Muslims would have the right to remove them. Administrative and other issues, regarding which there are no clear orders in the Shari'ah, would be settled only with the consensus of Muslims. If the law of God needs interpretation no special

group or race but all those Muslims would be entitled to interpret (*ijtihad*) who have achieved the capability of interpretation.

(Mawdudi 1969: 130)

'Sovereignty', defined as the highest unlimited power, rests with God. There-fore, when Mawdudi states that 'sovereignty belongs only to God. He is the lawgiver. Any person, even a prophet, is not entitled to issue orders or with-draw the orders [of God]', then no legislation in a state can be passed without first reference to God. This, however, presents us with a series of difficulties. To begin with, there is some disagreement, as we have noted, over the extent of the nature of God and whether He can, should or does personally intervene in the everyday world. Further, the Quran is simply not replete with detailed legislation to provide sufficient guidance, especially given it was revealed to a seventh-century Arabian audience which seems hardly comparable to the complexities faced by a twenty-first century society.

What political theory can be found in the Quran is in relation to the status of the Prophet Muhammad as a figure of authority who ruled over a state and a people. Mawdudi regards Muhammad as the ideal political ruler and the state of Medina as the perfect model of an Islamic state. He makes reference to this time as a 'golden era' because it was, he argues, a time when indeed religion and politics were as one. This time period is extended by Mawdudi to also include the rightly-guided caliphs (632–61). Mawdudi's vision of the caliph is not unlike that of Plato's Philosopher-King: as one who has knowledge of what is good and will as a result do what is good. It is worthwhile quoting Mawdudi at some length for his vision of what the caliph once was:

> He was not just the president of the state but the prime minister as well. He attended the parliament himself, presided over its meeting and fully participated in its debates. He was responsible for the affairs of his government and accounted for his personal affairs as well. He had neither an official party nor an opposition party; the entire parliament acted as his party as long as he followed the right path, and the whole parliament acted as the opposition party if he followed the wrong path. Each member was free to oppose or support his decisions; even his own ministers used to oppose him in the parliament. Nevertheless, the president and his cabinet got along very well; no one ever resigned from his office. The calipha was answerable not only to the parliament, but to the entire *qaum* [nation] for all his activities, even concerning his private life. He faced the public five times a day in the mosque and addressed them at Friday prayers. People could find him in the streets and muhallas, and anybody could stop him to ask for his rights. Not only could the members of parliament question him on prior notice but anyone could ask him questions at public places.

(Mawdudi 1969: 345)

This is certainly a very idealistic picture and that is also, of course, the very problem with such a picture, for history does not seem to give us a form of government like this as ever existing in reality. In fact, Mawdudi himself is forced to conclude that '[i]t can only become practicable when society has been fully prepared in accordance with the revolutionary principles of Islam' (Mawdudi 1969). In practice, Mawdudi's theo-democracy would be more theocracy than democracy for whereas in principle the emphasis on consultation may suggest democracy, it is the issue of who would be entitled to engage in the consultative process that undermines any kind of inclusiveness. No mention here is made of non-Muslims, who would not be entitled to take part in the political process, but Mawdudi would not include women either (see Chapter 7). The powers of ***ijtihad*** (independent reasoning) would only be for those Muslims 'who have achieved the capability of interpretation'. According to Mawdudi's own calculations, the percentage of Muslims with any true knowledge of Islam is not more than 0.001 per cent! Therefore, although Mawdudi acknowledges the importance of ijtihad in political and legal decision-making, those he regards as suitably eligible to engage in ijtihad would be a very small minority, because when

> laws are made with the will of the people, experience has shown that the common people themselves cannot understand their interests. It is a natural weakness of human beings that in most matters relating to their life they consider some aspects of the matter and overlook others; generally their judgement is one sided.
>
> (Mawdudi 1969: 132)

This distrust in people to be able to make decisions in the state-making process needs to be taken seriously, for not only is it a theme that, as we have noted, has cropped up in the history of philosophy since Plato's time, but it is also a view that is shared by a number of serious Muslim scholars to this day; and it does present us with a real dilemma of aligning what is evidently good about democracy with the concerns of many Muslims that God's commands must be obeyed and Islamic values upheld both at a personal level and a social level.

It is not an uncommon feature of religion for the world to be perceived in both the concrete real time of contemporary events and, at the same time, a universal framework that defies time and place. As the great American anthropologist Clifford Geertz (1926–2006) has remarked, ideologies bridge 'the emotional gap between things as they are and as one would have them to be, thus insuring the performance of roles that might otherwise be abandoned in despair or apathy' (Geertz 1973: 205). Mawdudi certainly stands out as a representative of how Islamic ideology is applied to the everyday world. In one respect, he is faced with a religion that millions engage in on an everyday level in contemporary India, whilst he is also confronted by an ideology, a series of paradigms of the Quran, Muhammad, the rightly-guided caliphs and Medina, in which all present a form of utopia that seems out of sync with the world as it happens to be. The literal Greek translation of 'utopia' is 'no-place', and whilst there may be many good reasons for striving to make a society better and to have a vision of what society could be like, there also needs to be a recognition that society – consisting as it does of human beings – is in a constant process of change. The problem with attempting to create a utopia is that it can result in a state that is ideological, impotent and static. Plato's speculations on a utopia are not made with any reference to any past historical precedent. This is not always the case: for example, the Genevan philosopher Jean-Jacques **Rousseau** (1712–78), in his *Discourse on the Origin of Inequality* (published in 1755), presents us with a 'hypothetical history' of Man in a pre-social condition:

> I see an animal less strong than some, and less active than others, but, upon the whole, the most advantageously organised of any; I see him satisfying the calls of hunger under the first oak, and those of thirst at the first rivulet; I see him laying himself down to sleep at the foot of the same tree that afforded him his meal; and behold, this done, all his wants are completely supplied.
>
> (Rousseau 2004: 4)

Unlike the English philosopher Thomas **Hobbes** (1588–1679), who saw the state of nature as an arena of conflict and brutality, Rousseau's 'savage man', who is taken back much further in history than Hobbes' man, does not live in a state of fear and anxiety, as he is in a position to fight or flee from other creatures. It is only when Man is removed from his natural condition that the fear of death becomes a real concern, and '[i]n proportion as he becomes sociable and a slave to others, he becomes weak, fearful, mean-spirited, and his soft and effeminate way of living at once completes the enervation of his strength and his courage' (Rousseau 2004: 28). However, Rousseau does not then conclude that Man should therefore *return* to the state of nature in which he once existed. In fact, Rousseau believes that any attempt to do this would result in disaster for the human race and, instead, he argues for a greater role for nature within the modern world. Whilst Mawdudi is in line with Rousseau in arguing that Man should live in accordance with nature, the former's reliance upon a re-creation of a society of the past seems incongruous for the modern world. For Mawdudi, the utopia of Medina was a concrete reality in the not-so-distant past, and it follows logically that such a phenomenon can occur again in the future. Whilst there could be no prophet, of course – for Muhammad was the final prophet – there could be a leader, a 'sheikh', with considerable authority. Mawdudi argues that, as Islam is the one and true religion and Medina was its incarnation on earth, governed by the Prophet of God, this was a society governed by the laws of God/nature (God being the creator of nature and the harmony within it). Man is a natural being in the sense he is a religious being. The Quran is full of such references, which state that Man, by turning away from God, is also turning away from his own true nature. As the renowned American anthropologist, Ernest Gellner (1925–95), pointed out, 'Islam is the blueprint of a social order' (Gellner 1979: 12). To be a Muslim is to live in an Islamic state, for ultimate authority rests in divine order. A political order living under sharia is, therefore, the realization of a utopia.

For Mawdudi, and for many Muslims generally, the meaning of the Latin term *religio* (to bind) is taken very seriously, for the binding of Man to God has political as well as personal implications simply because Islam, as exemplified in the Quran and in the life of the Prophet, concerns itself with all aspects of human society. In contrast to Christianity, where salvation effectively lies in the acceptance of Christ as the Messiah as manifested in sacramental rituals such as baptism and matrimony, for the Muslim salvation is living one's daily life. The everyday decisions he or she makes are religious acts:

> Christianity is essentially a mystery which veils the Divine from man … In Islam, however, it is man who is veiled from God … Islam is thus essentially a way of knowledge; it is a way of gnosis (ma'rifah) … Islam leads to that essential knowledge which integrates our being, which makes us know what we are and be what we know or in other words integrates knowledge and being in the ultimate unitive vision of reality.
>
> (Nasr 2001: 21, 22)

However, as Patrick Bannerman points out in his work *Islam in Perspective*:

> For Muslims, there is an added complexity in that the era of Rashidun, the 'Golden Age' of Islam, has become an idealized state in which pristine and pure Islam sprang forth, like Aphrodite from the waves, completely furnished with all the impedimenta of a fully fledged state and society – law, philosophy, administrative machinery, economic principles, etc. Yet as many authorities, including Muslim authorities, have conclusively demonstrated, the evolution of the impedimenta of a fully fledged state and society took place over a period of some three centuries or more following the Golden Age. Furthermore, the period of the Rashidun was itself one of the most innovative in the history of Islam.
>
> (Bannerman 1988: 61)

Mawdudi strived for what he called the 'intellectual independence' of Islam, for an Islam that is pure and unsullied by external cultural influences, for an Islam entirely divorced from foreign '-isms' such as Marxism, communism, capitalism, secularism and so on. For Mawdudi, Islam is a self-contained '-ism': it is Islamism and does not need or require external influence or guidance. This concept of intellectual independence derives to some extent from Mawdudi's readings of Muhammad Iqbal and his concept of khudi ('selfhood', see Chapter 5), which Mawdudi interpreted as Islamic self-assertion against alien '-isms', although Iqbal was not averse to Western ideas. As he says in *The Reconstruction of Religious Thought in Islam*, 'Approach modern knowledge with a respectful but independent attitude and … appreciate the teachings of Islam in the light of that knowledge, even though we may be led to differ from those who have gone before us'. However, Mawdudi was aware that one concern with Iqbal's concept of the khudi – which emerges in an evolutionary manner not unlike that of Nietzsche's Übermensch – is that it begs the question why such an individual, such a 'self' would feel any inclination to acquiesce in the ethical requirements of Islam. Iqbal did not seem to regard a clash as inevitable at all; he maintained that Islamic ethical values would be parallel to the values all humans share. But while this may be argued at a very general, abstract level, it is more complex when we get to the everyday practice of making ethical decisions about real-life situations. This kind of clash between the assertion of the existential self and the everyday world of practical ethics is a topic that Sartre, for example, never satisfactorily resolved, falling back on a form of Kantian categorical imperative or perhaps an emphasis on moral character reminiscent of Aristotle. Similarly, Nietzsche's 'creator of values' has raised questions as to the moral character of these Übermensch, and Nietzsche's own understandable resistance to any attempt to declare a 'table of values'. It is for these reasons that Mawdudi was unwilling to put trust in the individual self to be morally responsible for his or her own actions.

Mawdudi viewed Islam as an independent ideology, completely un-reliant upon other cultures or belief systems. If it so happened that another 'alien' culture possessed the same views as Islam in its politics, science, economics etc., this was not because Islam had been influenced by these external views. In fact, as Islam originated at the beginning of Time, it came before all other beliefs and so its views came before all others. That is to say, if it is argued that Islam is democratic, this is not because of what has been learnt from examples of democracy in other states, but because Islam has always been democratic. Democracy has just been 'forgotten' because the teachings of the Quran are being neglected and need to be revived. This is also the case with science: scientific discovery in the West did not conflict with Islam; it *is* Islam. Although Mawdudi's politics is backward-looking historically, this was because he saw Islam as originally revolutionary and dynamic, and therefore, by looking back, Mawdudi is actually calling for a return to that dynamism which, he believes, has been lost in this modern world. However, as we have seen, it is difficult to believe this Islamic state would really be as 'dynamic' as Mawdudi hoped.

The individual versus the state

Mawdudi's outline for an Islamic state is an authoritarian one to the extent that political coercion would be needed in order to implement Islamic ideology in all aspects of life. In all of his writings, Mawdudi has demonstrated a worrying distrust of the individual. His objective is not to organize a society on the basis of equity and justice – which would seem entirely 'Islamic' in spirit – but to interpret the sovereignty of God as the submission of the individual will to the coercive power of the state apparatus. The fact that it may be conceivable to organize a society on a level that would allow individual free will is a concept that Mawdudi distrusts entirely:

> It is obvious that to organise collective life, in all circumstances there is a need for coercive power, which is called the state. No one has ever denied this need except for the anarchists, or communist theory, which contemplates a stage when humanity would not need a collective state. All these are idealistic contemplations which cannot be supported by observation and experience ... Human history and the knowledge of human nature show that the establishment of civic life is essentially dependent on a coercive power.
>
> (Mawdudi 1969: 67)

Mawdudi concludes that in order to be a good Muslim, and, by definition, a good human being, it is necessary to live in an Islamic state. As has been shown here, he bases this argument on an examination of the past, a time when he saw religion, society and politics united under one *Weltenshauung* ('world-view'). What has also been demonstrated is that this reflection of the past is something of a distorted one. However, even if one is prepared to acknowledge that such a time did exist in the past – and here we are confronted with the classical 'is-ought' dilemma – why does it follow that we must therefore replicate this in the modern world? One thinker who has questioned this is Mohamed **Talbi**. Born in Tunis in 1921, he was educated there and then went on to study in Paris, and here we have another example of a scholar who is very familiar with the fields of the Islamic sciences, but also prepared to incorporate Western ideas.

Talbi, like Mawdudi, places the Quran at the centre of his understanding of what it means to be a Muslim, yet Talbi's interpretation of the Quran differs considerably from that of Mawdudi; for in his exploration of the text he found considerable evidence for a kind of critical reasoning, individual freedom and a pluralism of values that seems so lacking in the more conservative approach to the text as represented by Mawdudi.

Talbi, importantly, makes a distinction between universal ethical principles contained within the Quran and more detailed time-bound injunctions that were meant by God only for the particular situations of their revelation. Therefore, in his view, 'the timeless "wheat" of revelation must be separated from its time-bound "chaff"' (Talbi 1989). This, Talbi argues, is essential if we are to avoid the possibility of imposing a static ideology by applying rules formulated in seventh-century Arabia upon a society for which they are not appropriate. Talbi identifies as a central ethos of the Quran its timelessness and its ability to be relevant for different cultures and different times. However, this flexibility and universal relevance has, in Islamic history, frequently been buried by Muslim conservative scholarship, which, if anything, is often more conservative today than it was during the medieval period.

In Talbi's article 'Religious Liberty: A Muslim Perspective' (1989), he argues for placing the Quran in context when we attempt to determine Islamic ethical and political values. Talbi considers the relationship between Man and God by quoting the Quran: 'He first created man from clay, then made his descendants from an extract of underrated fluid. Then he moulded him: He breathed from His Spirit into him; He gave you hearing, sight, and minds.' (32:7–9). This passage presents Man as dual in nature, from a lower perspective of matter ('created man from clay'), but also able to transcend the material because he possesses God's 'Spirit'. This has significant political and ethical consequences for, whilst in the material sense we are all unequal, what all human beings do possess is the 'breath' of God: the same sacredness and entitlement to be vice-gerent on earth. Compare this with Mawdudi, who understands vicegerency as applicable only to those who are qualified as true Muslims. Here, Talbi argues, 'from a Quranic perspective we may say that human rights are rooted in what every human is by nature, and this is by virtue of God's plan and creation. Thus the cornerstone of all human rights is religious liberty.' For Talbi, this liberty extends to all, including ***dhimmis*** (non-Muslims) and even apostates. This latter belief conflicts with the conservative view that conversion from Islam to another religion is tantamount to treason and could well result in the death penalty. Talbi, however, points out that this view of apostasy rests largely on the precedent set by the first rightly-guided caliph, Abu Bakr, who, in the context of the apostasy wars being fought at the time, associated apostasy with rebellion and the risk of the very survival of the fragile burgeoning Islamic community after the death of the Prophet. In addition, this belief relies upon the hadith 'Anyone who changes religion must be put to death', which may well sound as definitive as you can get, but, as Talbi points out, this hadith is usually mixed in the books of hadith with rebellion and highway robbery and also, according to Talbi, 'we have many good reasons to consider it a forgery'. In the Quran there is no mention of the death penalty required against the apostate; punishment is to be left to God's judgement in the after-life.

The important point here is that Talbi cites examples of mistaken and ill-conceived attempts to inflict time-bound ideals on societies so radically different from their original context. For Talbi, religion should actually be divorced entirely from politics as, he argues, there is no concept of the Islamic state to be found in the Quran, and, even if there was, this does not mean that such a concept can be legitimately applied to the modern world and its concerns.

Even if it could be argued that the Quran does contain political directives, and that Muslims are required to adhere to these directives today, it still remains unclear what these values might be. Talbi engages in hermeneutics (see Chapter 9) to propose a spirit of the Quran that encompasses the principles of freedom, human rights and pluralism, and he argues that the best way to promote these Quranic values in today's society is expressed through democracy. Here, Talbi is not arguing that democracy is a political system contained within the Quran, but rather that democracy is the best way to adhere to what Quranic values are in the Quran. Therefore, Talbi would not be against any other political system per se – even Mawdudi's 'theo-democracy' – provided it is the best system on offer for dispensing the Quran's principles. Talbi would also acknowledge that it may well be the case that in the future a better political system than democracy (or some other form of democracy) may well come along but, until that time, what we have now is the best on offer. There are, of course, some scholars who would go much further and argue that democracy is, as a political system, inherently Islamic, making reference especially to the ancient Arabian (and Quranic) custom of **shura** ('consultation') whereby it is incumbent upon leaders to consult before making any decisions (although this consultation would usually be amongst a small number of the great and the good only), but Talbi rejects the association between shura and democracy because social and economic conditions, and our understanding of what is meant by democracy today, bear no resemblance to how shura was originally applied. As such, the use of shura in the past does not serve as a historical precedent at all.

As we shall see later in this book, Talbi is by no means a lone voice in his call for a contextualization of Islam and the use of hermeneutics. His ideas reflect those of a number of important modern scholars, although it is still a relatively new approach in Islamic scholarship. There is still perhaps some way to go yet, if it will ever be possible, before any agreement has been reached as to which common Quranic ethical principles can provide a foundation for an Islamic political outlook. However, some scholars have argued that Islam is at a crucial point in its history in this respect. For example, the American social anthropologist of Islam, Dale F. Eickleman, in his article 'Inside the Islamic Reformation', makes the assertion that Islam is undergoing something of its own Reformation, which may in future have the same impact on the Islamic world that the Protestant Reformation had on the Christian world. As he says himself, 'We will look back on the latter years of the twentieth century as a time of change as profound for the Muslim world as the Protestant Reformation was for Christendom' (Eickleman 1998: 86). Of course, this now being the twenty-first century, Eickleman's prediction has not quite come to fruition, but perhaps there are certain features of, for example, the Arab Spring that suggest an emergent individualism which is much more critical of official and traditional interpretations of belief and practice, although it has also resulted in greater fanaticism in some respects. Eickleman cites the contemporary Syrian civil engineer Muhammad Shahrur, whose book *The Book and the Qur'an: A Contemporary Interpretation* (1990) has sold many thousands of copies despite an official ban in much of the Middle East. Like Talbi, Shahrur tends towards democracy as his political form, for the same reasons. Eickleman sees this reformation as a depoliticization of Islam that will be more personal. Whether this proves to be the case we will have to wait and see, but it does highlight that it is difficult to talk of 'one Islam'; and it can, perhaps, help us both to understand that Islam is not a monolithic identity – nor is it totally monopolized by a conservative view – and to critique the rarely questioned view that there is no separation between the religious and secular in Islam. It may well be less helpful to make a comparison with the European Protestant Reformation, however, for – although there may well be certain common features, especially the emphasis on a personal interpretation of the holy scripture and the resultant call for individualism – the specific situation that gave rise to the Protestant Reformation, and what it was reforming against, was very different from what is occurring today. In addition, Islam has its own uniqueness and requirements, and any kind of reformation that does occur would cater for Muslims.

One important Islamic thinker who also calls for an Islamic reformation is Tariq **Ramadan** (b. 1962), who in many ways represents the kind of scholar that embraces many different traditions. He was born in Geneva in Switzerland. As he says himself, 'I'm always telling people I'm Swiss by nationality, I'm a Muslim by religion, I'm an Egyptian by memory and I'm a European by culture.' Ramadan is the son of Said Ramadan and Wafa Al-Bana, who was the eldest daughter of Hasan al-Bana, the founder of the Muslim Brotherhood (see Chapter 8). Ramadan studied philosophy and French literature and has a doctorate in Arabic and Islamic studies. His PhD dissertation was titled 'Nietzsche as a Historian of Philosophy'.

In his work *Radical Reform* (2009), Ramadan urges Muslims not to isolate themselves from the West, but rather to fully engage with it, challenging those traditionalists who argue defensively against reform as a foreign import and deviation from Islam. There is, he argues, no conflict between being both a Muslim and a European, and it is quite possible to embrace the laws of a European country and still be a good Muslim, as he emphasizes the differences between religion and culture, arguing that being a citizen of a country and being a religious believer are two different things and should not be confused. Ramadan argues that authentic reform is inherently Islamic and is grounded in the textual sources and intellectual tradition. Western Muslims, instead of looking back to an Arabic Islam, should create a 'Western Islam', in the same way there is an 'Asian Islam' and an 'African Islam', thus emphasizing that Islam is more personal and less monolithic. Therefore, Muslims should look to the textual sources, to the Quran primarily, and interpret them in the light of their own cultural background.

Modernity, 'Westoxification' and the self

Whilst Sunni Islam may be regarded as more pragmatic in political matters on the whole, it is Shia Islam that is politically more esoteric and theoretical in its approach. This is no more evident than in modern-day Iran, which is an example of a society that has undergone a number of political transformations in a relatively short period of time and where, recently, a number of intellectuals have called for no less than an epistemological revolution.

Before we can consider the philosophical thought underlying Iranian political theory, we need to have some background, going back to its colonial period to understand why Iran has reacted against what it sees as the threat of Western modernity. During the nineteenth century, Iran was frequently little more than a pawn in the 'Great Game' of Russian and British empire-building, and suffered terribly as a result, experiencing poverty and political instability. The Russians occupied northern Iran in 1911; the British occupied much of western Iran during World War I and stayed there until 1921. In that year Reza Khan (1878–1944), the prime minister of Iran, declared himself Shah after a coup. The Shah initiated a vast modernization programme, although he was forced to abdicate in 1941 by Britain and the USSR,who were troubled by his links to Germany. The new Shah was Mohammed Reza Pahlavi (1919–80), although, during World War II, Iran was once more occupied by Britain and Russia. In 1951, Mohammad Mosaddegh (1882–1967) was democratically elected prime minister, and he was popular with the people when he nationalized the nation's petroleum industry, much to the concern of Britain and America, who relied on these oil supplies. In 1953, America, with support from Britain and with the concurrence of the Shah, organized a successful operation to overthrow Mossaddegh, the first time the US had – openly anyway – overthrown an elected civilian government of a state. Following this, the Shah became close allies with Britain and America and modernized Iran, under what was called the White Revolution, which effectively 'Westernized' Iran, although his rule became increasingly autocratic, corrupt and repressive.

By the mid 1970s this oppression led to growing domestic unrest and, in 1978, major demonstrations against the Shah resulted in the Iranian Revolution. The Shah fled the country in January 1979, and the Grand Ayatollah Ruhollah Khomeini (1902–89) took the reins of government as both religious and political leader, presiding over an Islamic revolution that attempted to rid Iran of all Western influence, as well as all possible opposition to the clerical regime. Back in 1963, Khomeini had publicly protested against the White Revolution. He was arrested for his involvement and, in 1964, sent into exile, first to Turkey and then on to Iraq. In the Shia religious centre of Najaf in Iraq, where he spent the next 15 years, Khomeini was able to sermonize against the Iranian regime and these powerful lectures were taped and distributed in the streets of Tehran. His lectures were published as *Islamic Government: Guardianship by the Clergy*, which formulated the role of the clergy in government with specific reference to the contentious concept *vilayat-i faqih* ('guardianship by the clergy', see below). During the 1970s, Khomeini became a central figure for militant religious opposition to the government, with many of his supporters suggesting that he was the 'Hidden Imam'. Khomeini was expelled from Iraq, and he took refuge in Paris until his return in 1979. Since that time there has been an uneasy relationship between the clergy and the state, and it is fair to say that currently Iran is undergoing something of an identity crisis, with various prime minsters sometimes arguing for greater democracy, freedom of expression and friendship with the West, while at other times they are more insular, autocratic and suspicious. It was during the turbulent period of the 1960s and 1970s especially, however, that philosophical thought on the nature of the state and authority was prevalent and lively, although also considered to be of continued relevance today.

At the centre of the philosophical call for an epistemological revolution is, some might say surprisingly, the German philosopher Martin **Heidegger** (1889–1976), who was to be a major influence on such Iranian intellectuals as Ahmad Fardid, Jalal Al-e Ahmad, Ali Shariati and Dariush Shayegan. Heidegger's philosophy is enormously complex, but here an attempt will be made to explain some salient points in order to highlight the arguments expressed by the above-mentioned Iranian thinkers. What these thinkers do, on the whole, share is an anti-Western rhetoric, which is also coupled with a view of philosophical 'authenticity' that is found in the writings of Heidegger. This quest for authenticity is coupled with an aim for fundamental and universal truths, and, for this reason, it is hostile to democracy, which is seen as synonymous with diversity.

Heidegger himself is an inheritor of the philosophical views of Nietzsche and Kierkegaard. Nietzsche, for his part, was critical of Christian morality and Western modernity, which he saw as symptomatic of a spiritual crisis in Europe during his time. Nietzsche highlighted the faith in democracy especially as causing the decline, which resulted in mediocrity rather than 'great culture'. Nietzsche, although not in any way a detailed political theorist, nonetheless called for a radical epistemological transformation that would inevitably have political consequences. Heidegger shared this view, deploring democracy and arguing for a new culture for politics and society. He saw the move towards modernity as soulless, and it is unfortunate that in Heidegger's case he naively saw the National Socialists as representative of this new spiritual revolution, coupled as it was with a German nationalism that Heidegger shared. Leaving aside Heidegger's own misguided political views, in a broader sense his philosophy can be seen as a critique of modernism and what it represents, and in this respect is not unfamiliar to the Muslim intellectuals who also engaged in an anti-modernist critique. For Heidegger, and indeed other German intellectuals, a distinction was made between *Kultur* and *Zivilization*; the former involves the cultivation of the spirit, while the latter is representative of Western decadence as characterized by materialism, as well as the political values of liberalism, individualism and democracy.

Heidegger's major work *Being and Time* is, amongst other things, an attempt to rescue us from this demise into decadence and spiritual emptiness. This would require a total transformation of values. Putting this in the Iranian context, we can see from the brief history of the country in the twentieth century why many have developed a hostility towards the West, perhaps not so much geographically speaking, but as an ideology, a belief that upholds democracy and materialism as essential goods. During the Iranian Revolution, the people of Iran effectively turned their backs on the material gains of 'Westernization' and preferred to put their support in religious leadership.

Heidegger, in a substitute for Western secularism and its perceived soulless rationalism, presents a utopia that is somewhat mystical and semi-religious, and therefore it is not surprising that it might appeal to the Iranian intelligentsia, given that many already saw Shia Islam as considerably more 'spiritual' than its

Sunni counterpart. Heidegger both looks forward and looks back, for he argues that the West needs to 'return' to its forgotten origins of Hellenic culture; the past is an essential part of us and it shapes our future, yet we have fallen into a state of alienation with our past. While the idea of being alienated from our traditions is not new with Heidegger (Marx and Weber argued the same), what is significant is that this alienation is inauthentic. Our selves have been uprooted from our tradition, from our very being, which is our hidden spiritual life. Modern society is inauthentic because it has allowed us to forget our Being and gives us emptiness in return, or what Heidegger called nihilism. 'Being' was a spiritual concern for Heidegger, which he believed concealed the essential grounding for Man.

The dominant Western tradition, therefore, is inauthentic, and so authenticity must be restored. This idea took hold amongst the Iranian intelligentsia during the 1979 revolution. The Shah was seen as nothing more than a puppet of American and British interest, and his White Revolution was the imposition of an 'alien outside' that tears the people from their Being. The most important philosopher in Iran to first identify the Heideggerian critique with what was occurring in Iran was Ahmad **Fardid** (1912–94). Fardid studied philosophy at Tehran University, the Sorbonne in Paris and the University of Heidelberg in Germany, and so it is no surprise that he studied the works of French existential figures as well as the German Heidegger. Fardid refashioned Heidegger's philosophy to fit the Iranian context, and argued that Iran's spiritual essence had been submerged by Western technological nihilism. He presents a dualism whereby there is opposition between the inauthentic West and the authentic essence of the 'Orient', which represents holy scripture and divine revelation. This idea was developed by Jalal Al-e **Ahmad** (1923–69), who coined the term 'Westoxification' (*gharbzadegi*). Ahmad had, in his time, been a Marxist, then a nationalist, then a Sartrean existentialist before embracing Islam, and his work *Westoxification*, written in 1962, became a blueprint for revolutionary change amongst the Iranian intelligentsia. While recognizing that the West itself was 'diseased' by modernity, this disease had spread to Iran, and so the people must look to a 'true' Iranian culture, an 'authentic' Islamic identity, to relieve itself of the toxicity of the West. Ahmad did not, however, wish to get rid of modernity, but rather to transfigure it: 'I am not speaking of rejecting the machine or of banishing it, as the utopians of the early nineteenth century sought to do … it is a question of how to encounter the machine and technology.' There is nothing wrong with technology as such, but it is our attitude towards it when we allow it to rule over us: 'the god of technology had for years exercised absolute rule over Europe mounted on the throne of its banks and stock exchanges, and it no longer tolerated any other god, laughing in the face of every tradition and ideology'. The only remedy, therefore, is not the abolition of technology, but for its subservience under the rule of Shia spiritualism. This does not involve a 'return' to old, pre-modern and tribal ways, but rather to reconfigure tradition so that it can accommodate modernity whilst being authentic.

Ahmad was certainly the most influential philosopher in Iran in the 1960s, but it was Ali **Shariati** (1933–77) who dominated the intellectual scene in the 1970s. Shariati was born in Mazinan in eastern Iran in 1933. He was initially educated in Mashhad, where his father, Muhammad Taqi Shariati, a one-time cleric who chose to become a teacher, established the Centre for the Spread of Islamic Teachings to propagate the progressive element of Islam. The purpose of this centre was to educate youths who saw Islam and modernity as compatible, but nonetheless rejected secularism as an option. Consequently, the centre was resistant to not only secularists, but also to the conservative ulama of the time. Ali Shariati, from an early age, was an active member of the centre and has written of the importance of his father in the formation of his own ideas. Shariati not only studied Persian literature, but also foreign literature, as well as poetry and philosophy. He graduated from Mashhad's Teacher Training College in 1952 and began teaching at a high school, while also writing, with the publication of *A History of the Development of Philosophy* in 1956; and, if that was not enough to take up his time, he enrolled as an undergraduate in Persian literature at the University of Masshad. Important in the development of his own philosophy was that his role as a teacher, as well as a university student and his activities at his father's centre, meant that Shariati was in very close contact with the young and intelligent class of Iran who, in more cases than not, seemed disillusioned with the state of their nation at the time and its cultural colonization by the West. Shariati's writings reflect this concern, and he considers how the people can respond to this. He recognized that a spiritual vacuum existed amongst the youth of Iran, who were not only disenchanted with Western materialism but, although prepared to look to Islam for answers, also disappointed by the quietist conservatism of the ulama and, for that matter, their lecturers. Shariati argued that Shia Islam is a distinct school of thought, and he is to be credited with giving it a modern and fully articulated revolutionary ideology that learns from concepts of modernity but does not simply imitate them, in particular by borrowing categories from, especially, Marxism, while at the same time insisting that these have been inherent within Islam from the beginning.

The events that were occurring in Iran at the time, including the coup that was organized with support from the US and Britain, left a great impression on Shariati, who coined the term *Zar-o Zoor-o Tazvir* ('wealth, coercion, deceit') to describe the capitalist elite, the intrusions of the US and Britain and the obscurantist policies of the official clergy. Shariati proved to be a brilliant scholar at the University of Masshad, and was able to do graduate studies at the University of Paris in 1960. This was another formative experience in Shariati's thought: he was both attracted by the intellectually enlightened ideas of the Parisian, whilst being equally appalled by the decadence of Paris. The intellectual environment, however, allowed him to encounter the works of French and European sociology and philosophy. This was during a period of intense student radicalism and he was particularly influenced by Third World movements. He attended lectures by the French scholar of Islam and history Louis

Massignon (1883–1962) as well as other Marxist scholars. Shariati, in his writings, certainly shows an appreciation and understanding of Western ideology, while also looking to Shia Islam for additional dimensions such as love, redemption, reward, resurrection and eternity, which he believed were lacking in the West. He was also not just a thinker, but was politically active, supporting Algerian and other liberation movements, joining the Confederation of Iranian Students and the (Iranian) National Front and becoming editor of its newsletter, 'Free Iran'. He advocated revolutionary armed struggle against the Iranian regime and he supported the uprisings that took place in Tehran in 1963 against the increasing capitalism and corruption. His ideological views at this time reflected most strongly those of the revolutionary militant French West Indian political theorist and philosopher Frantz Fanon (1925–61), perhaps the leading anti-colonial thinker of the twentieth century, who was nonetheless highly controversial in defending the right of colonized people to engage in violence in their struggle for independence. Interestingly, although Shariati was largely critical of the ulama in Iran because of their unwillingness to engage in politics at all, he does praise Ayatollah Khomeini as an exception. For his part in the 1963 riots, Khomeini was exiled to Turkey and then to Iraq.

Shariati completed his doctorate and returned to Iran in 1964, where he was immediately arrested because of his anti-government activities. He spent two months in Khoy prison in Azerbaijan and, after his release, he inevitably struggled to get a teaching position until he obtained a post teaching history at his *alma mater* the University of Masshad in 1966. By all accounts he was a very popular teacher. He made frequent lecture trips to Tehran, giving talks at the debating institutions known as *Husayniya-yi Irshad*. *Husayniyas* ('centres for religious education'), named after the martyred Imam Husayn, and were common institutions in Iran. They were usually located next to a mosque and, whereas the mosque was usually restricted to congregational prayers and other more formal religious practices, they welcomed speakers on often controversial religious issues, so the government kept a watchful eye upon them. Not surprisingly, Shariati's popular talks resulted in his arrest once more in 1973, although he was allowed to leave for Europe in 1977. He died in Britain in the same year under suspicious circumstances: the British coroner reported that he had died of a massive heart attack, whilst his supporters blamed SAVAK, the Iranian secret police.

Shariati appreciated the popular appeal of Marxism in his time, but he argued that Islam was more humanistic in its values, while also possessing an inherent sympathy with the masses. Shariati looked to the Islamic sources, and he interpreted the role of Man as God's vicegerent on Earth as a reference to all people, rather than a small minority or, again in Mawdudi's understanding, those elite who are suitably qualified to be called 'Muslim'. Therefore, God's vicegerency was synonymous with power to the masses, to *al nas* ('the people'). Shariati saw the umma in Marxist terms as a class-free people. In his work *The Sociology of Islam*, Shariati uses a term we have come across already (Chapter 5): the '**theomorphic man**', a 'Perfect Man' who possesses the qualities of truth, goodness and beauty, a rebellious spirit who combines the virtues of Jesus, Caesar and Socrates. As we have seen, this concept of the theomorphic being owes much to Arabi's concept of the Perfect Man and draws upon Sufi concepts of the Perfect Man (insan-al-kamil), which were also developed by the Indian poet and reformer Muhammad Iqbal, as well as Nietzsche's Übermensch. Shariati's criticism of the West is summed up neatly in the following passage:

> Both these social systems, capitalism and communism, though they differ in outward configuration, regard man as an economic animal … Humanity is every day more condemned to alienation, more drowned in this mad maelstrom of compulsive speed. Not only is there no longer leisure for growth in human values, moral greatness, and spiritual aptitudes, but this being plunged headlong in working to consume, consuming to work, this diving into lunatic competition for luxuries and diversions, has caused traditional moral values to decline and disappear as well.
>
> (Shariati 1980: 13)

What is interesting concerning the above quote is that although capitalism and communism are rivals and very different in so many ways, this is only in their 'outward configuration'. Here Shariati demonstrates the view that historical reality is divided into two layers: a surface layer, where rival ideologies appear antagonistic, but also a deeper, concealed layer of metaphysical truth, where they are in reality one. Shariati sees Islam in the same way, with a surface layer of difference, diversity and nihilism, but with an underlying 'soul' of social inclusion and higher spiritual values. Here Shariati also demonstrates a familiarity with Heidegger, whom he admired as a 'religious' thinker, arguing that politics is, or rather should be, an ontological enterprise, a quest for authenticity and unity rather than the pursuit of various '-isms'.

This is a utopian, but also Heideggerian vision that foresees the coming of a dark and dispirited world where mankind is alienated from itself, but which can find salvation through a spiritual rebirth. For this salvation, Shariati looks to Islam, but this is not a backward-looking return to the Islamic source material, in the Mawdudian way; instead, he examines the concerns of people in the modern world and how Islam can imbue those concerns with its own spirit, which, Shariati states, shows 'a fundamental bond, an existential relation (between man and the world), in regarding the two as arising from a single (sublime) origin'.

In more practical terms, Shariati argued in his influential pamphlet *What Is to Be Done?* that there would be a revolution undertaken by a militant band of intellectuals, rather than the ulama. Whilst the conservative ulama were offended by his teachings, Khomeini, without openly acknowledging his debt to Shariati, would frequently employ slogans created by Shariati, which gave the impression amongst his followers that Khomeini was far more liberal in his outlook than he turned out to be. However, it was no doubt due to Shariati's inspiration that Khomeini rebelled against the general view of most of the clergy that they should not play a part in politics. It is interesting that whereas Ali Shariati saw the Perfect Man as an empowerment of the masses in an existential sense, Khomeini saw it in a hierarchical elitist sense, and many of his followers saw Khomeini as this Perfect Man, if not the Mahdi (the 'messiah' or, rather, the return of the twelfth imam: see glossary) himself, an observation Khomeini neither denied nor admitted to. In Khomeini's writing and his lectures he argued that for Islam to be rejuvenated it must look to the Perfect Man for spiritual and political leadership. Criticizing the Shah, Khomeini argued that a monarchical state is incompatible with Islamic ideals, and he also rejects nationalism in favour of Islamic universalism, although this inevitably is Shia in character.

In the absence of a Perfect Man to guide them, Khomeini argued that the clergy should step into the breach and not merely advise the government, but take over the government and rule directly. This doctrine of 'rule by the jurists' (vilayat-i faqih) had little Quranic support, as well as being rejected by virtually all of the Shia clergy. However, for Khomeini, the concept of rule by jurists was a logical conclusion to the much more widely held view that an Islamic state, if it were to be truly Islamic, must be governed by Islamic principles, enshrined in the sharia. If the sharia is meant to be a complete guide for all, then, logically, there is no need for human legislation whatsoever. In practice, however, new concerns and issues arise on a day-to-day basis which sharia is not specific enough to address adequately, in which case experts are required to interpret sharia so that it can be applied to specific circumstances. Shia Islam has a long tradition of independent reasoning, or 'ijtihad', and Khomeini argued that those best qualified for ijtihad are the jurists, the mullahs. Khomeini presents a view of his Republic of Iran not unlike Plato's hypothetical 'Republic': a state ruled by Philosopher-Kings who, naturally, should rule as they have access to moral truths. Similarly, the 'Guardians', or the ayatollahs, had access to God's law by nature of being the most learned. It is an additional boon if one amongst them is suspected of being the Perfect Man with near infallibility in his decision making, and, as mentioned above, it was this eponym that was sometimes attached to Khomeini.

Shariati, for his part, never lived long enough to see the Iranian Revolution. In his latter years, no doubt affected by the time he had spent behind bars, Shariati became more concerned with issues related to freedom. In his *Revolutionary Reconstruction of the Self* he states that total freedom is to be equated with Islamic emancipation. This notion of freedom should not be understood in the liberal democratic sense of the term, but in the existential sense of freedom of the self. This freedom undoubtedly has a political narrative – in the same way it does for Nietzsche, Heidegger and Sartre – but it is also about one's personal response to one's place in the world. Therefore, political liberation was closely tied to a mystical enlightenment of the self, which can be achieved through reflecting upon the spiritual aspects of life.

Further reading

Axworthy, M. (2013), *Revolutionary Iran: A History of the Islamic Republic*, London: Allen Lane.

Jackson, R. (2010), *Mawlana Mawdudi and Political Islam: Authority and the Islamic State*, Abingdon: Routledge.

Ramadan, T. (2005), *Western Muslims and the Future of Islam*, New York: Oxford University Press.

——(2009), *Radical Reform: Islamic Ethics and Liberation*, New York: Oxford University Press.

Shariati, A. (1980), *Marxism and Other Western Fallacies: An Islamic Critique*, Jakarta: Mizan Publishing.

7 Ethical dilemmas

The extent to which the religious and secular can be separated according to Islamic sources is open to considerable debate, as we have seen in relation to politics in the previous chapter. However, this does not prevent many Muslims who strive, nonetheless, to provide a comprehensive religious-moral system in which Islamic values are embedded at all levels of society, so that all human institutions, whether they are political or cultural, are subject to the will of God. Consequently, the important question that needs to be considered is whether such striving for an ethical philosophy from Islamic sources is really possible in the modern world, given the rapid changes and new ethical dilemmas that continue to arise. It would not be possible to pay attention to all the ethical issues in the twenty-first century, but it will certainly help to see how Islamic paradigms work in practice by focusing on specific contemporary moral issues.

The problem of suffering, evil and health

If you ever have an occasion to visit a Muslim country you will likely come across the term '*inshallah*' used, frequently, at the end of a sentence. It means 'if God will it' and, though seemingly thrown in somewhat casually, has major philosophical and moral implications in term of our actions and responsibility to ourselves and to others; for it suggests a kind of fatalism, that no matter what we as human beings do, ultimately we have no power, and the results of our actions rest with God. This is a subtle deterministic orthodoxy, which, however, is starting to be questioned in today's more individualistic, existential and choice-oriented world. In this section I wish to consider how this increasing awareness of the power of the human to overcome difficulties – rather than passively submit to fate – has an effect on the issue of human suffering.

When we talk of acts of moral evil, we mean what humans inflict upon other humans (or other creatures). For example: torture, murder, stealing, bullying (physical or mental) and so on. Here the moral responsibility rests with the person who engages in the act, who may or may not feel remorse and guilt as a result of these actions. What we call physical or natural evils include tsunamis, plagues, earthquakes, disease and the like. These actions are not – at least directly – a result of human actions (natural disasters may indirectly be a result of what humans are doing to the environment). A point here needs to be made concerning human disease: if a person succumbs to a disease as a result of, say, an epidemic or some other cause over which that person has no control, then this is regarded as a physical evil. However, if a person is ill or diseased as a result of, say, bad eating habits, or smoking, or driving dangerously, then it is a moral evil because that person has inflicted suffering upon himself, which may also cause suffering to others. According to traditional Islamic thinking, natural evil reminds us that human beings are frail creatures, subject to the will of an all-powerful God whose actions remain mysterious. In terms of moral evil, the fact that a person feels guilt and remorse as a result of their actions is a demonstration of God's moral code acting upon human conscience.

Human beings can, and indeed will, suffer from both natural and moral evils, and so we need to consider how Islam can respond to a given fact of life that all of us experience, though, for some, to a much greater extent than others. The Quran has something to say concerning moderation: 'Children of Adam, dress well whenever you are at worship, and eat and drink (as We have permitted) but do not be extravagant: God does not like extravagant people' (7:31). Both physical and moral suffering is here seen as self-inflicted due to an overindulgence of God's bounty, a result of eating too much or engaging in other sensual pleasures to excess. This is supported by various hadith which report that the Prophet Muhammad condemned those who lack moderation in their consumption; he advised people to look after their health, including engaging in physical exercise, for physical and psychological well-being – though a divine gift – cannot be taken for granted. However, this is all very well if we have in fact been given health in the first place, but what of those who do suffer from illness that is not of their own choosing, for example, a disease that is inherited genetically? Suffering that is not a result of human actions raises questions concerning the goodness and justice of God and the extent to which God is to blame for this kind of suffering. This religious attitude to suffering also affects how illness and suffering is treated or alleviated, especially if the subject of the suffering sees his or her pain as an expression of God's power which the individual has no way to comprehend and must remain humble, compared with a secular medical response which sees the human as powerful and able to conquer this pain, at least to some extent. For a devout Muslim, such an attitude can smack of hubris for it displaces God's will.

Technology can achieve much and, in the future, will achieve more, especially in terms of extending a person's lifespan and alleviating physical suffering (mental suffering is another matter). However, this can also be seen as conflicting with God's plan to give us all a specific lifespan and to allot a time when we die: 'Everyone on earth perishes; all that remains is the Face of your Lord, full of majesty, bestowing honour' (55:26). Whilst technology certainly has not reached the stage of preventing all on Earth from perishing, it may delay it, although, of course, it may also result in causing the Earth to perish *sooner* than God has planned. What has hopefully been demonstrated throughout this book is the importance for Muslims of God's omnipotence, and so anything that attempts to infringe upon this power may be seen as suspiciously Frankensteinian, even in the case of helping human beings' physical condition, for humans are only stewards of the body, not owners. Nonetheless, the philosophical quandary of resolving the conflict between God's power over all created things, including human destiny (*qadar*), and God's justice when confronted with, for example, the suffering of children and the innocent is one that all Muslims need to consider. This quest for understanding and for an 'Islamic' position on such matters is made more difficult because Islam does not have the equivalent of the Vatican Council in Catholicism. There are inevitably contrasting views amongst not only Sunni and Shia theologians, but amongst the theologians themselves within these respective traditions. Historically, the Islamic response to the existence of evil has been incredibly diverse, with Asharite views emphasizing God's will, which resulted in absolving humans of any moral responsibility, to the extent that the Umayyad caliphs blamed their own somewhat dubiously moral actions on the will of God rather than on themselves. The Mutazalite and Shia view, on the other hand, has tended to blame humans for moral evil.

The Quran does not contain within it a coherent moral code, as we have already seen, and so it is no easy task to determine a 'Quranic' response to suffering and evil. For example, consider these two verses:

> No misfortune can happen, either in the earth or in yourselves, that was not set down in writing before We brought it into being – that is easy for God – so you need not grieve for what you miss or gloat over what you gain.
>
> (57:22)

> By your Lord, they [the hypocrites] will not be true believers until they let you decide between them in all matters of dispute, and find no resistance in their souls to your decisions, accepting them totally – if We had ordered, 'lay down your lives' or 'Leave your homes,' they would not have done so, except for a few – it would have been far better for them and stronger confirmation of their faith, if they had done as they were told and We would have given them a rich reward of Our own and guided them to a straight path.
>
> (4:65–68)

Any interpreter of the first passage would consider all actions as the will of God, and so there is no point lamenting over one's suffering or, in contrast, congratulating oneself or others for successes in life. However, this is very different in the second passage where the 'hypocrites' – those who pledge a nominal and pragmatic allegiance to Islam but do not really have faith in their hearts – are masters of their own fate: they can *choose* to follow God's will or turn away from it. How is the believer meant to respond to these conflicting views of God? Consider another Quranic quote, which occurs when those who, after converting to Islam, still experienced suffering in battle, although they had expected to be immune now they were under God's power:

> Why do you [believers] say, when a calamity befalls you, even after you have inflicted twice as much damage [on your enemy], 'How did this happen?' [Prophet], say, 'You brought it upon yourselves.'
>
> (3:166)

The above quote is supported by the following: 'It was not God who wronged them [the disbelievers]; they wronged themselves' (3:117). The emphasis on these passages does suggest greater human responsibility for their actions.

One feature that comes across in a number of passages attributes human evil to disbelievers or hypocrites. This is not so much to say that disbelief is in itself an evil, but that the consequences of disbelief – disobeying God's will which, because it issues from God, must be good – logically means that one is immoral. Disobedience towards God, the highest authority, is a grave sin (*kabira*) that results in divine punishment in this world, the next or in both, unless atoned for. Offences against one's equals are a minor sin (*saghira*), which is disapproved of by God and requires the offender to seek forgiveness. In practice, of course, it can be rather difficult to distinguish when an act is against God and when it is against an equal; if you steal from another person you are obviously committing an offence against that person, but also committing a sin in the eyes of God. It is these kinds of ambiguities that make it difficult for the interpreter.

One interesting hadith that is often quoted is '[t]here is no disease that God has created, except that he has also created its treatment.' This seems to counter the view that those suffering from disease, or those witnessing such suffering, should passively accept this as God's will. Rather, given that God has created a treatment it is human responsibility to seek out this treatment. It is no coincidence, therefore, that Muslims were among the first in the world to build hospitals, or that scholars paid particular attention to medical texts amongst the Greek and Persian works that were discovered. In the Muslim prayer of thanksgiving, not only do the believers give thanks to God for all his blessings but also '[t]o You belongs praise for all the good affliction with which you have inured me.' The idea of a 'good affliction' is that through suffering we evolve spiritually, a notion not uncommon in Christian theodicy with the concept of evil as 'soul-making'. Importantly, this does not mean that suffering is welcome and passively accepted, but rather it is identified, and all attempts are made to heal the suffering so that the person can continue to live life a spiritually better person. In this sense, health and illness are seen not as isolated physical experiences, but as psychological and spiritual ones too. Having said all that, whereas Christianity has, over the years, developed sophisticated theodicies in attempts to address the imbalance between God as all-good and the facts of human nature as one of suffering, in the case of Islam, the late Rev. Kenneth Cragg (1913–2012) is correct when he says that Islam 'ignores or neglects or does not hear these questions [about the injustices in human society] … It does not find a theodicy necessary either for its theology or its worship' (Cragg and Speight 1987: 16). In comparison with Christianity, Islam still has some way to go, although to some extent the question can be asked whether the believers really regard such debate as necessary, given the emphasis on submission to God and an acceptance of His will, together with a belief that suffering is, quite simply, an acknowledgement that we cannot take health and justice for granted.

Abortion

Within the Muslim world, the practice of contraception has a long history, and it has moral implications when considered in the light of the termination of potential life. This, however, must also be evaluated against the issue of the right of a woman to have power over her own body, and so it is up to her as to when or if she wants a baby. However, it is a virtual consensus amongst the jurists that the husband should be asked permission if contraception is to be used, and this has also been considered a mutual thing: a man must get permission from his wife should he wish to use contraception. Culturally there is the added pressure that having children is regarded as a sign of having entered manhood and, indeed, womanhood, although the statements of jurists on these matters is concerned mostly with temporary contraception on the basis that a man has the right to have offspring at some point in time. Therefore, we are talking here of endorsing family planning, rather than having no family at all, and there are a number of hadith in which the Prophet encouraged large families.

Whilst the *temporary* prevention of potential life is permissible, what of the termination of actual life? Partly the problem here is the issue of how 'life' is defined and when it begins. A much-quoted passage from the Quran is the following: 'Do not kill your children for fear of poverty – We shall provide for them and for you – killing them is a great sin' (17:31). Contextually, this passage is a reference to the custom of infanticide, especially of baby girls, at this time (see also 81:8). Nonetheless, the passage incorporates the ethical principle of protecting the weak against self-interest. The 'weak' in this case may well be babies and children, but in Islamic tradition there is no permission given to abort a foetus, even if it is found to have a genetic disease or some other abnormality. This is made more complicated by the fact that Islamic tradition is unclear when life as such begins, with no distinction made between an embryo and a foetus, and so the question of when one has possession of full human rights remains disputed, given that the various law schools differ on these matters. The Quran does not refer to abortion as such, only to the sanctity of life, and so the best that can be determined from the scripture is that life is precious, and killing the weak and innocent is a serious crime. Recognition that there are biological stages of development can help to determine when life begins. In the Quran, the Meccan sura 23:12–14 states:

> We created man from an essence of clay, then We placed him as a drop of fluid in a safe place, then We made that drop into a clinging form, and We made that form into a lump of flesh, and later We made that lump into bones, and We clothed those bones with flesh, and later We made him into other forms [infancy, childhood, maturity].
>
> (23:12–14)

The significance of this passage is the recognition that life as such does go through various stages of development, although this does not help in determining when one becomes a person with accompanying legal status. What is more helpful in this respect is a hadith by Bukhari (one of the more reliable hadith collectors) that is given considerable status by both Sunni and Shia legal scholars, in which Muhammad is reported as saying:

> Each one of you in creation amasses in his mother's womb [in the form of the drop, the *nutfa*] for forty days; then he becomes a blood clot for the same period; then the angel is sent with a mandate [to write down] four things [for the child]: his sustenance, his term of life, his deeds, and whether he will be miserable or happy. [Another authoritative version then adds the following] Then the angel is sent to breathe into him the spirit (*al-ruh*).
>
> (Bukhari)

Leaving aside the predestination issues here, jurists have tended to identify the time when the angel breathes in the spirit as the moment of ensoulment and therefore the foetus has the identity of personhood. The actual timing of this event varies amongst traditions from the 40th, 42nd, 45th, or 120th day! However, this does not result in consensus that ensoulment is the beginning of legal rights, for some would argue that abortion is not permitted *before* that time, going back as far as the 'drop' (*nutfa*) stage as part of human creation, i.e. the zygotic stage. However, there is a consensus that once ensoulment has occurred, abortion is unlawful (unless the mother's life is in danger or in the case of rape or incest), although when ensoulment occurs is still debatable. For all, though, 120 days is the maximum. The reason for the importance of ensoulment is that traditions state that before ensoulment the foetus is not yet a human being and therefore will not be resurrected on the Day of Judgement, but this does conflict with another tradition which refers to the foetus being in heaven, although it does not state at what stage of foetal development it is.

Morally, the issue of the legal status of the unborn is growing in importance with stem cell research and the use of embryos. The following passage in the Quran (41:53) has relevance here: 'We shall show them Our signs in every region of the earth and in themselves, until it becomes clear to them that this is the Truth. Is it not enough that your Lord witnesses everything?' The 'signs' here are God's creation – nature – which operates in an orderly and purposeful way according to God's plan. This passage is essentially a condensed design argument, with nature as evidence of the existence of God. But if scientists are in a position to improve on nature by producing healthier children or clone better people, then how does this affect God's plan and nature's order?

An important principle that is often invoked in ethical matters is **maslaha**, which means 'public good'. It is a recognition that the traditional sources of the Quran and the Sunna cannot always address societies that are in a constant state of change, and that to some extent one should rely on human reason to decide what is best for human beings. The term was used by the Andalusian lawyer Imam Abu Ishaq al-Shatibi (d. 1388), who argued that we need to look at the relationship between humans for social solutions, rather than the relationship between humans and God. One of the key founders of Islamic modernism, the Egyptian jurist Muhammad Abduh (*c.* 1849–1945) also recognized it as an important basis for reconciling modernism with tradition. The term 'maslaha' has become prominent in recent years on the issue of Islamic finance, especially in an attempt to reconcile the ban on interest rates with what is best for the prosperity of the Muslim community. Here, then, is introduced a social dimension to moral responsibility. Given that advances in biotechnology and medicine can be viewed as being of considerable benefit to the Muslim community, then the principle of maslaha needs to be considered in making moral decisions, especially as neither the Quran nor the Sunna has anything to say directly concerning these new technologies. However, this principle also needs to adhere to another principle that may or may not conflict with it, the so-called 'No harm, no harassment' (*la darar was la dirar fi al-islam*) rule. By 'harm' (*darar*) what is meant is 'detriment, loss' and this refers to the individual person. Therefore, an important moral consideration of any action is that it should not result in the detriment or loss of a person's property, dignity or personal interest. 'Harassment' (*dirar*) means literally 'harming, injuring or hurting in return', and so there should be no requital or revenge undertaken. In effect, no law or moral decision should be made that results in harm for anyone in society, whether intentionally, unintentionally or as a result of revenge. This principle, it should be kept in mind, is not always strictly applied, and it will depend on how complicated a case happens to be, for there is yet another principle, called the 'right of discretion' (*taslit*) of an owner over all his possessions, that can come into play under certain given circumstances. Here the 'greater good' is 'a major consideration'. For example, if you wish to donate your kidney to save your child's life, although you are harming yourself, as you have ownership over your own body the right of discretion may allow you to do this. However, this may not always be the case: one example comes from a hadith in which a man who owned a property would walk through a neighbour's garden to get to it on regular occasions. This upset his neighbours and the Prophet determined that the principle of 'no harm, no harassment' overruled the 'right of discretion'.

Coming back then to the use of biotechnology for the benefit of the community, this will need to be considered in terms of the harm it does to individuals. Muslim jurists have, therefore, denied the use of medical treatment which is experimental on this principle, even if it may result in the 'greater good' overall. However, although this concern for the health of the individual should be lauded, there is also the pressing need to alleviate the suffering from poverty and disease of so many, a large proportion of which occurs in Islamic countries, in Africa especially. The decision to refuse experimentation on the basis of 'no harm' can also result in passivity, given these kinds of decisions are usually made by a small elite in non-democratic countries and involve little debate on these ethical issues. As one example, when Dolly the sheep was cloned in 1997, this resulted in incredible public interest and debate amongst the scientific community in the Western world, yet the Muslim world remained virtually silent on the matter, at least in the sense of debate concerning how this related to Islamic ethics.

Cloning

One very interesting comment comes from a leading Egyptian scholar, Yusuf al-Qaradawi (b. 1926), who was asked whether he thought human cloning was interfering in the creation of God and opposing God's will. He responded with:

> 'Oh no, no one can challenge or oppose God's will. Hence, if the matter is accomplished then it is certainly under the will of God. Nothing can be created without God's will facilitating its creation. As long as humans continue to do so, it is the will of God. Actually, we do not raise the question whether it is in accord with the will of God. Our question is whether the matter is licit or not.'
>
> (Sachedina 2009: 201)

Some thought-provoking points here: first, this is, at least, somewhat more enlightened than the remarks of some other Muslim judges at the time, who declared that cloning is the work of Satan! Second, there is no conflict perceived between what Man achieves and the plan of God, which, logically, makes sense given that Man is part of God's plan. And, third, the concern with whether the matter is 'licit or not' reflects the more general Islamic preoccupation with legal matters, rather than moral concerns. Qaradawi is nonetheless concerned about the effect technology can have on human life, stressing the importance of family for the development of a human being.

Cloning and other technological advances in medical science are also regarded with suspicion by many Muslim jurists because they see them to be Western imports and, therefore, just more attempts to impose Western ideas to the detriment of Muslim ethical values, hence Qaradawi's concern for the possible effect on family values, which is seen as reflected in the Quran and the hadith. Having said that, Islamic tradition encourages the pursuit of knowledge 'even as far as China' and science is seen by some scholars as not against the laws of nature, but rather uncovering the laws of nature, citing such Quranic passages as: 'Have you not considered how God has made everything on the earth of service to you?' (22:65). Much of the concern regarding cloning is based on the possibility of the technology being abused, which is symptomatic of human frailty more than anything else, as reference to another Quranic passage takes note: 'Do you not see those who, in exchange for God's favour, offer only ingratitude and make their people end up in the home of ruin?' (14:28).

Ending life

We have seen above that regardless of what science or technology may say regarding when life begins, and therefore when one becomes a 'person', for the purpose of Islamic philosophy, what matters primarily is what the Islamic sources say about the matter. The same can be said regarding when life comes to an end: medical science has technical definitions of death, but, again, for Muslim ethics, the concern must centre on what the textual sources can reveal here. For the believer, God is the giver of life and death, and death occurs when the soul departs from the body. Naturally, this is not a matter for empirical science to be able to determine, and the medical world sees it as its obligation to keep a body functioning for as long as it can. In Islam, however, destruction of the physical body is seen as another stage in the journey towards God:

> Do not say that those who are killed in God's cause are dead; they are alive, though you do not realise it. We shall certainly test you with fear and hunger, and loss of property, lives, and crops. But [Prophet], give good news to those who are steadfast, those who say, when afflicted with a calamity, 'We belong to God and to Him we shall return.'
>
> (2:154–56)

Death of the physical body is the intermediate period before the next stage in the journey – the Day of Judgement – when the dead will be resurrected and will be held accountable for the life that they led on earth; hence this acts as a reminder that the actions one engages in during one's lifetime will be reckoned and that there is a world to come. For this reason, life must be valued and made the most of so that one can fulfil God's purpose, and so to look to hasten death is a sin. The Quran is clear here: 'No soul may die except with God's permission at a predestined time' (3:145); 'It is God who gives life or death; God sees everything you do' (3:156). Death comes at an appointed time; even if a person finds this life so unbearable – whether as a result of severe poverty or suffering from an illness – this life is seen as transitory and must be borne with as much dignity as one can. This is also tied to the view that we do not have ownership over our own bodies, only stewardship, and so we are tasked to look after the body.

This seems unequivocal. However, as so often in moral issues, there can be occasions when values come into conflict. As we have seen above when considering the use of biotechnology, the principle of maslaha – the public interest – needs to be weighed against the principle of 'no harm, no harassment'. In the case of the right to die too this must be a consideration when someone is suffering so much that the harm being caused through suffering could outweigh the rule that one cannot die before the 'appointed time'. The question then arises as to whether it is permissible to engage in mercy killing (active euthanasia) or letting die (passive euthanasia). Legally speaking, it should be pointed out that sharia does not permit assisted dying, but passive assistance is permitted when it involves giving pain-relief treatment that could, as a result, shorten life. This is because the primary aim here is to reduce the 'harm and harassment' of the person rather than to directly end the person's life. This also applies in the case of withdrawing treatment for this is allowing nature (God-given) to take its course rather than delay the inevitable. What is important here, ethically speaking, is the *intention*, which in both these cases is not aimed at the person's death. For this reason, the giving of a lethal injection is not permitted in sharia.

Homosexuality

In some Muslim countries the practice of homosexuality carries the death penalty, and there are examples where sentences have been carried out. Is the prohibition towards homosexuality in Islam absolute? Some scholars argue that you can be gay and Muslim, but the sexual act itself is wrong in the same way that sex outside marriage for heterosexuals is considered a sin. This is not dissimilar to the view that is upheld by the Catholic Church, that the homosexual act is in violation of divine and natural law. However, people tempted by homosexual desires, like people tempted by heterosexual desires outside marriage, are not actually sinning until they act upon those desires. In Catholicism this moral basis is founded on the Bible, particularly the well-known account in Genesis 19 when two angels, in disguise as men, visit the city of Sodom. The two angels are given shelter and hospitality by Abraham's nephew, Lot. During the night, however, the men of the city demand that Lot hand these two men over for homosexual intercourse. The angels blinded the men, and Lot with his family fled the city before the town is destroyed by fire 'because the outcry against its people has become great before the Lord' (Genesis 19:13).

Given the importance of the Quran as a source for ethical guidance it is necessary to see what the Muslim scripture has to say on the matter. The Quran also gives the account of the twin cities of Sodom and Gomorrah in a number of passages (for example: 11:77, 54:37) and so this also seems to portray homosexuality as a sin deserving of God's punishment.

Muslims who are gay and actively so may also look to the Quran as a source, citing passages that emphasize the diversity that exists amongst His creation, although these make no specific reference to the diversity of sexuality. Concerning the references to Lot, the same approach by some progressive interpreters of the Quran mirrors that by interpreters of the passage in the Bible (and Rabbinic commentary). That is to say, God condemned the people of Sodom for other reasons such as the lack of hospitality, intimidation, the intention to rape and the widespread promiscuity that existed. However, others argue that the Quran is very specific here. Consider the following passage concerning the event at Sodom: 'We sent Lot and he said to his people, "How can you practice this outrage? No one in the world has outdone you in this. You lust after men rather than women! You transgress all bounds!"' (7:80,81). At first glance this may seem as direct as you can get, but the subtleties of Quranic interpretation take note of references here to 'No one in the world has outdone you in this' and 'You transgress all bounds!' which can be interpreted as condemning the *excessiveness*, the promiscuity, rather than the act itself.

As regards hadith, this is less ambiguous in many passages. Here are just a couple of examples from two different respected hadith-collectors:

> Narrated by Ibn 'Abbas: The Prophet cursed effeminate men; those men who are in the similitude (assume the manners of women) and those women who assume the manners of men, and he said, 'Turn them out of your houses.' The Prophet turned out such-and-such man, and 'Umar turned out such-and-such woman.
>
> (Sahih Bukhari 7:72:774)

> Narrated by Abdullah ibn Abbas: If a man who is not married is seized committing sodomy, he will be stoned to death.
>
> (Abu Dawud 38:4448)

But even these passages are not definitive, like many other hadith that refer to the 'crimes of the people of Sodom', which, as we have seen, can mean many things other than consenting homosexual acts. In the case of the first passage, this is not a reference to the homosexual act, even if it may be seen as rather closed-minded in other respects. As for the second passage, it could be seen as critical of sex outside marriage, rather than sodomy as such, for it does not say you cannot commit sodomy *if married*.

Supporters of the view that Islam does not condemn homosexual acts will argue in the broader context of the veracity of hadith per se, in contrast to the divine authority of the Quran, which raises even broader issues over what sources can be relied upon to determine Islamic values and what, therefore, constitutes the essence of Islam. Are we, therefore, picking and choosing hadith to suit a particular belief, or are we saying that, given the unreliability of some (or many) hadith, then they are to be regarded as unreliable in a wholesale way? Even if perceived criticisms of homosexuality are open to interpretation, the problem is that one cannot find any reference in the traditions – Quran or hadith – that *affirms* homosexuality. What is interesting is that there are a number of hadith that make reference to '*mukhannathun*', variously translated as 'effeminate ones' or 'men who resemble women', and so it was not unknown for transgender to exist in Arabia at the time; and there are hadith that also suggest that Muhammad was not adverse to the presence of these mukhannathun – some being entertainers and musicians – amongst his companions, and even to be present with his wives.

In Islamic history it is interesting to note that as far back as 1858 the Ottoman Empire decriminalized homosexuality, and the Ottomans have a very strong tradition of love poetry, much of which concerns one man's love for another man. Given this is an Islamic empire, how could it justify such an attitude towards homosexuality? Pragmatically speaking, an empire as vast as that of the Ottoman needed to be accepting of diversity within its boundaries – in terms of religious beliefs and cultural beliefs – and perhaps this can be seen as the very nature of Islam that allows for multiplicity. Having said that, it has been argued that this openness to homosexuality was the preserve of a small minority of the Ottoman elite who were, on the whole, probably not very observant, pious Muslims anyway.

The question of whether it is possible to be a gay Muslim is obviously related to so many other factors, in particular how the sources are to be interpreted. Nonetheless, there are Muslims who are gay and who do not believe they are sinning or need to stop being Muslim in order to practise homosexuality. In 2012 a gay Islamic scholar, Ludovic-Mohammed Zahed, who is married to a gay man, opened an inclusive prayer room on the outskirts of Paris that is described as 'gay friendly'. As he says on the BBC website article 'Gay-Friendly "Mosque" Opens in Paris', 'Many gay men don't go to the mosque because they don't want to be recognised … They don't want to be ostracised because they wear earrings or because they're effeminate or they're transgender, something that's pretty obviously rejected in many mosques in France.' Evidently this points to the existence of many gay people who are Muslim and wish to worship freely. Whether Islam will be able to accommodate this in the future will be interesting to see as it gets at the very heart of what the religion stands for ethically and morally.

The rights of women

This writer hesitates to devote so few words to such a massive subject as women in Islam. However, it is the very fact that this *is* such a massive subject and has, as a result and thankfully, produced a large and growing number of excellent scholarly works on women and gender in Islam – in terms of ethics, philosophy, theology, sociology etc. – that allows one to confidently point the reader to this corpus. Here, then, a brief philosophical treatment of some of the main issues and voices that have arisen in recent years will have to suffice.

One such voice, indeed probably the best-known Muslim feminist, is Fatima **Mernissi** (b. 1940). Mernissi was born in Morocco and belongs to the first generation of Moroccan women to be in a position to access higher education. She studied political science at the Sorbonne and at Brandeis University in

Boston, where she earned her doctorate. The role of women in Islamic society is a human rights issue, and therefore a moral issue, and Mernissi's research focuses on the role of women in Islam by questioning the validity of the source material that makes claim to the restricted role of women, in particular hadith. Her monograph, *Beyond the Veil*, published in 1975, is a seminal work. In another of her works, *The Veil and the Male Elite: A Feminist Interpretation of Women's Rights in Islam*, originally published in English in 1991, Mernissi says:

> 'Can a woman be a leader of Muslims?' I asked my grocer who, like most grocers in Morocco, is a true 'barometer' of public opinion.
>
> 'I take refuge in God!' he exclaimed, shocked, despite the friendly relations between us. Aghast at the idea, he almost dropped the half-dozen eggs I had come to buy …
>
> … A second customer, a schoolteacher whom I vaguely knew from the newsstand, stood slowly caressing his wet mint leaves, and then hit me with a hadith that he knew would be fatal: 'Those who entrust their affairs to a woman will never know prosperity!'
>
> (Kurzman 1998: 112, 113)

It was at this point that Fatima Mernissi realized the power of hadith to silence any debate, such is the high regard they possess. The reader will, by now, be aware that in tackling many issues in Islamic philosophy, the importance of the sources is key, and although Mernissi's work may come under the rubric of sociology or anthropology, it also has important philosophical implications. Mernissi set out to investigate the vast religious literature and did something that we are so often afraid to do: adopt a critical approach to these works. For Mernissi, her research is within the context of a broader claim that Islam was originally an egalitarian project that was intent on liberating women, but was derailed by the vested interests of Meccan men, who were more at ease with pre-Islamic traditions.

Here I will provide a brief summary of Mernissi's investigation into this one hadith, although it obviously has implications for many other hadiths and for the whole 'science of hadith'. Mernissi found that the quote 'Those who entrust their affairs to a woman will never know prosperity' was uttered by the Prophet Muhammad and was heard by one of his Companions by the name of Abu Bakr (not the same Abu Bakr who became the first caliph). According to Abu Bakr, the Prophet pronounced the hadith after hearing that Persia now had a woman ruling over them.

Mernissi emphasizes that the reason why this hadith is so powerful is that it is recorded in the collection of hadiths by Bukhari, who is regarded as the most reliable of the hadith collectors, to the extent that if Bukhari cites it then it *must* be true. This hadith is considered 'sound' (*sahih*), which, according to the Muslim jurist Shafi'i (767–820), requires that each reporter recorded in the hadith should have a reputation for trustworthiness and should understand what he or she is communicating, as well as report it verbatim.

So how trustworthy *is* this narration? Now, Mernissi notes that 'Abu Bakr must have had a fabulous memory' (Kurzman 1998: 115) as he recalled the quote 25 years after the death of the Prophet. This, however, does not in itself make the quote invalid, for it is a short quote – surely not that difficult to remember – and as Arabia had a strong oral tradition it would not have been unusual for people to be able to recall much longer passages than this, given that some could recite the whole Quran from memory. However, Mernissi digs much deeper than this and looks at the life of Abu Bakr: a man who had once been a slave and had risen in the ranks to be a respected figure in the Muslim community. Without going into the details here, Mernissi argues forcibly that Abu Bakr was something of a political opportunist: 'Abu Bakr had a truly astonishing memory for politically opportune hadith which curiously – and most effectively – fitted into the stream of history' (Kurzman 1998: 118). And so it is really not what Abu Bakr remembered, but the fact that he seemed to have a habit of recalling various hadith at moments that would help to demonstrate his own allegiances.

An important feature of the science of hadith is that it is not enough to be someone who happened to know the Prophet Muhammad personally. In addition, they must also be people of impeccable intellect and moral fibre. Does Abu Bakr fulfil this? As Mernissi points out, 'If we apply this rule [lying in their relations with other people] to Abu Bakr, he would have to be immediately eliminated, since one of the biographies of him tells us that he was convicted of and flogged for false testimony by the caliph Umar ibn al-Khattab' (Kurzman 1998: 119).

As Mernissi also states, 'this "misogynistic" hadith, although it is exemplary, is not a unique case' (Kurzman 1998: 120), and she goes on in her study to demonstrate that many other hadith are not as trustworthy as supposed. Questioning the veracity of the Quran is one thing, given that it is regarded as divine in origin, but hadith are not divine: they are very much a human product, and if it can be shown that the 'science' of hadith collection is not as scientific as supposed – that the accounts given by these human beings are debatable – then the whole status of hadith needs examining.

This does not mean that the Quran should not be *interpreted*. An important feminist interpreter of the Quran is the African-American Muslim scholar Amina **Wadud** (b. 1952 in the US, previously Wadud-Muhsin). Amina was actually born with the name Mary Teasley, and her father was a Methodist minister. In 1974, however, she changed her name to Amina Wadud to reflect her conversion to Islam two years previously. She received an MA in Near Eastern studies and a PhD in Islamic studies from the University of Michigan in 1988. As part of her doctorate programme she studied philosophy at the prestigious Al-Azhar University in Egypt. Aside from her writings, Amina Wadud is currently very active in addressing mixed-sex congregations and even leading Friday prayers in the US. The latter activity has caused considerable debate (and threats to her life) over whether women can be imams, an issue in Islam that is as controversial as priestly ordination for women in the Roman Catholic Church.

As Wadud states in *Quran and Woman*: 'My objective in undertaking this research was to make a "reading" of the Qur'an that would be meaningful to women living in the modern era' (Wadud 1999: 1). Here, then, is summed up Wadud's belief that the Quran must be, and can be, meaningful for a contemporary audience, and for this to be the case, Quranic verses need to be interpreted in relation to specific historical circumstance. Here I shall look at just one example where Wadud does this.

One important and contentious passage from the Quran that Wadud cites is the following:

> Husbands should take good care of their wives, with [the bounties] God has given to some more than others and with what they spend out of their own money. Righteous wives are devout and guard what God would have them guard in their husband's absence. If you fear high-handedness from your wives, remind them [of the teachings of God], then ignore them when you go to bed, then hit them. If they obey you, you have no right to act against them: God is most high and great.
>
> (4:34)

There is so much to dissect from this passage alone, and Wadud notes that '[t]his is classically viewed as the single most important verse with regard to the relationship between men and women.' Wadud notes that many men interpret this passage as proof that God created man above woman when, notably, it states that 'God has given to some more than others' the 'some' are the men (husbands) and the 'others' are the women (wives), but Wadud emphasizes the 'some' here, stating that all that the Quran is doing is pointing out the historical fact that some men have more money and material possessions than women and therefore are responsible to take care of wives who have less. Presumably, in situations where the women have greater material wealth, they are equally obliged to take care of their husbands.

Translations are key here. In the above quote I have used the recent translation by Abdel Haleem (considered a moderate Muslim), who translates *qawwamuna 'ala* as 'take care of', whereas Pickthall translates it as 'in charge of' and Mawdudi translates it as 'manages the affairs of'. These are significant differences. No doubt the reader has noted in the Haleem translation the phrase 'then hit them'. Again, this has been variously translated as 'beat' (Mawdudi) or 'scourge' (Pickthall). In the Yusuf Ali translation it says 'beat them (lightly)', and so he has added notes in parentheses that are not in the original. Another translation by Ahmed Ali goes: 'As for women you feel are averse, talk to them suasively; then leave them alone in bed (without molesting them) and go to bed with them (when they are willing).' Here 'hit' or 'beat' has been omitted altogether. Yusuf Ali's insertion of 'lightly' may be an attempt to 'lighten' the 'hitting'. For example, the Assembly of Muslim Jurists of America (AMJA) is made up of religious scholars, most of whom have their doctorates in Islamic law or other Islamic subjects; they are qualified to write fatwas (religious rulings or opinions), and one of the scholars has stated the following: 'Hitting women as a disciplinary remedy is a last cure and a final resort. It is the end of a stage of a gradual curative program. Doctors of Quranic exegeses unanimously have stated that hitting, if needed, must not be harsh, and they likened it as hitting by a tooth stick' (Al-Sawy 2005). Hitting with a 'tooth stick', or toothpick as we would call it today, may seem odd, but in seventh century Arabia a toothpick, called a *siwak*, was a twig taken from the shrubs that existed in Arabia at that time.

Wadud points out that the 'hit' or 'beat' solution is the last resort. The first is a 'verbal solution' ('remind them', which is a discussion on what the duties and responsibilities of the husband and wife are according to Islam that could take place between husband and wife or include independent arbiters in a dispute), while the second, refusing to share a wife's bed, Wadud sees as a 'cooling-off period which would allow both the man and the woman, separately, to reflect on the problem at hand'. As regards the last resort, Wadud states that the verb *daraha* 'does not necessarily indicate force or violence' and that the reference 'should be taken as prohibiting unchecked violence against females ... [T]his is not permission, but a severe restriction of existing practices.' However, this does not seem to discount violence altogether, but is rather a condemnation of *excessive* violence. From a historical perspective they may well be seen as progressive in relation to the practices of the time, but it hardly fits with modern feminist views or the ethical concerns raised by beating one's wife!

Ultimately, Wadud struggles to escape the fact that hitting, whatever 'hitting' may mean, women is enshrined in the Quran and therefore a divine law, and the various linguistic contortions seem unconvincing. However, a further option is the question as to whether a verse such as 4:34 can be seen as past its expiry date and therefore can be considered as abrogated. This would be contentious theologically as it argues that revelation can be changed following the death of the Prophet Muhammad. Wadud's more recent scholarship seems to be heading in this direction with *Inside the Gender Jihad* (2006):

> Since we live in the time when at least the conceptualization of women's complete agency and equality between women and men is conceivable, then we must dance the delicate dance between text and agency to assert a movement of complete gender justice. I have already argued significantly that the text can be interpreted with egalitarianism in mind; I now propose one step that some consider even beyond that. *We are the makers of textual meaning.* The results of meaning-making is the reality we establish from those meanings to human experiences and social justice.

(Wadud 2006: 204)

Wadud places her own emphasis with the sentence '*We are the makers of textual meaning*', implying that readers can intervene and say 'no' to a text that conflicts with Quranic principles of justice and human dignity.

What has stronger grounds is to argue for women's rights through legal argumentation. In the case of marital discipline, although it is the case that Islamic law recognizes a husband's right to discipline his wife, the husband is also subject to liability for any injuries that he inflicts upon her. In fact, the law here tends to be in support of the wife's accusations, for the onus is on the husband to provide evidence that he did not harm his wife. If he cannot provide this evidence, then he is required to provide financial compensation, and the wife also has good grounds for divorce. From a moral perspective, how the Muslim husband who beats his wife is perceived is worth being taken into account, with the Prophet Muhammad as the paradigm of how a good Muslim should behave. Muhammad never hit a woman; he said that the best men are those who do not beat their wives and, in the case of one hadith, he says the following: 'How does anyone of you beat his wife as he beats the stallion camel and then embrace (sleep with) her?' (Al-Bukhari).

The rights of non-Muslims

Historically, as Islam spread beyond the Arab boundaries in a relatively speedy manner, it was not long before the Arab Muslim had to confront the issue of how non-Muslims (and non-Arabs) were to be treated. The term *dhimmi* is given to non-Muslim groups that existed within Islamic states. In some cases this could constitute a majority and so it raises serious questions for the caliphs concerning the rights of dhimmis within the community. During most of the period of the rightly-guided caliphs, the Rashidun, only Arabs could be Muslims, but generally Muslims lived peaceably with non-Muslims, especially as most of the people they encountered were *ahl al-kitab* ('People of the Book'). The Arabs at this time thought that only descendants of Ishmael could be Muslim, and so conversion was not encouraged. The People of the Book were accorded dhimmi status, which was also financially rewarding for the Arabs as dhimmis had to pay a 'protection' tax from which Muslims were exempt. During this time the Arab Muslims, once they conquered a territory, lived in separate garrison towns, *amsar*. These amsar were effectively Arab enclaves, 'untainted' by foreign mores.

Even though a number of countries came under Muslim rule as a result of force or jihad, the teachings of the Quran were observed to the extent that Islam was never imposed by compulsion. With a few exceptions, dhimmis have been allowed to pursue the religion of their choice, and in many cases, as we have seen with the example of Andalusia, their situation was improved under Islamic rule, enjoying lengthy periods of tolerance and prosperity, as well as holding high positions in administrations, courts and economic activities. However, they did suffer discrimination from time to time, notably after the reign of the Abbasid caliph al-Mutawakkil (r. 847–61) who, in 850, made a decree requiring all dhimmis to wear clothing that would distinguish them from Muslims. He also destroyed their places of worship, had demonic effigies nailed to the doors of their homes and businesses and prevented them from having any power in government matters. Notoriously he ordered the ancient, sacred and mighty Cypress of Kashmar to be felled in order to use it for beams for his new palace in Samarra. It is said that the cypress, believed to be 1400 years old at the time of al-Mutawakkil, was planted by the prophet Zoroaster in honour of the conversion of the Persian King Vishtaspa to Zoroastrianism. The Zoroastrians offered to give huge sums of money to al-Mutawakkil in an attempt to save the tree, but the caliph would not budge. However, a Turkish soldier murdered him on the very night the fallen tree arrived on the banks of the Tigris, and so he never got to see it for himself. Things were to get worse for dhimmis under the reign of the third Fatimid (Shia Muslims) caliph al-Hakim (966–1021), who is known in Western literature as the 'Mad Caliph', largely due to his order for the destruction of the Holy Sepulchre in Jerusalem in 1009. Whether he was actually insane is open to dispute, but he was certainly none too favourable towards dhimmis. In 1004 he decreed that the Christians could no longer celebrate Epiphany or Easter. He outlawed the use of wine and other alcoholic drinks, which, aside from a hardship for those non-Muslims who liked to drink, also presented difficulties for Christians and Jews where wine is used for religious rites and festivals. In 1005, Hakim ordered that Jews and Christians follow *ghiyar*, 'the law of differentiation', whereby Jews had to wear a wooden calf necklace and Christians an iron cross. In the public baths, Jews must replace the calf with a bell. In addition, the women had to wear two different coloured shoes, one red and one black. During the latter years of his reign, Hakim relaxed his hostility towards non-Muslims, preferring to target Sunnis.

Even in cases where non-Muslims have been tolerated, this needs to be tempered by the fact that this toleration is due to dhimmis belonging to a separate community under the protection of the respective Muslim ruler. On the whole, Islamic states have tended to pursue an isolationist policy towards dhimmis who, as noted, have to pay a 'protection tax'. Ideologically, an Islamic state cannot by definition integrate with those that do not share Islamic values, for then it would cease to be an 'Islamic' state and would, instead, be more pluralistic. For a state to be Islamic, the law of God – as evidenced in the Quran – must prevail, and so any other source of authority – whether it is the Bible, the Torah or a secular source – can only be accepted to the extent that it agrees with the Quran. Uniformity of conduct under the law of God has to take precedence over national integration, which would then need to accommodate ideals of ethnicity and pluralism that may be seen as anti-Islamic unless, of course, these ideals can be shown to be Islamic (see Chapter 9). However, as the political scientist P.J. Vatikiotis (1928–97) has pointed out:

> Surely, the essence of secularism, apart from the separation between religion and state, is the acceptance of the proposition that there is no finality to forms, no exclusive possession of absolute and indivisible truth. A corollary of this is the recognition of alternative notions about man and the world and, more significantly, the toleration of these alternative views.

This implies scepticism, not certitude towards absolutist assertions, and experimentation with alternative forms.

(Vatikiotis 1987: 98)

This 'finality of forms' is best expressed through Mawdudi's writings, and also Mawdudi represents a conservative strand within Islam that is concerned that any giving in is a slippery slope that threatens that 'finality'. As an example, Mawdudi condemned newly converted Muslims who occasionally eat pork. When Mawdudi heard that Muslims in China who had recently converted would still on occasion eat pork, he notes that as the Quran states that the eating of pork is unacceptable, this cannot be permitted. Whilst this may well adhere to the strict letter of Quranic law, the lack of leniency and flexibility can be very short-sighted, given that historically Islam was able to spread across the world as a result of allowing a degree of cultural diversity. At issue here is the extent to which Islam sees 'non-Islamic' traditions and beliefs as a threat to Islamic values, rather than embracing this difference, and here we have a contrast between the conservative and liberal elements of the tradition.

To say that non-Muslims are 'tolerated' is not the same as saying they are 'integrated'. We have seen in Chapter 6 that Mawdudi's views on the Islamic state express his concern for the solidarity and superiority of an Islamic nation against those that promote other political systems, and this 'us versus them', Islam versus jahiliyya outlook results in less accommodation for any kind of religious and ethnic diversity within state boundaries. The dhimmi is 'tolerated' more as a member of a separate community, rather than fully fledged citizens. In *First Principles of the Islamic State*, Mawdudi guarantees protection of 'life and limb, property and culture, faith and honour' (Mawdudi 1967: 66) for dhimmis, and he states that Islam gives them equal rights with Muslims in all 'civil matters'; that is, criminal and civil law are the same for both Muslims and non-Muslims. In addition, dhimmis, Mawdudi states, can follow their own laws and customs, and this includes being allowed to make and sell (to fellow non-Muslims) alcohol and to raise and sell pigs. However, the non-Muslim cannot be the head of an Islamic state, nor a senior member of its national government. Government participation for the dhimmi is limited to the extent that he or she (although, in Mawdudi's cases, probably just males) does not affect the ideological (i.e. Islamic) basis of the state. The non-Muslim cannot preach beliefs that are contrary to Islam: that is, they cannot hold, entertain or publish opposing or differing views and beliefs.

A concrete example of the conflict that can arise between Islamic state ideology and those that may not be entirely allied to these views is Mawdudi's remarks during the Court of Inquiry into the anti-Ahmadiyya riots of 1953 when Mawdudi – as well as the ulama – declared that apostasy is punishable with death in Islam, declaring that Islam is not only a matter of personal faith, but part of the social order. Hence, a change of faith is equivalent to an attack on society, which is effectively saying an act of treason has been committed. The Ahmadiyya movement itself was founded by Mirza Ghulam Ahmad

(1835–1908) in India at the end of the nineteenth century. Ahmad proclaimed himself to be a *mujaddid*, a 'reformer of the age', as well as being the promised messiah that was foretold by the Prophet Muhammad. Ahmad and his followers saw themselves as representatives of the true Islam, and their missionary activity was an attempt to revive an Islam that they saw to be threatened at the time. They are, nonetheless, considered to be non-Muslims by the majority of orthodox Muslims. In 1924, some Ahmadi missionaries in Afghanistan were brought to trial on charges of apostasy. They were found guilty and executed. The Ahmadiyya to this day continue to be discriminated against in Pakistan.

Ultimately, the position of non-Muslim depends on what kind of society one envisions, and we come back yet again to that key philosophical question: How can one be a 'good person'? Translated into Islamic terms, this is synonymous with 'How can one be a good Muslim?' and Does this require a Muslim to live within the boundaries of a monolithic Islamic state governed by Islamic laws? The traditional Mawdudian camp would answer, 'Yes', to the latter, but we have seen that this is not the only Muslim voice out there. As the Muslim Indian scholar Humayn Kabir (1906–69) points out, 'Where you have a completely homogenous, monolithic society, the chances of survival of that society or community are always less than those of an heterogenous society in which there are many centres of power, many ways of expression' (Kurzman 1998: 145). There are certainly, therefore, pragmatic reasons to argue for heterogeneity, but can this be supported by the Islamic sources? We shall see in Chapter 9 that a case can be put forward for a vision of Islam that is pluralistic in terms of ethical values, and this emphasis on its universal aspects can be carried into the attitudes towards non-Muslims in any community. The Malaysian political scientist and activist Chandra Muzaffar (b. 1947) has himself borne witness to the religious tensions and conflict in Malaysia between the Muslim population, which comprises a slight majority, and the non-Muslim Chinese and South Asians. As he states:

> One of their [Islamic political groups'] more important intellectual commitments was the quest for common principles that could unite Muslims and non-Muslims – a commitment which conforms to Quranic ideals. In this connection, no Muslim group in Malaysia has ever bothered to embark on such a mission, though, at the level of social philosophy, there are many outstanding similarities between Islam and aspects of Chinese culture and Hindu thought.
>
> (Kurzman 1998: 160)

Important in the quote above is the argument that Islam should be more concerned with inter-religious dialogue in determining what common values all religious believers share. Presumably it could also be argued that non-believers also share common values that are essentially *human*. This call for universalism is a noble one, though those suspicious of it would argue that this simply dilutes Islam and submerges its identity. We can refer back to Muhammad Iqbal here (see Chapter 5), however, who saw Islam as a universal religion, which envisaged all mankind as a unity. Rather than a religion that is narrow and static, it is – or should be – evolutionary and dynamic.

Further reading

Kurzman, C. (1998), *Liberal Islam: A Sourcebook*, New York: Oxford University Press.

Mernissi, F. (2003), *Beyond the Veil: Male-Female Dynamics in Muslim Society*, new edn, London: Saqi Books.

Sachedina, A. (2009), *Islamic Biomedical Ethics: Principles and Application*, Oxford: Oxford University Press.

Wadud, A. (1999), *Qur'an and Woman: Re-Reading the Sacred Text from a Woman's Perspective*, 2nd edn, New York: Oxford University Press.

8   Jihad and just war theory

Just war theory in the non-Islamic sense

Historical background

Many ethics students will no doubt be familiar with just war theory in the Western philosophical and theological tradition, but perhaps not so many are aware that legal and ethical discussion of war and peace has existed in the Islamic tradition for some considerable time as well. For example, the influential *Law of Peace and War*, which was written by the Dutch jurist and philosopher Hugo Grotius (1583–1645) in 1625, was based on the ideas expressed by the Spanish jurists Francesco de Vitoria (*c.* 1483–1546) and Francesco Suarez (1548–1617), who acknowledged their debt to Islamic law. Having said that, just war theory in the Western world has a very long tradition too, going back to the writing of the great legalist and philosopher of the Roman empire, Cicero (106–43 BC), who proposed three basic rules:

1. There must be a just cause for war (for example, to repel an attack).
2. There must be a formal declaration of war by someone of authority (for example, a king or emperor), which allows for the opponent to attempt to prevent war.
3. War must be conducted justly (for example, unarmed civilians should not be harmed).

These are certainly rudimentary and, therefore, allow for a large degree of ambiguity in their interpretation, but it is a start and, significantly, there is an awareness that a distinction needs to be made between what rules should be followed *before* one actually becomes committed to war, known by the Latin term **jus ad bellum** ('justice of resorting to war'), and what rules should be followed once opponents are *involved* in war, referred to as **jus in bello** ('justice in war'). As the first Christians were pacifists, the issue of just war did not arise, but when the Roman emperor converted to Christianity, the relationship between religious belief and state policy became intermingled. The Church, in theory at least, became the moral harbinger and so was compelled to declare its position on war. St Ambrose (*c.* 330–97) and St Augustine (354–430) are regarded as the first to write on this within the Christian tradition, although largely drawing from what already existed in Roman law. Augustine, however, added to Cicero's list, including a rule that the rights of conscientious objectors to not fight must be respected. This might well seem ahead of its time, given that conscientious objectors were imprisoned as late as World War I. However, Augustine restricted this right to religious professionals only.

There have been a number of important thinkers on just war theory during the Middle Ages, significantly Thomas Aquinas, who added more conditions. Also the Second Lateran Council of 1139 banned crossbows, bows and arrows and siege machines! Since that time, of course, the development of technology and the massive changes socially, economically and politically have resulted in a number of changes in just war regulation.

Modern **jus ad bellum** *rules*

There are a number of hurdles that need to be overcome if one is to argue for starting a just war today. Considered the most important is the Just Cause Principle, which effectively states that there must be a good reason for going to war. An inevitable problem with this is the question, What would constitute a good reason? Answers go back to Cicero, who states that being attacked by a foreign power is sufficient cause. Also considered to be good reasons are to come to the aid of a friendly nation that has come under attack, or if a large number of people of a nation are suffering (ethnic cleansing, poverty etc.) as a result of government action; in these cases, another nation can intervene.

Another important rule is the Legitimate Authority Principle. For a war to be considered just, a lawful authority – those who have been given a mandate to act on behalf of the nation, as opposed to dictators or private organizations – must undertake it. A third rule is the Good Intentions Principle, which in modern terms includes such acts as intending to establish justice rather than, say, to colonize or take revenge. Fourth is the Likelihood of Success Principle, simply because to engage in a just war (i.e. to establish justice) against the odds of succeeding will only result in more unnecessary suffering. A fifth, related, rule is the Principle of Proportionality, by which going to war will result in the likelihood of more good than evil. The sixth is the Last Resort Principle: all other avenues for a settlement of the dispute should have been explored before war is committed.

Modern **jus in bello** *rules*

Once war has been declared, the rules to be followed during the conflict are usually under two basic principles: Proportionality and Discrimination. The first principle is usually with reference to specific campaigns or battles during the war, in which the military leaders should take account of the Principle of Proportionality before engaging in an action. An action that may result in a high number of causalities but result in little territorial gain (the Battle of the Somme in 1916 may well be one example of this) would be considered unjust here. Regarding the Principle of Discrimination, the war must discriminate amongst its targets, focusing on military personnel and objects (airports, bridges etc.) whist avoiding unarmed civilians, hospitals, schools and so on.

Just war in action: 9/11

On 11 September 2001, four commercial airplanes were hijacked by 19 people, who declared an allegiance to the terrorist group al-Qaeda. These four planes were intended to be flown into targeted buildings in the US as a suicide attack. Two of the planes, American Airlines Flight 11 and United Airlines 175, were flown directly into the two towers of the World Trade Center in New York City, resulting in the collapse of the these buildings. A third plane, American Airlines Flight 77, was crashed into the headquarters of the US Department of Defence, known as the Pentagon. The fourth plane's intended target was the US Capitol in Washington DC, but this crashed into a field near Shanksville, Pennsylvania after a failed attempt by the passengers to take back control of the plane. As a result of these attacks, some three thousand people died, including all the passengers and the hijackers of the four planes, although the vast majority died in the World Trade Center.

How does just war theory apply to these events? In terms of *jus ad bellum*, considered the most important rule is the Just Cause Principle. Do the attackers have a good reason for their actions? Of course, no doubt the attackers themselves, and their leaders, do believe they have good reason, and the problem is in establishing any kind of objectivity here. Mentioned above is Cicero's view that a good reason is if your nation is under attack, but there is no 'nation' – or group of nations – here as such and, even if there were, there was no physical attack upon these nations by the US at that time. However, this does raise some interesting questions that will need to be explored much further later on, because it relates to the fundamental way in which the world is changing and how the old criteria of 'nation' and 'military invasion' are becoming very grey areas in the twenty-first century. For instance, battles take place often between ideologies rather than nations, and what constitutes an attack can be interpreted in many different ways, not simply as an invading military force, but, for example, a corruption of a culture's values (including religious beliefs). Therefore, American culture could be seen as a threat to Islamic culture. However, if one does want to be more traditional than this and argue that these acts could hardly be considered 'acts of war', many Muslim groups frequently cite the support the US gives to Israel (through military equipment and intelligence for example) – which does, in turn, commit military acts against Palestine – as effectively constituting an attack on a friendly nation. This view of 'a friend of my enemy is my enemy' is the same logic the US used after the 9/11 attacks to invade Afghanistan.

What this raises here is that determining just cause is notoriously difficult and inevitably subjective. Further, even if it were possible to argue that the 9/11 attackers did have just cause, it is required that they fulfil *all* the *jus ad bellum* principles in order for it to be regarded as morally justified. In term of *jus ad bellum*, one important rule referred to above is the Legitimate Authority Principle. The attackers, by declaring their affiliation with the group al-Qaeda, can not be identified with any particular nation state, and so there is no political leader who has been given a mandate by the people to rule. The Likelihood of Success Principle is extremely difficult to gauge, given the intentions of the attackers remain unclear and it is uncertain how far in the future one needs to look in order to measure this, or by what standards. Therefore it is extremely difficult to apply either of these rules to this act at all. In terms of what might be applicable, the Last Resort Principle may be more fitting for it may be argued that for people to sacrifice their own lives in such a horrific and demonstrative manner was only because all other avenues had failed. However, this is only an assumption and by no means conclusive. It may well be that the attackers – or rather their leaders – had made serious and determined attempts to negotiate with the US over whatever reasons were given for the attack, but at this moment in time there is little reason to believe that was indeed the case. What of the Principle of Proportionality? The year 2001 is still relatively recent historically, and at this moment in time it is difficult, not to say somewhat gruesome, to see this act as anything other than evil, and from which no good whatsoever has come. Whether this view will change in the future is another matter, but, ultimately, to argue that the act was proportional because good will come out of it a thousand years hence seems like a very weak justification. The Good Intentions Principle is another subjective rule, although the attackers and their leaders would certainly have argued the case for justice here, for they would not have engaged in it if they had felt themselves that it was an evil act; rather, for them it was a just act in order to alleviate what they perceived as the evil committed by the US and its allies.

As regards *jus in bello*, this makes the case for the attackers even weaker. Taking the principle of Discrimination first, whereby one should discriminate in terms of targets, and focus on military personnel and objects whilst avoiding civilians, this was blatantly not the case here on two counts: in the case of the 227 civilians who lost their lives in the 'weapons' used, i.e. the passengers on the airplanes, and the 3,000 other civilians that were killed as a result of the attacks on the ground, although it may be argued that the Pentagon qualifies as a military target. The Principle of Proportionality in terms of territorial gain is effectively nil. Whether 'gain' should be measured in other ways – say, in terms of highlighting grievances – is another issue and also difficult to determine.

Therefore, attempts to apply these rules of just war to just one particular case result in it being problematic for a number of reasons. It is not a simple case of stating that the 9/11 attack was 'unjust' because it fails to satisfy all the criteria, unless we are also prepared to question the criteria itself as suitable. Also, it would be extremely difficult – if not impossible – to find any war in history that would satisfy all these principles. For example, many would cite World War II as a clear-cut example of good versus evil and thus satisfying the Just Cause Principle, amongst others, but it was very difficult to gauge in terms of Likelihood of Success and also some historians have argued that not all other attempts at a peaceful settlement had been explored before Britain declared war on Germany, which brings into question the Last Resort Principle.

Further, there were a number of occasions during World War II (*jus in bello*) that would conflict with both principles of Proportionality and Discrimination. The most obvious example was the atomic bombing of the two Japanese cities of Hiroshima and Nagasaki in August 1945. Within the first four months of these bombings, around 200,000 people died as a result of the effects, with roughly half of these occurring the first day. This kind of bombing makes no discrimination between military or civilian, women, men or children. The argument is often made that it was proportional as it resulted in the end of the war and, therefore, the prevention of more deaths if the war was to continue, but it is questionable whether it was necessary to drop two bombs, and both on such highly populated cities, in order to get the point across to Japan what would happen if they did not surrender. More conventional bombings that also did not discriminate would include the Coventry Blitz, in particular the raid on 14 November 1940, which was intended to destroy Coventry's factories (including munitions) and industrial structure and in this respect may qualify as a military target, but the bombing – involving over 500 German bombers – was so intense, many residential areas were also destroyed and civilian lives lost. Another well-known example often cited as morally dubious is the bombing of the German city of Dresden, which took place in the final months of the war. It consisted of four raids between 13 and 15 February 1945 involving 3,900 tons of high explosive bombs and the killing of about 25,000 people. Whilst it has been argued that Dresden was a major military and industrial target, a number of other scholars have argued that many targets were of no military significance at all.

Just war theory in the Islamic sense

The home of war and the home of peace

Given, then, that no war truly qualifies as 'just', the best, it can be argued, that can be hoped for is the extent to which those involved in war, or in considering going to war, strive to adhere to these principles as much as possible. However, a further issue here is whether or not these principles are – or should be – universally accepted. To what extent do these principles apply to Islam, or are they 'Western' and therefore non-applicable? The Muslim scholar Bassam Tibi states: 'The Western distinction between just and unjust wars linked to specific grounds for war is unknown in Islam' (Hashmi 2002: 178). He goes on to argue that if it is a war against unbelievers then this is ethical justification in itself. Therefore, the definition of a just war is one that involves the dissemination of Islam, and an unjust war is when non-Muslims are attacking Muslims. This view is based on a particular concept of the world as a dualistic one, divided up between what is called the 'home of Islam' (***dar al-Islam***) – or the 'home of peace' (***dar al-salam***) – and the 'home of war' (***dar al-harb***). While the notion of a 'home of war' is not Quranic, reference to the 'home of peace' is: 'But God invites [everyone] to the Home of Peace, and guides whoever He will to a straight path' (10:25). This 'invitation' to join the home of peace, Tibi argues, was historically much more forceful: 'If non-Muslims submit to conversion or subjugation, this call (*da'wa*) can be pursued peacefully. If they do not, Muslims are obliged to wage war against them' (Hashmi 2002: 177). This vision of the world as being in a permanent state of war is not one that all Islamic scholars share. Also, how the term 'war' is understood in Islam in two distinct ways. The first is the word ***qital***, which is better translated as 'fighting' or 'battle', and so refers to war in the literal sense; and this form of war is seen in Islam as a last resort, especially if non-Muslims get in the way of the spreading of Islam. The distinction between the home of peace and the home of war sees war in this sense metaphorically, as a permanent state between Muslims and non-Muslims. **Jihad**, in this respect, is seen as 'striving' to make the world a peaceful place – that is, entirely the home of peace – but, in this striving, jihad may result in qital because of opposition to the spread of Islam in its mission for peace. However, **dawa** need not be seen in a military way, especially in the modern world. The late Grand Sheikh of Al-Azhar, Jad al-Haqq (1917–96) provides a more tolerant understanding of jihad:

> In earlier ages the sword was necessary for securing the path of *da'wa*. In our age, however, the sword has lost its importance, although the resort to it is still important for the case of defence against those who wish to do evil to Islam and its people. However, for the dissemination of *da'wa* there are now a variety of ways.
>
> (Hashmi 2002: 184)

Haqq points out that not only can other, peaceful means be used to engage in dawa, such as the use of modern forms of communication (the media), but that Islam does not set out to enforce its religion upon others in the first place. As passages in the Quran such as 2:256, 'There shall be no compulsion in religion', and 109:6, 'To you your religion and to me mine', illustrate, it may well be that Islam is not a missionary religion at all. In this way, the 'invitation' to join Islam, or the home of peace, is one that a non-Muslim is perfectly within his or her rights to refuse without any feeling of compulsion. This is not like an 'invitation' by the mafia to be given 'protection'. What Haqq is doing is placing Islam within a modern-day context and, inevitably, and as with so many of the ethical issues being considered in this book, an understanding of a just war is dependent upon how one relates to the original sources. An Islamic fundamentalist response would be much different.

Jihad in the Islamic sources: the Quran

As with all Islamic philosophy, an Islamic ethics of war begins with what the Quran has to say on the matter. The term 'jihad' appears in the Quran 35 times, but its meaning is ambiguous in most cases, for the word literally translates to 'struggle' or 'striving' and not, as many assume, 'holy war'. When referring to the notion of a literal war, in terms of actual military engagement, the Arabic word used is 'qital', which literally means 'fighting', whereas the term 'jihad' has a number of different meanings. For example, it can mean any of the following:

- Jihad of the heart (*jihad bil qalb/nafs*), which concerns combatting evil within oneself. According to a well-known hadith (see below), this was regarded as the 'greater jihad' (*al-jihad al-akbar*).
- Jihad by the tongue (*jihad bil lisan*), which is concerned with speaking the truth and spreading the word of Islam.
- Jihad by the hand (*jihad bil yad*), which refers to choosing to do what is right and to combat injustice and what is wrong with action, although not necessarily of an aggressive kind.
- Jihad by the sword (*jihad bis saif*), which refers to *qital fi sabilillah* (armed fighting in the way of God, or holy war), the most common usage by Salafi Muslims and offshoots of the Muslim Brotherhood (see below). According to hadith this was regarded as the 'lesser jihad' (*al-jihad alasghar*).

This is further elaborated upon by scholars such as Amir Ali, who presents 12 senses of jihad which can be found in the Quran and hadith:

1. recognizing God and loving Him the most (9:23,24);
2. resisting pressure from parents, peers and society (25:52);
3. keeping to the straight path (22:78);
4. striving for righteous deeds (29:69);
5. conveying the message of the Quran with courage (41:33);
6. defending Islam and the umma (22:39,40);
7. helping non-Muslims who are allies (8:58);
8. removing treacherous people from positions of power (8:58);
9. defending Islam through pre-emptive strikes (2:216);
10. striving to spread the message of Islam without external hinderance (2:217);
11. freeing people from tyranny (4:75);
12. after freeing people from tyranny, creating a society that is just and equitable (4:58; 5:8; 7:181; 16:90).

In fact, the term 'jihad' used in the Quran in the 'lesser jihad' context can only be identified with any certainty in four cases. As for the other references, 11 are pacific, and the other 20 are ambiguous. Whilst, then, it cannot be denied that there are some 'warlike' passages in the Quran, another issue that needs to be borne in mind is whether this necessarily means that Muslims are therefore *morally obliged* to engage in war. After all, other religious texts are not entirely pacific. Consider the following from the Old Testament:

> Now go, attack the Amalekites and totally destroy all that belongs to them. Do not spare them; put to death men and women, children and infants, cattle and sheep, camels and donkeys.
>
> (1 Samuel 15:3)

Or this from the mouth of Jesus Christ in the New Testament:

> Think not that I am come to send peace on earth: I came not to send peace, but a sword.
>
> (Matthew 10:34)

This raises the question of how a religion's texts should be treated by its believers, and Jewish and Christian scholars have done much admirable work in this field in relation to such aggressive texts. So, indeed, has Islam, but the term 'jihad' has become so heavily loaded with meaning and given prominent media attention – in its negative, violent sense – that it is often forgotten that the word 'Islam' has the same root as '**salam**', which means 'peace', a word that occurs 129 times in the Quran!

In attempting to understand what the Quran has to say about war, and how this relates to what it has to say about peace, reference should be made to Abd al-Rahman Ibn Khaldun (1332–1406). Khaldun was a historian, philosopher, social scientist and jurist, and was possibly the first philosopher of history. His best-known work *Muqaddimah* (known as *Prolegomenon* in English) gives us guidance on the Islamic view of war, and the work was described by the British historian Arnold J. Toynbee as 'a philosophy of history which is undoubtedly the greatest work of its kind that has ever yet been created by any mind in any time or place'. Whilst we will not have space to consider the field of philosophy of history as such, Khaldun's comments on history's importance in providing us with philosophical insights are worth quoting:

> On the surface history is no more than information about political events, dynasties and occurrences of the remote past, elegantly presented and spiced with proverbs. It serves to entertain large, crowded gatherings and brings to us an understanding of human affairs ... The inner meaning of history, on the other hand, involves speculation and an attempt to get at the truth, subtle explanation of the causes and origins of existing things, and deep knowledge of the how and why of events. History, therefore, is firmly rooted in philosophy. It deserves to be accounted a branch of philosophy.
>
> (Khaldun 1958: 6)

Such observations of history, not to mention Khaldun's own experiences of conflict in the various regions of the world that he lived in, led him to conclude the following: 'wars and different kinds of fighting have always occurred in the world since God created it'. It is, 'something natural among human beings. No nation and no race is free from it.'

What is particularly interesting here is that Khaldun is pragmatic in his understanding of human nature: whilst we may *strive* for peace, it is also our nature to be prone to conflict and war. Keeping Khaldun's insights in mind here, how then should we regard the following passages from the Quran?

1. So [Prophet] as a man of pure faith, stand firm and true in your devotion to the religion. This is the natural disposition God instilled in mankind – there is no altering God's creation – and thus is the right religion, though most people do not realize it. (30:30)
2. [Prophet], when your Lord told the angels, 'I am putting a successor [*khalifah*] on earth,' they said, 'How can You put someone there who will cause damage and bloodshed, when we celebrate Your praise and proclaim Your holiness?' But He said, 'I know things you do not.' (2:30)
3. So, the devil tricked both and he brought both of them out from what they were in, and We said, 'Descend, you are all enemies of one another ... ' (2:36)

If we consider each in turn:

1. Two elements to this passage. First is that human beings have a specific nature, an 'essence', and this is given to them by God. This nature is devotion to religion and, if we understand this to mean Islam, then mankind is naturally disposed to salam, to peace. However, the second element here is that 'most people do not realize it', so whilst our nature is for peace, our ignorance of our nature leads to conflict.
2. The term '**khalifah**' has many meanings, but essentially it means 'caretaker' in the sense that mankind has been put on the earth to take care of it. This caused an uproar amongst the angels because whereas they obey God and do as He wishes mankind has the tendency to do the opposite. However, God's statement, 'I know things you do not', suggests that the conflict and violence humans engage in is all part of God's plan, whatever that might be.
3. This is a reference to Adam and Eve, who were tricked by the devil into disobeying God. As a result, mankind are 'enemies to one another'. However, there is an element of hope in that mankind's original state is one of peace and it is the turning away from God that has resulted in conflict.

The importance of dialogue and conflict resolution

Therefore, to take a pragmatic approach, a variety of beliefs and practices exist in the world, and this results in conflict and war. The Quran, however, does not suggest that peace can only be achieved when all people are Muslim, at least not Muslim in the sense of adherence to a specific religious tradition: the Islam with a capital 'I' that has its historical roots with the Prophet Muhammad. The Quran consistently associates itself with other religious traditions based in the belief that we are all effectively born 'muslim' because we are all born with our essence, our nature: it is only our environment that leads us astray. This presents an optimistic picture of a possible future of conflict resolution and how important it is to engage in dialogue with one's enemies, as the following demonstrates:

- Say, 'O people of the book, let us come to a common statement between us and you; that we do not serve except God, and do not set up anything at all with Him, and that none of us takes each other as lords beside God.' (3:64)
- There shall be no compulsion in religion. (2:256)
- Those who follow the Messenger, the unlettered prophet, whom they find written in what they have of the Torah and the Gospel, who enjoins upon them what is right and forbids them what is wrong and makes lawful for them the good things and prohibits for them the evil and relieves them of their burden and the shackles which were upon them. (7:157)
- To you your religion and to me mine. (109:6)

However, this optimistic picture of the future must be tinged by the present state of humanity and the pragmatic awareness of Khaldun that evil does exist in the world and force is sometimes necessary. Consider this passage:

> Believers are those 'who, whenever tyranny afflicts them, defend themselves'.
>
> (42:39)

Or this one:

> Permission to take up arms is hereby given to those who are attacked, because they have been wronged ... Had God not defended some men by the might of others, the monasteries and churches, the synagogues and mosques in which His praise is daily celebrated, would have been utterly destroyed. But whoever helps God shall be helped by Him.
>
> (22:39–40)

And then we have this one:

> Slay them wherever you find them. Drive them out of the places from which they drove you. Idolatry is worse than carnage. But do not fight them within the precincts of the Holy Mosque unless they attack you there; if they attack you put them to the sword ... Fight against them until idolatry is no more and God's religion reigns supreme. But if they desist, fight none except the evil-doers.
>
> (2:191)

In these passages there is an evident tension between the right for someone to practise his or her religious beliefs without hindrance and the attempts by others to deny this right. It is also not surprising that many are shocked when parts of one of these passages are left to stand on their own: for example, if someone were to quote just the first three sentences of the passage above, 'Slay them wherever you find them. Drive them out of the places from which they drove you. Idolatry is worse than carnage.' Yet what of the rest of the passage where it is said that one should not fight them unless they attack you at the Holy Mosque, or that fighting should stop if the aggressors desist from attacking you?

Jihad in the Islamic sources: the Sunna

Unlike Jesus, the Prophet Muhammad does not come across historically as quite so pacifistic, for he was as much a military leader as he was a spiritual one, engaged in conflict (**ghazwa**) with rival tribes. Also, Muhammad was brought up with an Arabic ethos that valued courage in the battlefield, although this is not the same as saying that war was glorified. The Arabic ethos of **muruwah**, which is at its strongest amongst the Bedouin tribes, encompasses such virtues as bravery, loyalty and honesty. The primary aim of ghazwa is to demonstrate these virtues, whilst avoiding as much bloodshed as possible, hence there were 'rules of the game' which prohibited fighting during specific months, the kill ing of civilians and gratuitous destruction. This ethos has its origins in jahiliyya, in the time before Islam, but was so highly valued that Arabic children from cities such as Mecca were sent to live amongst the Bedouin for a time to become acquainted with it, and Muhammad, as a boy, was no exception to this.

What is interesting to consider is the extent to which this ethos became a part of the Islamic moral framework, given the importance of Muhammad's deeds and words as a source for such guidance. It does seem that during the Meccan period of his Prophethood, Muhammad was averse to any kind of violence at all – even when his followers were physically attacked – and Muhammad comes across as more of a Gandhi-like figure than a military warrior. This was no doubt partly for prudential reasons – Muhammad and his followers were hardly in any position at that time to respond in kind – but it may also have been because of what comes across in various early (Meccan) Quranic passages referred to above that emphasize violence only as a last resort. Focus on Muhammad's more aggressive stance comes from the Medinan period when Muhammad was now effectively a head of state surrounded by enemies and the possibilities of non-violent resistance were limited. This period, from AD 622–32, saw Muhammad personally authorize over 70 military attacks on the ruling tribe of Mecca, the Quraysh, and its allies. These attacks varied from pitched battles to sieges to skirmishes. It was also during this time (so far as can be determined, for dating Quranic passages is speculative in many cases) that passages in the Quran became more belligerent. Despite these necessities of war, sources generally present Muhammad as a reluctant warrior who would always seek compromise and non-violent measures whenever possible, despite frequent protest from his own companions that he should be more aggressive towards his enemies. Perhaps the hadith that best sums up Muhammad's ethos towards war is the following from Bukhari: 'Oh people! Do not wish to meet the enemy, and ask God for safety, but when you face the enemy, be patient, and remember that Paradise is under the shade of swords.'

Hasan Al-Banna and Sayyid Qutb on Jihad

Whilst scholars such as Haqq are prepared to interpret jihad within a contemporary context, and thus can be seen as more revisionist and liberal in their approach, others are much more within the fundamentalist camp. One such radical group, the **Muslim Brotherhood** (*al-Ikhwan al-Muslimum*), was founded in 1928 by Hasan al-Banna (1906–49), henceforth referred to as **Banna**. Ideologically, Banna is associated with the *Salafiyya* (a movement of modernization that 'looks back' to the time of the Prophet Muhammad and the Companions for inspiration and guidance); he was a highly effective organizer as well as a charismatic leader who proved an inspiration for many Islamic movements that were to follow. Banna wrote a treatise on jihad in which he treats the Islamic sources, the Quran and hadith, in a very literal sense, as is the wont of fundamentalist groups, and he begins by quoting the Quranic verse 'Fighting is ordained for you, though you dislike it' (2:216), as well as 'Whether you are killed for God's cause or die, God's forgiveness and mercy are better than anything people amass' (3:158) and 'To anyone who fights in God's way, whether killed or victorious, We shall give a great reward' (4:74). Banna uses such passages to argue that fighting and death in the cause of God are condoned. Here we have a perfect example of making use of the Quran to suit one's own ideology, for Banna adopts a 'pick and mix' approach and completely ignores the more tolerant verses quoted above by Haqq. However, Haqq can likewise be accused of being selective in order to adopt a more moderate ideology, and so the problem one faces is whose understanding of the Islamic sources is right, if it is at all possible to be right or wrong on such matters. This is a topic that will be explored in more depth when we consider the issue of ethical pluralism in the next chapter. Whereas Haqq regards qital as a 'low jihad' (*al-jihad al-asghar*), to use Banna's words, Banna himself sees qital as 'high jihad' (*al-jihad al-akbar*) and the very essence of jihad, for he states, 'The great reward for Muslims who fight is to kill or be killed for the sake of Allah.' As he goes on to say: 'Allah rewards the umma which masters the art of death and which acknowledges the necessity of death in dignity … Be sure, death is inevitable … If you do this for the path of Allah, you will be rewarded' (Tibi 2007: 60).

Sayyid **Qutb** (1906–66) was an Egyptian active reformer and a leading Islamic intellectual who formulated a distinct ideology for the radical reform movement the Muslim Brotherhood. While the head of this movement was actually Banna, Sayyid Qutb is regarded as the intellectual ideologue of the movement. His writings are highly regarded as literary works. He spent a number of years in prison, where he concentrated on his writing, producing such well-known works as *In the Shade of the Qur'an* and *Milestones*. As part of Egyptian president Jamal Abd al-Nasser's campaign against the Muslim Brotherhood, Qutb was executed in 1966 on the charge of conspiracy against the government. His execution has given him the status of martyr (*shahid*). It in his work *Milestones* that he writes specifically of jihad, and it is important because this – along with other writings by Qutb – is frequently cited by fundamentalists today. As we have seen, much Islamic scholarship adopts a dualistic approach to the world as the home of peace and the home of war, with varying views on the relationship between these two. What Banna does with this, like Mawdudi (see below), is to use the term 'jahiliyya' ('age of ignorance', which is more commonly a reference to the time before the coming of the Prophet Muhammad and to the place of Arabia) to refer to any place that has non-believers, and so we now have the division between 'the world of believers' and 'the world of neo-jahiliyya'. What counts as 'jahiliyya', then, would include features of modernity and even those who may call themselves Muslims but would not satisfy the rigorous, orthodox standards of such fundamentalist groups as the Muslim Brotherhood. One interesting quote from Qutb's *Milestones* is the following:

> If we insist on calling Islamic Jihad a defensive movement, then we must change the meaning of the word 'defense' and mean by it 'the defense of man' against all those elements which limit his freedom. These elements take the form of beliefs and concepts, as well as of political systems, based on economic, racial or class distinctions. When Islam first came into existence, the world was full of such systems, and the present-day Jahiliyya also has various kinds of such systems.
>
> (Qutb 1990: chap. 4)

Returning to the conditions required in order to fulfil the prerequisites for a just war, then the Just Cause Principle could be applied here if it is considered just to defend one's beliefs against the threat of jahiliyya. As Qutb goes on to say:

> In the verse giving permission to fight, God has informed the Believers that the life of this world is such that checking one group of people by another is the law of God, so that the earth may be cleansed of corruption. 'Permission to fight is given to those against whom war is made, because they are oppressed, and God is able to help them. These are the people who were expelled from their homes without cause, except that they said that our Lord is God. Had God not checked one people by another, then surely synagogues and churches and mosques would have been pulled down, where the name of God is remembered often.' Thus, this struggle is

not a temporary phase but an eternal state – an eternal state, as truth and falsehood cannot co-exist on this earth.

(Qutb 1990: chap. 4)

This understanding of jihad as a form of justified defence relies upon certain premises. The fundamentalist approach places so much emphasis on the words of the Quran that it subsumes any willingness to engage in human critical reasoning. As Islam means submission to God's will, and not human will, then Muslims have a duty to follow the Quran by the letter. The Muslim Brotherhood, and like-minded organizations, see themselves as the vanguard of right-believing and right-acting Muslims ready to assume leadership of the Muslim world when the time is right. Muslims are eternally at war with non-believers and the only reason that this is not always translating into physical attack is because it is not currently in a strategic position to do so: restraint from physical war is a *strategy*, not a principle. The end of the path is, ultimately, a world consisting of believers (i.e. Muslims) only and hence the 'vanguard' is there to achieve the 'milestones' along this path.

Mawdudi on jihad

Mawlana Mawdudi has much to say on many topics (see, especially, Chapter 6), and his views continue to be regarded with some esteem by many Islamic scholars and laypeople alike. Mawdudi's attitude towards jihad represents a conservative strand in Islam that has influenced other commentators as well as radical and more militant groups. In his work *Jihad in Islam* (first edition 1930), Mawdudi starts by condemning those Muslims who adopt a more apologetic approach to jihad. Mawdudi criticizes apologists who, he argues, attempt a revision of history by regarding Islam as a historically peaceful religion in an attempt to allay the Western picture of jihadi Muslims as 'a marching band of religious fanatics with savage beards and fiery eyes brandishing drawn swords and attacking infidels wherever they meet them and pressing them under the edge of the sword for the recital of the Kalima [short passages recited from the Quran]'. Apologists were so 'taken aback' by 'this picture of ours painted by foreigners' that they 'started offering apologies in this manner – Sir, what do we know of war and slaughter. We are pacifist preachers like the mendicants and religious divines' (Mawdudi 1996: 1).

These apologists attempt to present a more palatable image of jihad, Mawdudi asserts, although they 'plead guilty to one crime, though, that whenever someone else attacks us, we attacked him in self-defence' (Mawdudi 1996: 3). Jihad, then, is only in response to a physical attack and, for the apologists, what is far more important, the 'greater jihad', is an internal struggle to have faith. Mawdudi, however, is less pacifistic here: 'Islam requires the earth – not just a portion of it – not because the sovereignty over the earth should be wrestled from one or several nations and vested in one particular nation – but because the entire mankind should benefit from the ideology and welfare programme or what should be truer to say from "Islam" which is the programme of well-being for all humanity' (Mawdudi 1996: 6, 7).

This view fits in with Mawdudi's belief that Islam is the *true* religion and, therefore, it follows logically that the whole planet should be Muslim. Nine years after the publication of *Jihad in Islam*, Mawdudi gave a public lecture called *Jihad fi sabil Allah* in which he reiterates these views:

> the objective of the Islamic Jihad is to eliminate the rule of an un-Islamic system, and establish in its place an Islamic system of state rule. Islam does not intend to confine this rule to a single state or to a handful of countries. The aim of Islam is to bring about a universal revolution. Although in the initial stages, it is incumbent upon members of the Party of Islam to carry out a revolution in the state system of the countries to which they belong, their ultimate objective is none other than a world revolution.
>
> (Mawdudi 1995: 12)

The year of this address, 1939, has significance when we consider that the world's religions seemed to be submerged under the pressure of such secular ideologies as Nazism, fascism and Marxist-Leninism. To argue for an Islamic 'world revolution' at that time seemed out of tune with events. But it was the fact that Islam was being 'attacked' by more secular ideologies that led Mawdudi to call for a resurgence and a revolution in the first place. Mawdudi's understanding of jihad is not as 'war' but rather as 'liberation' and he is not averse to 'borrowing' secular ideological terms and seeing them as essentially Islamic in origin. In terms of this 'world revolution', Mawdudi was thinking long term; this is not something that could occur overnight, or even in a life-time, especially given the seemingly waning state of Islam at that time. Mawdudi's historical picture of Islam begins with the 'liberation' from jahiliyya, the state of 'ignorance' that existed amongst the Arab peoples before the coming of the Prophet Muhammad. This jahiliyya is a world of paganism, polytheism, atheism, immoralism, injustice and violence. Therefore, jihad is perceived as the *opposite* of this, as a 'struggle' for peace and justice against a Hobbesian conception of Man as living a life that is 'brutish and short'. The original goal of holy war, Mawdudi argues, was not to force people to convert to Islam, but rather to liberate people from injustice (*fasad*) and civil war (*fitnah*).

Mawdudi's views on jihad connect very closely with his views on the Islamic state, which were considered in Chapter 6. Mawdudi's revolution called for the eradication of all governments and the eventual establishment of one united people, an umma, under the rule of God and His laws. This would, of course, mean that people could choose to be non-Muslims, but would nonetheless be living under Islamic rules. This is a logical consequence of a belief in one God with the existence of absolute, universal, perfect moral values.

Mawdudi goes further by dismissing the distinction between jihad as offen-sive and defensive by arguing that such a distinction is irrelevant. Jihad is a 'revolutionary programme' rather than a conflict between states, and it is at the centre of Mawdudi's call for an international (Islamic) Revolutionary Party, the 'party of God', of 'Hezbollah', engaged in a jihad against those who resist what Mawdudi saw as a logical and inevitable revolution. Mawdudi argued that there exists a tension in every society between the home of peace and the home of war, which would continue unless there is submission and acceptance of the will of God. Mawdudi, therefore, could not conceive of the possibility of a pluralistic state because the tension between Muslims and non-Muslims is synonymous with the tension between right and wrong: a state must strive towards being either morally good (living under the laws of God) or morally bad (living under secular laws). There cannot be two or more systems of beliefs or political parties.

Mawdudi's views are very black and white, but perhaps his most important contribution to the topic of jihad is giving the concept a more contemporary relevance by contrasting it with jahiliyya. Mawdudi imposes the paradigm of the Prophet Muhammad's jihad against the jahiliyya of the pagan Arabs upon contemporary events. This original approach takes jihad and jahiliyya out of their pure historical context and places them within a recurring struggle of good versus evil. The 'good' always remains the same, submission to God, but the 'evil' can change from one place to another, from one age to another. For Mawdudi, Islam and the Islamic state are synonymous, and his concept of jihad is not equivalent to 'war', but is the striving to achieve God's will on Earth.

However, the implications for those Muslims who do not live in an Islamic state, or, in other words, in the 'home of war', is that they are not really Muslims at all, but sinners. Mawdudi argues that all who claim to be Muslims must fulfil their duty to engage in jihad against un-Islamic systems and have them replaced by an Islamic way of life. In effect, to assert that one is a Muslim and yet to continue to live happily in a non-Islamic country is not really to be a true Muslim, so far as Mawdudi was concerned. Whilst Mawdudi may well have been thinking specifically of Muslims in India at this time, this would nonetheless include all Muslims across the world who find themselves in a similar situation. If an Islamic state is attacked by a non-Islamic state then all Muslims, no matter where they are from, should come forward and engage in jihad. In this respect, jihad is as important as daily prayers or fasting, and someone who displays any reluctance to engage in jihad is a sinner.

Just war theory applied to Islam

Certainly, as seen from the fundamentalist perspective, the 'clash of civilizations' thesis seems to hold a great deal of water, but not all scholarship accepts this dualistic 'us versus them' vision or sees notions of peace and war as so radically different from Western just war theory. Historically, matters concerning the conduct of war in Islam have been addressed, primarily, by legal scholars, rather than philosophers, and this often resulted in resorting to pragmatism – appealing more to the political needs of the state – rather than necessarily considering the moral merits in relation to the Islamic framework.

We return again to Khaldun's *Muqaddimah*, which makes a distinction between four different types of war. The first two kinds he calls 'illegitimate wars' and consist of, first, petty squabbles between rival families or tribes and, second, attempts at plunder from 'savage peoples'. What is of more interest is when Khaldun considers the situation that was more contemporary to him and this perceived struggle between the house of peace and the house of war. The third type of war, that between one Muslim and another, Khaldun classes as *fitna* ('trial' or 'test'), a civil war that tests the beliefs of Muslims when faced with a dispute. These, Khaldun argues, should be resolved quickly as Muslims should not make war against one another. This view can be contrasted with that of Sayyid Qutb, who effectively argued that if Muslims are fighting Muslims it may well be because one side, at least, are not 'Muslim' according to his strict principles, and it is therefore justified aggression. The term 'jihad', then, is reserved for war against non-believers only, and this is Khaldun's fourth type of war.

Another important thinker on jihad is Averroes, whose treatise *The Distinguished Jurist's Primer* goes into considerable detail concerning the grounds for war. It was, at the time, a given that Muslims are morally obliged to wage war in self-defence, but what was of greater debate was justifying war at a time when Islam was in a process of territorial expansion. Inevitably, as Islam and Muslims spread beyond Arabia and encountered non-Islamic states, the example of Muhammad – sources state that he sent letters to the rulers of Byzantium, Iran and Egypt inviting them to preach Islam in their countries – was used whereby the first encounter was an invitation to spread the word of Islam. If the ruler refused this invitation, then he was given the option of accepting incorporation within the Islamic realm, the house of peace, as a protected community that could still follow their own laws, beliefs and customs but would be required to pay a tax (*jizya*) for the cost of protection under the Islamic umbrella. If the non-Muslim ruler rejected this option, only then would the Muslim ruler have grounds for aggression and, in fact, was morally obliged to wage war against them.

Averroes points out that a major problem was, once engaged in jihad, at what point does it stop? What is evident here is that there is no suggestion that non-Muslims should be forced to convert to Islam, but also Averroes recognizes that the state of perpetual house of peace versus house of war is unsatisfactory, and so argues that it is sufficient for a nation to submit to subjugation to Muslim rule, leaving non-Muslims free to keep their own religion. This is on the premise that, in time, they would see the error of their ways and convert to Islam, which in fact would often be the case.

As the primary aim of jihad is to create a house of peace, and not purely territorial gain or plunder for the sake of it, it is important for Muslim armies to behave in a manner that provides a good example to those non-Muslims that have been conquered, given they will not be forced to convert but, it is hoped, will acknowledge Islam's superiority in a number of respects, not least as morally upstanding. In terms of *jus in bello*, then, a key passage of the Quran is 'Fight in God's cause against those who fight you, but do not overstep the limits: God does not love those who overstep the limits' (2:190). This, incidentally, comes immediately before the well-known 'sword-verse', 'Kill them wherever you encounter them' (2:191), and yet this former passage is often ignored by those (Muslim and non-Muslim alike) who argue that Islam is aggressive in nature. However, the command to not 'overstep the limits' (*la ta'tadu*) is generally considered to consist of those boundaries established by the Prophet and the Rashidun (the first four 'rightly-guided' caliphs). Traditions state that when Muhammad sent out a force to do battle he would insist on a number of restraints being adhered to, and the first caliph, Abu Bakr, according to his 'ten commands', carries this on:

> Do not act treacherously; do not act disloyally; do not act neglectfully. Do not mutilate; do not kill little children or old men, or women; do not cut off the heads of the palm trees or burn them; do not cut down the fruit trees; do not slaughter a sheep or a cow or a camel, except for food. You will pass by people who devote their lives in cloisters; leave them and their devotions alone. You will come upon people who bring you platters in which are various sorts of food; if you eat any of it, mention the name of God over it.
>
> (Aboul-Enein and Zuhur 2004: 22)

The above clearly lays out Principles of Discrimination and Proportionality that, by analogy (references to palm trees and camels may be time- and culture-specific, but presumably can in the modern world be applied to, for example, civilian factories and cars), can be applied to today. Having said that, there has historically been some dispute over when these restrictions should apply. The renowned eighth-century jurist of international law, Muhammmad al-Shaybani (750–805), reported that the founder of the Hanafi law school, Abu Hanifa (699–767), was concerned that if attackers abided by these principles then it would not be possible to engage in fighting at all, for he could not think of any city or territory of war in which none of these rules would be broken. Consequently, it was argued, the use of such tactics as catapults and flooding was allowed even if – as it was sure to – it caused the loss of life of women, children and old men, as well as the destruction of fruit trees! The view here is that discrimination should be exercised in war, but if collateral damage is unavoidable this is the fault of the enemy for making it impossible to avoid such damage. A modern-day equivalent would be the placing of a munitions factory in the centre of an area heavily populated with civilians.

The Quran also specifies conditions during war, for example on the treatment of prisoners: 'When you meet disbelievers in battle, strike them in the neck, and once they are defeated, bind any captives firmly – later you can release them by grace or by ransom – until the toils of war have ended' (47:4).

On the treatment of non-Muslims, residents of the house of war: 'If any of the idolators should seek your protection, grant it to him so that he may hear the word of God, then take him to a place safe for him, for they are people with knowledge' (9:6). And on the division of military spoils: 'Know that one-fifth of your battle gains belongs to God and the Messenger, to close relatives and orphans, to the needy and travellers … ' (8:41).

To conclude, there is still a great deal of work to be done on the issue of just war in Islam compared with that in the Western philosophical tradition, although hopefully it is evident from this chapter that the Islamic tradition is not as inherently averse to just war principles as some might think and, in fact, its principles, in a broad sense, do not differ greatly from the Western view.

Further reading

Hashmi, S.H. (ed.) (2002), *Islamic Political Ethics*, Princeton, NJ: Princeton University Press.
Kepel, G. (2009), *Jihad: The Trail of Political Islam*, London: I.B. Tauris & Co.
Mawdudi, M. (1996), *Al-Jihad fi al-Islam (Jihad in Islam)*, 15th edn, 1st edn 1930, Kuwait: International Islamic Federation of Student Organisations.
Qutb, S. (1990), *Milestones*, Indianapolis, IN: American Trust Publications.

9 Islam and shared moral values

From the broader perspective, an important question is the extent to which a commitment to one faith is synonymous with ethical exclusivity. More specifically, the reason for focusing on Islam as a faith commitment here is that, since the events of 9/11, Islam has been at the forefront of attention in terms of discourse on such important issues as tolerance, human rights and pluralism.

In 1992, the American political scientist Francis Fukuyama (b. 1952) published *The End of History and the Last Man*, which itself is an expansion of a 1990 essay, 'The End of History?' In the article, Fukuyama says the following:

> What we may be witnessing is not just the end of the Cold War, or the passing of a particular period of post-war history, but the end of history as such: that is, the end point of mankind's ideological evolution and the universalization of Western liberal democracy as the final form of human government.
>
> (Fukuyama 1991: 341)

Here, Fukuyama is presenting a Hegelian view of history as progressing towards universality and homogeneity. For Karl Marx, this end to history would result in communism but, for Fukuyama, it was liberal democracy and the triumph of capitalism. According to Fukuyama, other ideologies do still exist, of course, but they are no competition for the West and, he would argue, it is the responsibility of the West to maintain a league of civilized nations to police non-compliant nations until they are ready to enter the global community of liberal democracy.

In a response to this seminal book, another American political scientist, Samuel P. Huntington (1927–2008), wrote an article for *Foreign Affairs* in 1993 entitled 'The Clash of Civilizations?' which he then expanded into his 1996 book, *The Clash of Civilizations and the Remaking of World Order*. Since that time the notion of the 'Clash of Civilizations theory' has entered the mainstream of dialogue in not only politics, but history, philosophy, economics etc. In brief, it is the thesis that a people's cultural and religious identities – their 'civilizations' – will be the main source of conflict in the present and the future. Huntington was not the first to use the phrase 'clash of civilizations': the historian Bernard

Lewis (b. 1916) used it in 1990 in his article 'The Roots of Muslim Rage', and, in fact, one can trace the term as far back as 1926 with the book, *Young Islam on Trek: A Study in the Clash of Civilizations*, by Basil Mathews. What is interesting from these titles is that the clash of civilizations thesis seems to relate particularly to Islam, rather than to any other civilization.

There is a growing concern amongst Muslims and non-Muslims alike that there is this civilizational conflict between Islam and the West especially. Rather than being presented with the theological view of Islam as a member of the same family as the Judaeo-Christian tradition, we have conflict and difference. Whilst many Western scholars would support Samuel Huntington's 'Clash of Civilizations' thesis, it is evident that there are thinkers and movements *within* Islam that are also sympathetic to the view that Islam and the 'Other' are essentially incompatible. Because of the incredible diversity that exists within Islam itself, the reader will no doubt be aware by now that it is extremely difficult, if not impossible, to determine a consensus amongst all Muslims on any particular topic. This, to some extent anyway, should be applauded as it reflects the richness of the tradition and the fact that Islam – in line with other world religions – does not stand still and is interrelated to a vast array of varying cultural, moral and religious traditions. Nonetheless, as this book has consistently argued, if we are to make any use of the term 'Islam' at all, it is incumbent upon us to seek for at least some essential tenets that distinguish this particular religious tradition from any other. When considering the matter of Islamic human rights, then, the struggle to ascertain what this actually is will be a challenging one given these caveats.

The issue of Islamic human rights is an extremely important and topical one. Given the recent Arab Spring uprisings, vital moral questions concerning the rights of human beings to engage in freedom of thought and expression are closely linked to political struggles and calls for democratization. This, in turn, raises questions over whether Islam and democracy are compatible, which links here to the previous chapter on political philosophy.

Human rights

The very idea of an elaboration of *Islamic* human rights is a relatively recent one, and must be seen within the context of a backlash against Western colonialism, which imposed Western forms of human rights upon Islamic states. With the independence of Islamic nations from the colonial yolk comes a need to determine an Islamic identity, rather than simply adopting Western standards of human rights. If it be the case that Islamic notions of human rights happen to mirror Western notions, then perhaps that is because there is a recognition that certain human rights are universal and fundamental, regardless of cultural, religious or ethnic identity. In some circles there is a suspicion that for an Islamic state to endorse, say, the Universal Declaration of Human Rights (UDHR), this is equivalent to being servants of Western imperialism. However, if it can be demonstrated that international human rights are, at least in some respects, embedded *within* Islamic tradition, then this suspicion is unjustified. These suspicions, however, can be explained by, again, keeping in mind recent political events. For example, US government intervention in Afghanistan against the Taliban and in Iraq against Saddam Hussein were given moral credence by the US arguing that human rights were being violated in these countries by those concerned. The US government, therefore, maintained they were morally obliged to intervene to free the oppressed and to bring in international human rights. Therefore, for any Islamic country to defend international human rights at this time could be tainted by being associated with US foreign policy. This, however, seems to avoid the more fundamental point as to whether the Taliban and Saddam Hussein are truly representative Islamic moral agents. Therefore, as best as we can, we need to keep the contingent political motives separate from the search for universal moral codes and the question of whether or not Muslims and non-Muslims share a common humanity and common rights and freedoms.

Moral relativism

There is also an on-going debate about whether or not there is such a thing as universal human rights. The more existential approach here is that human beings do not have a human nature as such – each human being is his or her own 'project' to use Sartre's term – and, therefore, it makes no sense to argue for humans possessing an 'essence' in terms of rights and freedoms. In fact, Sartre himself did struggle with this from a moral standpoint, stating that, if nothing else, we are 'condemned to be free', although he actually went much further than that in arguing that human beings must act as if they are legislators for all mankind. This Sartrean shift to a form of Kantian ethics suggests a concern for moral relativism: that the moral code of one group is relative to the moral codes of that group. This does not mean that 'anything goes', for we are still bound by a moral code (whether it be family, nation and so on), but it does mean that the moral code of one group could differ from that of another group, and neither of these groups would be 'right' or 'wrong' because they could not be judged by any universal standard. Moral relativism has been used as a weapon by Islamic governments to argue that to abide by UN moral law would be against Islamic moral law. For example, in 1984, Iran's UN representative Said Raja'i-Khorasani argued that the Islamic Republic was in harmony with Islamic moral convictions and therefore the UN had no right to interfere. In fact, this trend for defending religious values against international human rights is growing, evidenced by the power of the Organisation of Islamic Cooperation (OIC), which will often vote as a bloc on the UN Human Rights Council. This, however, conflicts with the OIC's own charter, which states that fundamental human rights are compatible with Islamic values.

Opposed to this moral relativism, however, are those who would argue that Islam is in accord with human rights because there are certain basic rights that all human beings possess, and this is recognized at the core of Islamic tradition.

It is important to stress here that this is not Islam *responding* to human rights issues and 'updating' its belief system, but rather that basic human rights have always existed within the Islamic tradition. If anything, it is a *going back* to how Islam was and a recognition that Islamic states are failing in their moral duty to uphold these basic Islamic principles. The fault, then, is not Islam; it is politics. For example, the human rights lawyer Shirin Ebadi, who won the Nobel Peace Prize in 2003, has argued that Islam and human rights are compatible – despite, ironically, such proclamations endangering her own life – and that those who endorse relativism are using this as an excuse to violate human rights. It should also be pointed out that all Muslim states have joined the United Nations and many have contributed considerably to the development of international human rights organizations and initiatives.

International human rights: a brief history

In terms of the Western world, the idea of an actual formulation of human rights is also a relatively recent phenomenon, largely produced by the focus on humanism in Renaissance and Enlightenment thought. In concrete terms we have the American Declaration of Independence of 1776, the Bill of Rights that was added to the US Constitution in 1791 and the 1789 Declaration of the Rights of Man and Citizen, which resulted from the French Revolution. These are important because they represent something of a 'paradigm shift' in how humans are perceived: not as mere instruments of the state – the idea, which goes back to the ancient Greeks such as Plato and Aristotle, that the state comes first and the individual is nothing without the state – but a more 'bottom-up' approach in which the rights of the individual come first and the role of the state is to protect those rights, not to deny them. This paradigm has become standard amongst Western nations and there is now a vast range of bodies assigned to protect these rights, the most prominent being the UDHR.

The UDHR regards many human rights as absolute; that is to say, there can be no rationale for curbing them. These include the right to equality before the law; freedom of thought, conscience and religion (including the freedom to change your religion); and the right to work. In terms of other human rights these may only be curtailed if they conflict with the freedom of others or with the morality and general welfare of a democratic society.

And so when we talk about human rights, we mean it in the sense that it has been formularized as a set of principles. In this respect it is a relatively recent phenomenon, even in the Western world. This is not the same as saying that human rights may well be *implied* within certain traditions. Therefore, to say that human rights exist within the Islamic tradition and have done so since the beginning of Islam (i.e. human rights exist in the Quran) is not the same thing as saying that Islam produced an actual formal document that outlines individual human rights in seventh-century Arabia. Not unlike Western societies before the eighteenth century, Islamic societies did not focus on the rights of the individual generally speaking, although certain elements of

Islam – most notably Sufism – do possess a more individualistic and existential character.

As we have seen in previous chapters, certain Islamic philosophers – for example, Alfarabi and Averroes, as well as the rationalist Mutazilites and the Kharijites, who split away from the mainstream because of their insistence that the leader of the community should be elected – have, in the past, strived to assert humanistic values, and that one's moral status should be determined by the light of reason, but such efforts have been met with resistance from the more conservative theologians. Such resistance prevented the possibility of an Islamic Enlightenment in this respect, if ever such a possibility were to arise. The emphasis, rather, was not on the rights of the individual, but on a pious Muslim's duty to obey God's law without question. Any attempt to assert one's individual freedom, therefore, was tantamount to questioning God and, therefore, heretical.

The conservative approach

How one approaches the Islamic sources does, as we have seen, depend upon one's own ideological inclinations and we have already divided these (see Chapter 8) into, very roughly, the liberal Muslim and the conservative Muslim. I say 'roughly' because using such labels as 'liberal' and 'conservative' may help to some degree, but hinder to some extent too. Here, 'conservative' is a reference to Muslim thinkers who are more tied to the traditional Islamic sources and less inclined to embrace non-Islamic ideas. This is not to suggest that human rights is exclusively a 'liberal' construct, but rather that conservatives would look for the source of human rights within the traditional sources.

It has already been noted in the previous chapter how important Mawlana Mawdudi is in terms of the more conservative element; and as he wrote a pamphlet entitled *Human Rights in Islam* (published in 1976), it is appropriate to refer to him in this chapter. Mawdudi argues that human rights actually originated with Islam and that, therefore, the West has nothing to teach Islam regarding human rights. In 1981, a document was published called the Universal Islamic Declaration of Human Rights (UIDHR) with the support of the Islamic Council, a private organization affiliated to the Muslim World League, which is based in Saudi Arabia. Whilst one should praise Islamic political leaders for being prepared to engage in the human rights debate, the results of this document are problematic. One might suppose that having the acronym 'UIDHR' brings it close in spirit to the UDHR, but this would be misleading, as the links with conservative Saudi Arabia might suggest. Emphasis is placed upon duties and obligations to God rather than on the rights of the individual. Like Mawdudi, the UIDHR claims that human rights are Islamic in origin: 'Islam gave to mankind an ideal code of human rights fourteen centuries ago.' Therefore, human rights are placed within the context of being restricted by sharia. This makes human rights considerably less 'universal' because it allows individual nations to circumscribe human rights on the basis of how they interpret sharia. This is not helped by the fact that the important intricacies of the Arabic UIDHR document are disguised in the English translation. For example, in the English version you have the following: 'all persons are equal before the Law and are entitled to equal opportunities and protection of the Law' (Article 3.a). This, at first, seems perfectly in harmony with the UDHR. However, note the word 'Law' here: in the Arabic (which it is stated must be given precedence) the 'Law' equals 'sharia'. And so what the principle is really saying is that humans have rights according to sharia, which, in many countries, denies equality for women and non-Muslims. There are many other examples of such discrepancies between the English and Arabic versions, but the point to be made here is that we need to be careful when various bodies proclaim themselves to be upholders of human rights in the way that it is understood in the West or when they assert that the Islamic codes of human rights pre-date those of the European Enlightenment.

Liberal Islam

On the more 'liberal' side is Soroush (see Chapter 5). He has often been critical of the government and now teaches Islamic philosophy and theology in Tehran. It is this Iranian context that is key to Soroush's political philosophy, for he witnessed first-hand a political order that suppressed individual human rights. Whilst the Iranian government claimed to rule according to Islamic principles, Soroush argued that its concern was with keeping its citizens under a tight rein rather than true adherence to Islamic principles. The importance here is that true religious belief requires the individual to believe out of choice, not out of fear or mere blind obedience. Freedom, therefore, is a necessary condition of faith:

> True believers must embrace their faith of their own free will – not because it was imposed, or inherited, or part of the dominant local culture. To become a believer under pressure or coercion isn't true belief.
>
> (Wright 2008: 268)

Soroush argues that God created Man to be free, although freedom in turn has its faults as it allows humans to engage in deceit and to sin. However, the cost is worth it. Soroush is not, it should be noted, saying that the West is free and the Islamic world is tyrannical, for a distinction needs to be made between internal and external freedom. By 'external' he means the actions one engages in that seem to make us free, for there is no denying that many Western countries are 'freer' in the sense of freedom of movement, political action and so on. However, Soroush believes that Islam, and especially Sufism, has much to teach us all about internal freedom. Ultimately, we can all learn from each other. This idea of freedom is not dissimilar from the kind of freedom that Jean-Paul Sartre wrote of in *Being and Nothingness*, making a clear distinction between empirical freedom and ontological freedom. When Sartre controversially says that 'the slave in chains is as free as his master' he is, of course, well aware that, empirically speaking, the slave is nowhere near as free as his master, but, from an ontological perspective, the slave still is 'condemned to be free' in terms of having *choices*, limited though they may be. The kind of freedom that existentialists talk about is a sense of personal freedom that is neither political nor metaphysical but has very much to do with how we think of ourselves, how we behave, how we think about our behaviour. The idea is that freedom has to do with making choices, with deciding how you are going to live your life, with facing the consequences of your choices. Freedom is often connected with reason: to be free is to act rationally, and Soroush shares that rational tradition with the Mutazilites. That devoutly religious Christian existentialist Søren **Kierkegaard** (1813–55) has a nice little aphorism that summarizes this view: he says with reference to the Denmark semi-revolution in 1848: 'people hardly make use of the freedom they do have, like freedom of thought, instead they demand freedom of speech as compensation' (Balk 2012: 117). This is reminiscent of Soroush, who accused the West of being too concerned with such external freedoms as freedom of speech, which, as a result, is a freedom that is abused and results in excessive sex and violence. Therefore, it is not so much the *possession* of external freedoms, but your *attitude* towards them that matters.

Mawdudi is very critical of Western thought and wants to ring-fence the Islamic world – which he regards as entirely self-sufficient – against what he sees as the corruption of the West. Soroush, on the other hand, argues that truth and knowledge are not exclusive to any one tradition: all sources of knowledge can contribute to understanding, and it is understanding that should be the true goal of all pious Muslims. The Islamic sources are, of course, valuable for our ethical knowledge, but this does not deny the importance of non-Islamic sources. This attitude to the West may well be to some extent reflected in Soroush's own biography. Whereas Mawdudi, the product of an India under Western rule that witnessed the decline of Muslim power as a result, saw the West as the enemy to be resisted, Soroush in Iran suffered less from Western imperialism. Although it was by no means absent, Iran was always in a much stronger position to resist Western incursions, and it did so with some success historically. Soroush is not only writing from another geographical location, but from another time period, which saw Iran reject American power during the Islamic Revolution of 1979. Soroush also studied in England, and Western philosophers such as Kant and Hume have influenced his philosophy.

For Soroush, toleration towards non-Muslims was essential to human rights. For someone to be intolerant of other people's beliefs is to make the intellectual error of confusing the person with their beliefs, for it is quite possible both to disagree with a person's beliefs and to find the holder of those beliefs blameless, respectable and even commendable. For example, Soroush cites Ghazzali and St Francis of Assisi as two individuals who are 'praise-worthy' and 'honourable' despite the fact that their religious beliefs differ so widely. The very fact that there are many diverse religions suggests, for Soroush, that such diversity is all part of God's plan, whereas Mawdudi would see this as human beings diverging from the true path. For the conservative, the true path is Islam; for the liberal, the true path is diversity, although Soroush himself would not call attention to difference of belief merely because it is the 'liberal' thing to do, but rather because it tells us something about human nature. Therefore, although human rights are certainly not the exclusive property of liberals, a conservative Muslim is by definition tied to Islamic sources, which logically means that diversity (which presumably would include having the right to be non-Muslim or to be an apostate) as a 'right' is difficult to defend, though perhaps not impossible.

Looking to the sources

Here we have examples of how different Islamic scholars can see their religion in very different ways. But how can going back to the sources really help us to determine what the attitude to Islam is in terms of such human rights issues as tolerance towards other people's beliefs? There are numerous verses in the Quran that seem to point towards religious tolerance, notably the following:

> We have assigned a law and a path to each of you. If God had so willed, He would have made you one community, but He wanted to test you through that which He has given you, so race to do good: you will all return to God and He will make clear to you the matters you differed about.
>
> (5:48)

> If your Lord had pleased, He would have made all people a single community, but they continue to have their differences.
>
> (11:118)

> People, We created you all from a single man and a single woman, and made you into races and tribes so that you should get to know each other.
>
> (49:13)

Soroush believes that greater globalization is a good thing for Islam as it allows Muslims to encounter more readily the beliefs of others and, in turn, to learn more about themselves. Others, however, see globalization as a threat to Islam. Yet, as the Muslim philosopher Fazlur **Rahman** (1919–88) notes, the Prophet Muhammad 'recognised without a moment of hesitation that Abraham, Moses, Jesus, and other Old and New Testament religious personalities had been genuine prophets like himself' (Rahman 1980: 164). For Muhammad, references to People of the Book include all divine revelations. Therefore, from the very beginnings of Islam, there has been an interaction with other beliefs and practices, and, as we have seen in previous chapters, many Muslim thinkers have been open to the ideas of other cultures, despite the opposite tendency to resist such things.

When we talk of Islamic ethical values, there is the difficulty over what counts as specifically 'Islamic' in origin and what does not, for the arrival of Islam in the seventh century inherits an indigenous (i.e. Arabic) system of beliefs (and there are, of course, additional issues here as to what extent any belief is indigenous), as well as engaging in an interaction with other value systems as Islam spread beyond its Arabic borders. We have already come across the term jahiliyya, which usually, although not exclusively, refers to the time prior to the arrival of Islam. Geographically speaking, it refers to Arabia and to the people that inhabited that region at the time. It is a period of 'ignorance' in that the people were unaware of the message of God, although the term also suggests that the people of jahiliyya possessed an inherent barbarity resulting from a lack of order and the ethical guidance that Islam brings. The absence of Islam, therefore, is synonymous with an absence of a coherent belief, of a unity, of literacy and so on. Whilst the term jahiliyya, then, has a specific reference to the time and place of pre-Islamic Arabia, it also, as we have seen (see Chapter 8), has been extended to other times and places; for, as the reformist Sayyid Qutb, notes: 'If we look at the sources and foundations of modern modes of living, it becomes clear that the whole world is steeped in Jahiliyya, and all the marvellous material comforts and advanced inventions do not diminish its ignorance' (Qutb 1990: 8).

Hence, jahiliyya becomes a reference to the modern world in general, which has turned its back on God's message of unity, peace and virtue by, instead, engaging in such things as the pursuit of excessive wealth and the exploitation of the weak. The term is used in the Quran to refer to a psychological state:

> While the disbelievers had fury in their hearts – the fury of ignorance – God sent His tranquillity down on to His Messenger and the believers and made binding on them [their] promise to obey God, for that was more appropriate and fitting for them.
>
> (48:26)

The reference here to God's 'tranquillity' can be seen as a change in attitude, replacing an age of turbulence and chaos with a unified spiritual and moral identity, a 'wholeness' in both the individual and the community. This portrayal of a pre-Islamic society that was 'barbaric' and chaotic may, however, be questioned historically, for evidence points towards a society that was much more complex than supposed. In fact, it is hard to believe that Arabia, with its harsh conditions, would have functioned as well as it did, or survived at all, if it did not have a degree of complexity, a structure of authority and a rigorous moral code to guide it. It would also be stretching credibility too far to accept that Islam, with its central concept of the umma and the paradigm of Muhammad and the state of Medina as guiding lights, could or did simply replace entirely the society that was already in place. Rather, over a period of some time (the length of which is debatable) the Islamic 'worldview' did transform Arabic authority, whilst continuities with the past continued to exist and were embedded within the Islamic worldview.

The Muslim philosopher of history Khaldun is an important contributor on this issue. In reference to the Bedouin of Arabia, he says, 'The leader is obeyed, but he has no power to force others to accept his rulings … There is scarcely one among them who would cede his power to another, even to his father, his brother, or the eldest member of his family' (Khaldun 1958: chap. 2).

Khaldun is a figure we came across in Chapter 8, when discussing jihad. He was born in Tunis and he went on to serve as tutor to the heir apparent of the then Muslim state of Granada in Spain and finished his career as a well-respected grand judge in Cairo. Khaldun's life experiences, however, were not limited to the royal courts: after defeat in a battle, which Khaldun led, he was forced to spend three years as a refugee amongst mountain tribesmen, and it is these experiences that add up to an insightful account of Arabic authority. For its time, Khaldun's work is radical in his application of philosophical method to the study of history in the belief that this could help us to understand how communities organize their lives. By this method, Khaldun hoped to build up a framework that would lead to a scientific account of how dynasties in the Middle East rise and fall. In his great work *Muqaddimah*, he begins with the sensible premise that 'the differences of condition among people are the result of the different ways in which they make their living' (Khaldun 1958: 1). He then goes on to contrast two ways of 'making a living' in Arabic society: that of the Bedouin and that of the city-dweller. In a way that is reminiscent of the French philosopher Rousseau's examination of the 'noble savage' transformed as he becomes a city-dweller, Khaldun traces what he perceives as the Bedouin's fall from purity and egalitarianism when he is likewise exposed to the city life. The Bedouin, through exposure to the comforts of the city and the authority of royal rule, may succumb and lose his strong sense of independence and individuality. This is all part of a cycle: the new migrants to the cities soften over time and are then subsequently easy prey to invasion from the more robust neighbouring tribes. Khaldun, therefore, stresses the importance of maintaining a strong Bedouin ethos, which religion can provide.

Ethical pluralism

The point here is that even pre-Islamic society should not be seen in such stark black-and-white contrast with the coming of Islam: the 'barbaric' that is then replaced by 'civilized' Islam. Recalling that Muhammad himself as a child spent time amongst the Bedouin, due to the city-dwellers' belief that the values of the Bedouin were worth preserving, the coming of the Prophet Muhammad was seen more as a warning that *traditional* values were eroding in Mecca than the need to introduce entirely new values. The fact that there is no 'church' in Islam means that it has inevitably accommodated a variety of moral standpoints, rather than impose one monolithic structure. As evidenced in the hadith, reference is often made to the pre-Islamic sunna; though sometimes as a rejection of certain of its values, it is also often an assimilation of those values to the Islamic worldview.

Therefore, on the one hand, Islam borrows heavily from its own indigenous Arabic moral values but, on the other hand, it also has been readily open to the ethical values of neighbouring cultures, most notably those of Persia, Greece and India, from a very early stage in Islamic history. Just for example, the writings of Ibn al-Muqaffa (d. *c*. 756), which consist of a number of moral fables that have been translated from Middle Persian literature, present images of moral character and precepts to imitate. For example, in one work attributed to him, *al-Adab al-kabir* (*The Major Work on Secretarial Etiquette*) importance is placed on friendship and surrounding oneself with people of sound moral character. Perhaps the best-known work of literature that raises the philosophical issue of moral character must be the tale *Hayy ibn Yaqzan* (*Alive, son of Awake*), named after the hero of this story. *Hayy ibn Yaqzan*, written by the Muslim Andalusian philosopher Ibn Tufayl (1105–85), was the first Arabic novel and anticipated such European works as Defoe's *Robinson Crusoe* and Rousseau's *Emile*. Hayy is abandoned as a young child on a remote and uninhabited island, where he is raised by a gazelle. The gazelle dies when Hayy is just seven years of age, but he survives by using his reason. For example, Hayy dissects the gazelle to find out what happened to her, and this causes the child to discover that the death was due to a loss of innate heat. It is this process of reasoned enquiry, in total isolation from other human beings, that leads Hayy into a journey for ultimate truth. As he grows older, Hayy becomes more reflective and, unlike the animals that he shares his habitat with who remain firmly within the physical world, he begins to question his existence and to speculate upon the metaphysical and God. In seven phases of seven years each, and solely through the exercise of innate faculties, Hayy goes through the gradations of knowledge discussed by the Muslim philosopher Avicenna.

Hayy then comes into contact with two other humans, Asal and his friend Salaman. These two had grown up on another island that followed the teachings of an ancient prophet. Salaman chooses faithfully to follow the commandments of his religion, in line with the majority of the believers. Asal, however, chooses the life of solitude and a more mystical, spiritual path. What is important here is that all three, Hayy, Asal and Salaman, found God, but in their very different ways. Despite this, when all three meet, their fundamental beliefs do not contradict each other, although they chose very different paths. Hence, the 'Truth' is essentially the same for all of us; even someone brought up on a desert island will know innately what is right and wrong.

What we have, therefore, is not a systematic formula of human rights, but nonetheless a solid body of literature that presents a set of applied ethics, which came to be known by the Arabic term *akhlaq*, essentially a person's moral disposition or character. The early Persian Islamic philosopher and historian Ibn Miskawayh (932–1030) wrote *Tahdhib al-akhlaq* (*Refinement of Morals*), which provides an extremely detailed treatment of ethical values from a number of traditions, not only pre-Islamic and Islamic, but also Greek, Persian and Indian, for he argues that the ethical values of these traditions are in accord with those of Islamic values.

Historical examples

For an audience today it is understandable to perceive a clear delineation between the world of Islam and this rather vague construct called 'the West', but such a division – however accurate it may be in reality – would seem very alien just a few hundred years ago, as it results primarily from the post-colonial period when Islamic nations felt a need to distinguish themselves from Western ideology and beliefs if they were to assert any identity of their own, hence the fact that those scholars who do tend to assert a distinctive Islamic ethics are also historically products of the post-colonial era (Mawdudi, Qutb and so on). The very fact that the boundaries between what is the 'Islamic' world and what is not were not always so clearly defined meant that what constituted Islamic ethical values and what did not was also somewhat indistinct. There are numerous examples that can be given here, but a couple of prominent cases would include Muslim rule in Andalusia in Spain, where Muslims, Jews and Christians intermingled, and during the Mughal reign in India, which not only included the three former religions, but also Hindus, Jains, Sikhs and Parsis. When Islamic rule came to an end in Spain with the conquering of Granada by Christians in 1492, the majority of Jews fled to Muslim North Africa to avoid forced conversion to Christianity. More recently, during World War II, Jews with French nationality in Vichy France were threatened with deportation (which would have meant the gas chambers), whereas Jews of Moroccan nationality were protected by Morocco's Muhammad V. The third Mughal emperor Akbar the Great (1542–1605) is an often-cited example of religious and moral tolerance, advocating the 'cult of reason' (*rah-i 'aql*), which required an open debate amongst all the religious traditions. Akbar even created his own religion, the 'Divine Religion' (*Din-i Ilahi*), with himself as the leader, which was intended to be a synthesis of different religious beliefs and practices, especially Islam and Hinduism. Akbar encouraged interfaith dialogue and religious diversity at a time when, in the Western world, religious groups were persecuted.

Whilst it would be an exaggeration to say that such an intermingling of different religious beliefs and moral codes resulted in mutual love and affection, it would nonetheless often result in a degree of tolerance towards one another. For example, in attempting to account for the decline of Buddhism in India, some scholars have explained this away as a result of hordes of Muslim warriors simply annihilating the defenceless, pacifist Buddhist community. Whilst this may well have been the case in certain districts and amongst certain groups of Muslim invaders – the Turks notably – there were also examples of a more benevolent rule, in Sindh in the early eighth century, for example. Also, this somewhat simplistic picture of Muslim invasions and intolerance does not

explain why Jainism and Hinduism survived whilst Buddhism did not. Therefore, the disappearance of Buddhism might be better explained by internal
factors, such as the gradual assimilation of Buddhism into Hinduism. Scholars
such as Kulke and Rothermund have pointed out that Indian culture was
enriched by the encounter with Islam, which as a result opened up new net-
works with West Asia, resulting in the transmission of new ideas to Europe
such as the Indian numerical system and, of course, the game of chess! During
the ninth and tenth centuries, Muslim rulers 'seem to have followed a policy of
peaceful coexistence with the Hindu population. It is said that the rulers of
Multan even carefully protected the temple of the sun god at Multan ... '
(Kulke and Rothermund 1998: 154).

Having said that, there have been occasions in history when this has not
been the case. Mention has already been made of the Kharijites, who would
not accept ethical pluralism amongst those who called themselves Muslims,
never mind other religious believers. Another example of this lack of tolerance
within the Muslim community itself is the *mihna* (inquisition) of 833–48.
Returning to India, the peaceful coexistence referred to above came to an end
when the Afghan ruler of the Ghaznavid empire, Mahmud of Ghazni (971–
1030), made a series of raids into northern India, resulting in the looting and
destruction of the holy places:

> The climax of these systematic campaigns was Mahmud's attack on the
> famous Shiva temple at Somnath on the southern coast of Kathiawar in
> Gujarat. After a daring expedition across the desert Mahmud reached this
> temple in 1025. Chronicles report that about 50,000 Hindus lost their
> lives in defending the temple. Mahmud destroyed the Shiva lingam with
> his own hands and then is said to have returned through the desert with
> about 20 million gold dinars (about 6.5 tons of gold).
>
> (Kulke and Rothermund 1998: 154)

Mahmud has had a lasting impact on Indian history and 'signifies the very
embodiment of wanton destruction and fanaticism – much like Attila and
Chingis Khan for the Europeans' (Kulke and Rothermund 1998: 154).
Mahmud would loot Hindustan (east of the Indus) on an annual basis in
order to turn his capital and birthplace, Ghazni, into one of the finest cities
of its day and surrounding his court with scholars and poets. Mahmud
was, therefore, both a patron of the arts and a destroyer of religious temples.
He ruled over an immense empire that covered what is today most of
Afghanistan, eastern Iran, Pakistan and northwestern India and was not
averse to killing Muslims whom he regarded as heretics as well, such as the
Ismailis.

In terms of other examples of intolerance, Alauddin Khiji, who reigned in
India from 1296–1316, is worthy of a mention. He fought successfully against
hordes of Mongol invaders and, indeed, proved to be as cruel in revenge as the
Mongols themselves. After an attempt to conquer Delhi, thousands of Mongol

prisoners were trampled to death by elephants while the sultan's court watched, and a pyramid composed of the heads of the Mongols was erected outside the Delhi city gates. Alauddin also invaded southern India, burning down cities and destroying great Hindu temples such as Srirangam. However,

> Although Ala-ud-din had the indisputable merit of having saved India from being overrun by the Mongols, the Hindus naturally disliked him because he oppressed them intentionally. Hindu historians have, therefore, criticised him just as they criticised Aurangzeb. But they tend to forget that Ala-ud-din was rather impartial in his oppression, his measures being aimed at Muslim courtiers just as much as against Hindu notables and middlemen.
>
> (Kulke and Rothermund 1998: 160)

One final example of extreme brutality is the notorious Timur (1336–1405), better known in the West as Tamburlaine, who saw himself as the scourge of Allah. Timur, a Turk, grew up in the Mongol Chaghaytay state in Samarkind. By 1387 he had conquered all the Iranian highlands and the plains of Mesopotamia. In 1395 he subjugated the old Golden Horde in Russia, and in 1398 he descended upon India and sacked Delhi:

> For three days Timur's soldiers indulged in an orgy of murder and plunder in the Indian capital. The Hindu population was exterminated; the Muslims were spared, although presumably their property was not. The deeds of these Turkish warriors shocked even Timur, who wrote in his autobiography that he was not responsible for this terrible event and that only his soldiers should be blamed.
>
> (Kulke and Rothermund 1998: 167)

For the sake of balance, therefore, it is important to keep in mind that Islamic rulers have not always been quite so enlightened. However, this may well be said of any civilization, whatever belief system it upholds, and these are always subject to being hijacked by power-hungry despots. What we all need to be wary of is attempting to use such historical examples as paradigms of what the religion truly represents. Whilst it is important to be aware of them, to high-light cruel sultans as examples of what Islam represents in a moral way is as perverse as arguing that the atrocities committed by Christian crusaders is what Christianity is all about.

The importance of hermeneutics

How is the modern reader meant to interpret the Quran? Can there be any agreement reached as to the fundamental tenets of the Quran? How is the reader – given that he or she comes from different time periods, cultures and beliefs – meant to make sense of the Quran? This question is at the root of hermeneutics. Since the existential theologian Rudolf **Bultmann** (1884–1976), the term hermeneutics is 'generally used to describe the attempt to span the gap between past and present' (Ferguson 1986: 5). Hermeneutics assumes that every reader of a text brings his or her own 'baggage' of beliefs, expectations and questions, to the extent that it would be 'absurd to demand from any interpreter the setting aside of his/her subjectivity and interpret a text without pre-understanding and the questions initiated by it [because without these] the text is mute' (Bultmann 1955: 251).

The Quran is considered to be literally the word of God, not a work that has been 'inspired' or 'influenced' by God. In this sense it has a timelessness and a universality. Having said that, all revelations are a commentary on a particular society; they address a specific audience in a specific language and so are part of that socio-historical and linguistic milieu. Making the transcendental into the earthly results in a degree of necessary interpretation. There has been some reluctance in Muslim scholarship (compared with, say, Christian scholarship) to pursue the question of temporal causality in the background of the Quran's 'Otherness', perhaps for fear that this will weaken the potency of its transcendental quality. However, although there is a reluctance to pursue the *implications* of such temporal causality there is nonetheless a general acknowledgement amongst Muslim scholars that the Quran needs to address itself within a social, cultural, historical and linguistic context if it is to be understood at all. As Mawdudi himself acknowledged: 'Although the Qur'an addresses itself to all of humankind, its contents are, on the whole, vitally related to the taste and temperament, the environment and history and customs and usages of Arabia' (Mawdudi 1988: 26, 27).

A perennial concern for the monotheistic religions is how to reconcile a timeless, immutable God with what appears to be progressive revelation (*tadrij*); that is, a series of revelations over periods of time, to different prophets and related to different contexts. The Quran was not transmitted as one whole text, but as a response to the demands of concrete situations. This is evidenced from parts of the Quran: for example, 'We have divided the Qur'an into sections so that you may recite it to the people with deliberation. We have imparted it by gradual revelation' (17:106); and when the unbelievers ask, 'Why was the Qur'an not revealed to him entire in a single revelation?' (23:52), the response is, 'We have revealed it thus so that We may strengthen your faith. We have imparted it to you by gradual revelation' (23:52).

Possibly the most renowned traditional scholar of *tadrij* is Shāh Walīullāh **Dehlawi** (1703–62), who developed a theory of the relationship between revelation and its socio-historical context. According to Dehlawi, the ideal form of religion corresponds to the ideal form of nature. The actualized manifestations of the ideal religion descend in successive revelations depending upon changing material and historical conditions. Every succeeding revelation reshapes the world into a new *Gestalt*, which embodies religion. According to Dehlawi, religion, through revelation, adapts its form according to the customs, faiths and practices of the recipient community. Dehlawi uses the analogy of God as the physician who prescribes medication according to the needs, temperament, age and so on of the patient. It follows that to attempt to apply the principles of the Meccan community of seventh-century Arabia to any modern society is rather like a physician prescribing the medicine for a young child to an adult. Nonetheless, the 'religion' remains, though in an altered form. The problem for interpretation, then, is determining what that religion is. This is echoed in the writings of the late Islamic modernist, Fazlur Rahman:

> It is strange … that no systematic attempt has ever been made to under-
> stand the Qur'an in the order in which it was revealed … by setting the
> specific cases of the … 'occasions of revelation', in some order in
> the general background that is no other than the activity of the Prophet
> (the *sunna* in the proper sense) and its social environment.
>
> (Rahman 1982: 137)

At the same time, Rahman argues, this hermeneutics must not lose sight of the Quran as a coherent whole, of its metaphysical element that acts as a backdrop to its injunctions. This cannot lead to absolute uniformity of interpretation, but will at least get rid of claims to inconsistencies and ambiguities by under-standing such verses in the light of the coherency of the whole text. Rahman sees these interpretative attempts occurring not only amongst individual scho-lars, but by teamwork as well. Through discussion and debate, the community at large can accept some interpretations and discard others. Further, time can allow for one-time interpretations to be replaced; they are not to remain dogma for future generations if the community feels it is no longer viable. Rahman feels that we have to adopt a fresh approach to the Quran, to get rid of our baggage, especially the reliance upon many unreliable hadith.

Religion creates unities: it is a binding force for communities, continuously reinforced through ritual, narratives, ceremonies and symbols. For Islam, the paradigm of the umma, the Muslim community, is central to the psyche of every Muslim. How that umma is perceived differs from one individual to another, of course. For some, it is seen as a spiritual community that transcends spatial and temporal boundaries, whilst for others it is a political imperative. The umma provides identity, yet identity implies exclusion. Identity need not, however, imply universality, and this is where many seem to misunder-stand the nature of the umma. One may have an identity as part of a community without sacrificing one's individuality or beliefs. However, there is a very thin line, it seems, between the imposing, totalitarian Platonic com-munity – where only one narrative is allowed to dominate – and a post-modernist, pluralistic, nihilistic existence, where there are many diverse narratives competing against one another. The umma, not unlike other ideo-logical communities, is capable of many expressions. In its essence – adopting a historical-critical and hermeneutic approach – the umma at least has the cap-ability of straddling that 'thin line' successfully. That is to say, a compromise between the Platonic and the nihilistic would not be 'alien' to the nature of the umma, but rather is akin to it.

The 'hermeneutics of suspicion'

The age in which we now live has given rise to a 'hermeneutics of suspicion', largely due to the contributions of those 'great masters' Marx, Nietzsche and Freud. Whereas scepticism questions the content of our beliefs, resulting in a questioning as to whether those beliefs are true or not, suspicion is concerned more with the motives and functions of our beliefs. A good definition of what is meant by 'hermeneutics of suspicion' is provided by Merold Westphal:

> the deliberate attempt to expose the self-deceptions involved in hiding our actual operative motives from ourselves, individually or collectively, in order not to notice how and how much our behaviour and our beliefs are shaped by values we profess to disown.
>
> (Westphal 1977: 13)

For Marx, the way we understand our world reflects the interests of the ruling class, whereas Freud's suspicion of religious beliefs is his view that they are essentially unacknowledged wish-fulfilments. For Nietzsche, when we cite examples of such apparent virtues as love, justice and altruism, these are merely expressions of the will to power for those without power. In the case of Nietzsche we have an example of religion working as a tool to gain power. More recently, the influence of Darwinism, evolutionary psychology and genetics has questioned further the motives of our human behaviour.

The 'hermeneutics of suspicion' is highly relevant to the debate on the nature of the umma as it raises the question of, on the one hand, the seeming subjectivity of the religious beliefs underpinning the umma and, on the other hand, the belief that we are essentially 'moral' people with values that we can acknowledge as noble and unselfish. It is even more relevant as much of this 'school' is concerned with 'text'. The basis of Islamic moral beliefs, of course, is with close reference to the 'text' of the Quran. The French philosopher, Paul Ricoeur, expresses his own concern for the seeming intrinsic subjectivity of the hermeneutics of suspicion and attempts also to create his own fine line between calling for an objectivity, yet at the same time remaining 'open' to interpretation. He saw the tradition in a positive light: 'Hermeneutics seems to me to be animated by this double motivation: willingness to suspect, willingness to listen; vow of rigor, vow of obedience' (Ricoeur 1970: 27).

It is this dilemma, the dilemma of interpretation, which the Islamic world is facing today. Ricoeur appeals to the text for both objectivity (nesting in some sense in the text itself) and openness (the reader's response to the text). Such approaches to interpreting text are not uncommon in religious traditions, and Islam – with its tradition of *tafsir* (interpretation) that can be traced to the beginning of the religion itself – has not been shy of interpreting the symbols and metaphors within the Quran whilst acknowledging an objectivity, an essence of the text. As the Quran itself states:

> It is He who has sent this Scripture down to you [Prophet]. Some of its verses are definite in meaning – these are the cornerstone of the Scripture – and others are ambiguous.
>
> (3:7)

However, the current media dominance of what is usually referred to as 'Islamic fundamentalism' has caused a dark cloud to cover Islam's traditional critical approach to its own tradition, to the extent that internally the Islamic world is fearful of recognizing its own ambiguities.

The problem of articulation

Robert Wuthnow has argued that all religions have a 'problem of articulation'. That is, if their ideas and practices do not articulate closely enough to their social settings, 'they are likely to be regarded by their potential audiences as irrelevant, unrealistic, artificial and overly abstract' (Wuthnow 1989: 3). However, if they 'articulate too closely with the specific social environment in which they are produced, they are likely to be thought of as esoteric, parochial, time bound, and fail to attract a wider and more lasting audience' (Wuthnow 1989: 3). An example from the Quran is its attitude to slavery:

> If any of your slaves wish to pay for their freedom, make a contract with them accordingly, if you know they have good in them, and give them some of the wealth God has given you. Do not force your slave-girls into prostitution, when they themselves wish to remain honourable, in your quest for the short-term gains of this world, although, if they are forced, God will be forgiving and merciful to them.
>
> (24:33)

As an immediate solution, the Quran accepts slavery on a legal plane because no alternative was possible. To have simply stated that slavery was to be abolished would have been an example of what Wuthnow meant by not articulating closely enough to the social setting: slavery was not even regarded as a moral issue, but an essential, pragmatic manner. However, if the Quran articulated too closely – essentially accepting the realities of slavery without the suggestion that there is a moral ideal to aim for – then it fails to have any universal, timeless element. Other examples can be found in the case of the Quran's views on women, divorce, inheritance, punishment and so on. Hence the need to keep in mind the eternal, enduring aspects of the Quran and the example of the Prophet – such as the stress on peace, hope, tolerance, justice, consultation, community etc. – and avoiding literalism of the text.

This 'problem of articulation' is often ignored by critics of Islam, as well as by the 'fundamentalist' element. To 'be' Muslim is not merely to memorize the Quran or to follow the beliefs and practices. It involves active engagement, self-reflection, reasoning and critical awareness. To this end, the tools of modernity can be used for good. A contemporary example of this is Al Jazeera TV, which has not only, through the mass media, been able to present alternative perspectives on world events, but discussion programmes on religious issues that are immensely popular. Such a force breaks the traditional monopoly of the often-conservative ulama by allowing members of the 'public' to engage in dialogue and to consider Quranic or legal texts in relation to the contemporary world, thus bringing the exercise of ijtihad – independent reasoning – to a more democratic standard.

Conclusion

Issues such as pluralism, tolerance and diversity are central to postmodern dialogue. The era of 'modernity' was marked by:

> belief in science, planning, secularism and progress. The desire for symmetry and order, balance and authority has also characterised it. The period is noted for its confidence in the future, a conviction that Utopia is attainable, that there is a natural world order which is possible.
>
> (Ahmad 1992: 6, 7)

This phase in history is usually perceived as a Western phenomenon, seemingly excluding the rest of the world. However, the rest of the world – due to the hegemony of the West – is naturally affected by any 'Western project'. Further, it seems both one-dimensional and erroneous to talk of a concept as specifically 'Western' or 'Other', keeping in mind the historical interaction between civilizations. There should be no hesitation in being prepared, therefore, to make full use of what are often referred to as 'Western' narratives in an attempt to understand the values and beliefs of a religion and/or culture not traditionally regarded as a product of the 'West'.

Postmodernist dialogue has raised suspicions concerning models based on rationality, with a resultant lack of the previous confidence in modernity. A reason-based model finds religious faith alien and conflicting and, indeed, any attempt to understand a faith will lead to misunderstanding by the 'outsider'. In talking of determining the 'essence' of a faith, in terms of its moral outlook, this suggests an approach to it from the point of view of objective neutrality. However, such an avoidance of 'ethnocentricity' is rarely achievable and is subject to extensive debate, for the tools for such analysis are in themselves products of a particular model of the world.

Attempts to apply absolute standards to any model sets aside such important criteria as states of consciousness, beliefs and inner motivation, which underpin a belief. Further, such analysis is in danger of ignoring the cultural and historical context of an event. Such an approach, the hermeneutical one, although layered with its own complications that must always be kept in mind, presents us with the most effective tool for understanding, unless we are prepared to either state that no evaluation of the 'other' is permissible, or that we embrace diversity for diversity's sake and assert that all belief systems, religious or otherwise, deserve equal respect regardless of their moral system.

The point here is that, historically, Islam *can* be intolerant, but it also *can* be tolerant. Within Islam itself – without having to look outside of the religion – the doors are certainly not closed to ethical pluralism by any means. Ethical pluralism, therefore, is not simply something that is the result of Western modernity; it has a much longer heritage than that. In addition, it is important to realize that ethical pluralism is not necessarily the antithesis of religious belief. Indeed, secularism, too, can be intolerant towards religious beliefs: for example, during the Ataturk era in Turkey, or more recent legislation in a number of European countries banning the wearing of the hijab.

Further reading

Fukuyama, F. (2012), *The End of History and the Last Man*, London: Penguin.

Huntington, S.P. (2002), *The Clash of Civilizations and the Remaking of World Order*, London: Free Press.

Mayer, A.E. (2012), *Islam and Human Rights: Tradition and Politics*, 5th edn, Boulder, CO: Westview Press.

Rahman, F. (1982), *Islam and Modernity*, Chicago: University of Chicago Press.

Appendix I: List of names

Islamic

Ahmad, Jalal Al-e (1923–69). Iranian philosopher.

Alfarabi (*c.* 872–951). Abū Naṣr Muḥammad ibn Muḥammad al-Fārābī. Latinized name 'Alpharabius'. Philosopher. Known to Muslims as the 'Second Teacher', with Aristotle being the first.

Alkindi (*c.* 801–73). Abu Yūsuf Ya'qūb ibn 'Isḥāq aṣ-Ṣabbāḥ al-Kindī. Latinized name 'Alkindus'. Considered the 'father of Islamic philosophy.

Alrazi (*c.* 864–925). Abu Bakr Muhammad ibn Zakariyā Rāzī. Latinized name 'Rhazes' or 'Rasis'. Persian philosopher.

Arabi (1165–1240). 'Abū 'Abdillāh Muḥammad ibn 'Alī ibn Muḥammad ibn 'Arabī. Andalusian philosopher and Sufi mystic.

Ashari (874–936). Abū al-Hasan Alī ibn Ismā'īl al-Ash'arī. Arab theologian, born in Basra.

Avempace (1085–1138). This is his Latinized name and is more commonly used. His Arabic name is Abû Bakr Muḥammad Ibn Yaḥyà ibn aṣ-Ṣâ'igh at-Tûjîbî Ibn Bâjja or Ibn Bajja for short. An Andalusian philosopher.

Averroes (1126–98). This is his Latinized name and is more commonly used. His Arabic name is 'Abū l-Walīd Muḥammad bin 'Aḥmad bin Rušd or simply Ibn Rushd. Philosopher and interpreter of Aristotle.

Avicenna (*c.* 980–1037). This is his Latinized name and is more commonly used. His Arabic name is Abū 'Alī al-Ḥusayn ibn 'Abd Allāh ibn Sīnā or simply Ibn Sina. Persian philosopher.

Banna (1906–49). Sheikh Hasan Ahmed Abdel Rahman Muhammed al-Banna. Muslim scholar and founder of the Muslim Brotherhood.

Basri (642–728). Al-Hasan ibn Abi-l-Hasan al-Basri. Early Muslim theologian.

Dehlawi (1703–62). Qutb-ud-Dīn Ahmad ibn 'Abdul Rahīm, though better known as Shāh Walīullāh. Scholar and reformer.

Fardid, Ahmad (1912–94). Iranian philosopher. Influenced by Heidegger especially.

Ghazzali (*c.* 1058–1111). Abū Ḥāmid Muḥammad ibn Muḥammad al-Ghazzālī. Latinized name 'Algazel'. Certainly one of the most influential Muslims on Islamic theology and philosophy.

Hanbal (780–855). Ahmad bin Muhammad bin Hanbal Abu 'Abd Allah al-Shaybani. Scholar and founder of Hanbali school of law.

Iqbal, Sir Muhammad (1873–1938). Philosopher, poet and politician.

Khaldun (1332–1406). Abd al-Rahman. Philosopher of history.

Khomeini (1902–89). Ruhollah Mostafavi Musavi Khomeini. Grand Ayatollah of Iran and religious thinker.

Mawdudi (1903–79). Sheikh Sayyid Mawlana Abu'l-A'la. Islamic politician and thinker.

Mernissi, Fatima (born 1940). Moroccan feminist.

Muhammad, Prophet (*c.* 570–632). Abū al-Qāsim Muḥammad ibn 'Abd Allāh ibn 'Abd al-Muṭṭalib ibn Hāshim. Believed by Muslims to be the prophet of God.

Nasr, Sayyed Hossein (b. 1933). Iranian philosopher.

Qutb, Sayyid (1906–66). Egyptian theorist and leading member of the Muslim Brotherhood.

Rahman, Fazlur (1919–88). Scholar of Islam.

Ramadan, Tariq (b. 1962). Swiss-born scholar of Islamic studies.

Rumi (1207–73). Jalāl ad-Dīn Muhammad Balkhī, though better known simply as Rumi. Sufi mystic and poet.

Sadra, Mulla (*c.* 1572–1640). Ṣadr ad-Dīn Muḥammad Shīrāzī, though usually referred to as Mulla Sadra. Iranian philosopher and mystic.

Shahrastani (1086–1153). Tāj al-Dīn Abū al-Fath Muhammad ibn 'Abd al-Karīm ash-Shahrastānī. Persian historian of religions and philosopher.

Shariati, Ali (1933–77). Iranian revolutionary.

Soroush, Abd al-Karim (b. 1945). Iranian reformer and philosopher.

Suhrawardi (1154–91). Shahāb ad-Dīn' Yahya ibn Habash as-Suhrawardī. Iranian Sufi mystic and founder of Illuminationist school of philosophy.

Talbi, Mohamed (b. 1921). Tunisian historian.

Wadud, Amina (b. 1952). American scholar and feminist.

Zayd, Nasr Hamid Abu (b. 1943). Egyptian Quranic scholar.

Non-Islamic

Aquinas, St Thomas (1225–74). Italian philosopher and theologian in the tradition of scholasticism.

Aristotle (384–322 BC). Greek philosopher and student of Plato.

Bultmann, Rudolf (1884–1976). German Lutheran theologian.

Descartes, René (1596–1650). French rationalist philosopher, regarded as the father of modern Western philosophy.

Epicurus (341–270 BC). Greek philosopher and founder of Epicureanism.

Hegel, Georg Wilhelm Friedrich (1770–1831). German philosopher and an important figure in the movement of German Idealism.

Heidegger, Martin (1889–1976). German philosopher, belonging to an early form of the existential tradition.

Hobbes, Thomas (1588–1679). English philosopher, best known for his political philosophy.

Hume, David (1711–76). Scottish empiricist philosopher.

Kant, Immanuel (1724–1804). German philosopher and a key thinker for modern Western philosophy.

Kierkegaard, Søren (1813–55). Danish philosopher, belonging to an early form of the existential tradition.

Malebranche, Nicolas (1638–1713). French rationalist philosopher.

Nietzsche, Friedrich Wilhelm (1844–1900). German philosopher famous for such ideas as the Will to Power and 'God is dead'.

Plato (*c.* 427–347 BC). Ancient Greek philosopher and student of Socrates.

Ricoeur, Paul (1913–2005). French philosopher known for his teachings in hermeneutics.

Rousseau, Jean-Jacques (1712–78). Genevan philosopher whose political philosophy influenced the French Revolution.

Sartre, Jean-Paul (1905–80). French philosopher, existentialist, novelist and playwright.

Appendix II: Glossary of terms

Abbasid Caliphate (750–1258). The reign of the caliphs that ruled from the capital of Baghdad.

al-insan al-kamil 'The person who has reached perfection' or, more simply, the 'Perfect Man'. Made with reference to the Prophet Muhammad specifically, but also considered the goal for Muslims to aspire to.

Asharism The school of theology founded by Ashari (d. 936).

dar al-harb The 'house of war' is a reference to countries that are not within the Islamic realm.

dar al-Islam The 'house of Islam' to distinguish this Islamic realm from the 'house of war'.

dar al-salam The 'house of peace', which is another term for the 'house of Islam'.

dawa Literally means 'issuing a summons', usually a term to describe proselytizing in Islam.

dhimmis Non-Muslims living in Islamic territory.

emanation Term used in Neoplatonism to describe the modes of being that derive from the Absolute being.

eudaimonia Greek term for personal well-being.

ex nihilo Latin term which means 'out of nothing'.

falasifah Philosopher.

falsafa Philosophy.

fiqh Islamic jurisprudence. It is the rulings and judgments that derive from sharia.

ghazwa Military expedition, battle, or raid.

hadith Sayings ascribed to the Prophet Muhammad.

Hanbalites School of law, which can be traced back to Ibn Hanbal (d. 855).

ijtihad A legal term to describe independent reasoning.

Illuminationism Persian Islamic philosophy that was influenced by Neoplatonic thought especially.

iman Belief.

Ismailism A branch of Shia Islam also known as 'Seveners'.

Jabarites An early Islamic school of philosophy that supported predestination.

jahiliyya 'Age of ignorance' with specific reference to the time before Islam, but also a reference to any peoples or places that are not considered Islamic.

jihad Literally 'struggle' which has many meanings, though most frequently associated with war.

jus ad bellum Latin for 'right to war'.

jus in bello Latin for 'justice in war'.

Kaba a cuboid-shaped structure in Mecca. It is the holiest site in Islam and the centre for pilgrimage.

kafir The name for an unbeliever.

kalam Literally 'speech' or 'words', but more generally the term used for Islamic theology.

khalifah The ruler of the Muslim community, usually translated as 'Caliph'.

kharijites Those who initially supported the fourth caliph, Ali, but then rejected his authority and subscribed to a particular view on what constitutes a good Muslim.

logos Pure intellect.

Mahdi In Shia Islam this is the twelfth Imam on his return.

maslaha Public good.

mihna Literally means 'testing' and refers to the Islamic inquisition in the ninth century.

mufti A scholar of Islamic law.

Mujahidin Literally meaning 'strugglers' or those engaged in jihad, it has come to have more specific reference to members of militant Islamic groups.

mumin Name for a believer.

Murjites An early Islamic school of philosophy.

muruwah Means 'courage', 'patience', 'endurance' etc., and is believed to be a quality that the Bedouin in particular possessed.

Muslim Brotherhood The Arab world's oldest Islamic movement, founded in Egypt in 1928.

mutakallim Theologian.

Mutazilites An early Islamic school of philosophy/theology which emphasizes rational thought.

Neoplatonism A mystical philosophy that has its origins in the third century.

Pir A title for a Sufi master.

Qadarites An early Islamic school of philosophy/theology that believed God endowed Man with free will.

qadi A judge.

qital The actual act of physical fighting.

Quran The holy scripture of Islam.

Ramadan The ninth month of the Islamic calendar.

Rashidun The 'rightly-guided', which refers to the first four caliphs.

Salafiyya Modern reformist movement that models itself on the early Islamic era.

salam 'Peace'.

sama Part of the Sufi ritual which may involve dancing, singing etc.

Sharia The body of Islamic law derived from the traditional Islamic sources.

Shia The 'party of Ali'; those who believe that Islamic leadership should be within the family of the Prophet Muhammad. Today they constitute about 10 per cent of the Muslim population.

shura Arabic for 'consultation'.

Sufi The mystical tradition within Islam.

Sunni The 'people of tradition' who represent about 90 per cent of the world's Muslim population.

tadrij Progressive revelation.

tafsir The act of interpretation.

takfir The practice of declaring someone an unbeliever.

tawhid 'Unity'.

theomorphic man Another term for 'Perfect Man', see al-insan al-kamil above.

ulama The class of Islamic scholars.

umma Meaning 'nation' or 'community', particularly the people of Islam as a whole, regardless of race or ethnicity.

Umayyad (661–750) The reign of the caliphs that ruled from the capital of Damascus.

via negativa From the Greek 'to deny'; a theological notion that God can only be understood by describing what He is not.

vilayat-i faqih A Shia notion of 'guardianship by the clergy'.

zakat Alms-giving.

Bibliography

Aboul-Enein, H.Y. and S. Zuhur (2004), *Islamic Rulings on Warfare*, Carlisle, PA: Strategic Studies Institute of the US Army War College.

Adamson, P. (2007), *Al-Kindī*, Great Medieval Thinkers, Oxford: Oxford University Press.

Ahmad, A.S. (1992), *Postmodernism and Islam: Predicament and Promise*, Abingdon: Routledge.

Al-Kindi (1974), *Al-Kindi's Metaphysics: A Translation of the Treatise on First Philosophy*, trans. by A.L. Ivry, Albany, NY: State University of New York Press.

Al-Sawy, S., Secretary General at the Assembly of Muslim Jurists of America (AMJA), in his reply to the question, 'Can A Husband Hit His Wife in the Face?' Question ID or fatwa no. 620, amajonline.com (23.4.2005).

Al-Shahrastani, Abu al-Fath Ibn 'Abd al-Karim (1923), *Kitab al-Milal wa al-Nihal*, ed. by William Cureton, in *Books of Religions and Philosophical Sects*, 2 vols, Leipzig: Otto Harrassowitz (reprint of the edition of London 1846).

Aminrazavi, M.A.R. (1996), *Suhrawardi and the School of Illumination*, Routledge Sufi Series, Abingdon: Routledge.

Aristotle (1987), *De Anima (On the Soul)*, trans. by Hugh Lawson-Tancred, London: Penguin.

Ashari, Abu al-Hasan (1905), *Risalah fi Istihsan al-Khaud*, Hyderabad: Deccan.

Austin, R.W. (1977), *Sufis of Andalusia: The Ruh Alouds and Al-Durrat Al-Fakhirah of Ibn Arabi*, Berkeley, CA: University of California Press.

Averroes (2001), *Decisive Treatise and Epistle Dedicatory*, trans. by Charles E. Butterworth, Provo, Utah: Brigham Young University Press.

——(1974), *On Plato's Republic*, trans. by R. Lerner, Ithaca, NY: Cornell University Press.

——(1961), *On the Harmony of Religion and Philosophy*, trans. by Charles E. Butterworth, Provo, Utah: Brigham Young University Press.

——(1921), *The Book of the Exposition of the Methods of Proofs Regarding the Beliefs of the Religion*, in *The Philosophy and Theology of Averroes*, trans. by Mohammad Jamil-Ub-Behman Barod, Baroda: Manibhai Mathurbhal Gupta.

Avicenna (1958), *Directives and Remarks*, ed. by Salayman Dunya, parts 3–4, Cairo: Dar al-Ma'arif.

——(1985), *Al-Najat (Deliverance)*, ed. by M. Fakhry, Beirut: American University of Beirut.

Axworthy, M. (2013), *Revolutionary Iran: A History of the Islamic Republic*, London: Allen Lane.

Balk, A.P. (2012), *Balderdash: A Treatise on Ethics*, Canberra: Thelema Publications.

Banerji, R. (2012), 'Gay-Friendly "Mosque" Opens in Paris', available at www.bbc.co.uk/news/world-europe-20547335 (accessed 11.7.13).

Bannerman, P. (1988), *Islam in Perspective: A Guide to Islamic Society, Politics and Law*, Abingdon: Routledge.

Barks, C. (2007), *Rumi: Bridge to the Soul*, London: HarperCollins.

Bultmann, R. (1955), *Essays, Philosophical and Theological*, London: SCM Press.

Chittick, W.C. (1989), *The Sufi Path of Knowledge: Ibn Al-Arabi's Metaphysics of Imagination*, Albany: State University of New York Press.

Cragg, K. and R.M. Speight (1987), *The House of Islam*, 3rd edn, Belmont, CA: Wadsworth Publishing Co.

Eickleman, D.F. (1998), 'Inside the Islamic Reformation', *The Wilson Quarterly*, pp. 80–89.

Fakhry, M. (2001), *Averroes*, Oxford: Oneworld.

Ferguson, D.S. (1986), *Biblical Hermeneutics: An Introduction*, London: SCM Press.

Fukuyama, F. (1991), 'The End of History?' in *Taking Sides*, 3rd edn, ed. by John T. Rourke, Guilford: The Dushkin Publishing Group. Originally in *The National Interest* (Spring 1990).

——(2012), *The End of History and the Last Man*, London: Penguin.

Gearon, E. (2011), 'The Arab Invasions', *History Today*, vol. 61, no. 6, pp. 47–52.

Geertz, C. (1973), *The Interpretation of Cultures*, New York: Basic Books.

Gellner, E. (1979), *Muslim Society*, Cambridge: Cambridge University Press.

Ghazzali, Abu Hamid (1980), *Freedom and Fulfillment: An Annotated Translation of Al-Ghazali's al-Munqidh min al-dalal and Other Relevant Works of al-Ghazali*, trans. by R.J. McCarthy, Boston: Twayne

Gibbon, E., (1994), *The History of the Decline and Fall of the Roman Empire*, ed. David Womersely, vols 5–6, London: Allen Lane.

Gilles, K. (2009), *Jihad: The Trail of Political Islam*, London: I.B. Tauris.

Hashmi, S.H. (ed.) (2002), *Islamic Political Ethics*, Princeton, NJ: Princeton University Press.

Huntington, S.P. (2002), *The Clash of Civilizations and the Remaking of World Order*, London: Free Press

Iqbal, M. (1920), *The Secrets of the Self*, trans. by R.A. Nicholson, Oxford: Macmillan. Also available at www.allamaiqbal.com/works/poetry/persian/asrar/translation/01secretsofthe-self.pdf

——(1989), *The Reconstruction of Religious Thought in Islam*, Lahore: Iqbal Academy.

Jackson, R. (2010), *Mawlana Mawdudi and Political Islam: Authority and the Islamic State*, Abingdon: Routledge.

Kashyap, S. (1955), 'Sir Muhammad Iqbal and Friedrich Nietzsche', *Islamic Quarterly*, vol. 2, no. 1, pp. 175–81.

Khaldun, Ibn (1958), *The Muqaddimah: An Introduction to History*, trans. by Franz Rosenthal, Abingdon: Routledge.

Kraus, P. (ed.) (1973), *Abi Mahammadi filii Zachariae Raghensis (Razis) opera philosophica fragmentaque quae supersunt*, Beirut: Pars Prior.

Kulke, H. and D. Rothermund (1998), *A History of India*, 3rd edn, Abingdon: Routledge.

Kurzman, C. (1998), *Liberal Islam: A Sourcebook*, New York: Oxford University Press.

LeBor, A. (1997), *A Heart Turned East: Among the Muslims of Europe and America*, New York: Warner Books.

Lyons, J. (2010), *The House of Wisdom: How the Arabs Transformed Western Civilization*, London: Bloomsbury.

McGinnis, J. (2010), *Avicenna*, Great Medieval Thinkers, New York: Oxford University Press.

MacLeod, R. (ed.) (2004), *The Library of Alexandria: Centre of Learning in the Ancient World*, London: I.B. Tauris.

Marrakushi, Abdelwahid (1881), *Al-Mujib fi Talkhis Akhbar al-Maghrib (The Pleasant Book in Summarizing the History of the Maghreb)*, ed. by R. Dozy, 2nd edn, Leiden: University of Leiden.

Mawdudi, M., 'The Spiritual Path of Islam', taken from a radio interview at http://jamaat. org. Transcription from the Sabr Foundation, available at www.islam101.com/sociology/spiritualPath.htm (accessed September 2013).

——(1967), *First Principles of the Islamic State*, 3rd edn, Lahore: Islamic Publications.

——(1969), *Islami Riyasat* (Islamic Rule), Lahore: Islamic Publications.

——(1980), *Human Rights in Islam*, 2nd edn, Leicester: The Islamic Foundation.

——(1988), *Towards Understanding the Qur'an*, London: Islamic Foundation.

——(1995), *Jihad fi Sabillah: Jihad in Islam*, trans. by Khurshid Ahmad, ed. by Huda Khattab, Birmingham: UK Islamic Mission Dawah Centre.

——(1996), *Al-Jihad fi al-Islam (Jihad in Islam)*, 15th edn, 1st edn 1930, Kuwait: International Islamic Federation of Student Organisations.

Mayer, A.E. (2012), *Islam and Human Rights: Tradition and Politics*, 5th edn, Boulder, CO: Westview Press.

Meisami, S. (2013), *Mulla Sadra*, Makers of the Muslim World, Oxford: Oneworld.

Mernissi, F. (1992), *The Veil and the Male Elite: A Feminist Interpretation of Women's Rights in Islam*, reprint edn, New York: Perseus Books.

——(2003), *Beyond the Veil: Male-Female Dynamics in Muslim Society*, new edn, London: Saqi Books.

Morris, J. (1986), 'Ibn Arabi and his Interpreters', *Journal of the American Oriental Society*, vol. 106, pp. 539–51.

Mujeeb, M. (1967), *The Indian Muslims*, London: Allen & Unwin.

Nasr, S.H. (2001), *Ideals and Realities of Islam*, Cambridge: The Islamic Texts Society.

Netton, I.R. (1999), *Al-Farabi and His School*, Abingdon: Routledge.

Nicholson, R.A. (1998), *Rumi: Poet and Mystic*, Oxford: Oneworld.

Nietzsche, F. (1969), *Thus Spoke Zarathustra*, trans. by R.J. Hollingdale, London: Penguin.

Qifti, Ali ibn Yusuf (1903), *Ta'rikh al-Hukama (History of Learned Men)*, ed. by Julius Lippert, Princeton, NJ: Princeton University Press.

Qutb, S. (1990), *Milestones*, Indianapolis, IN: American Trust Publications. Also available at http://web.youngmuslims.ca/online_library/books/milestones/hold/index_2.htm (accessed 12.7.13).

Rahman, F. (1980), *Major Themes of the Qur'an*, Minneapolis, MN: Bibliotheca Islamica.

——(1982), *Islam and Modernity*, Chicago: University of Chicago Press.

Ramadan, T. (1989), *Radical Reform: Islamic Ethics and Liberation*, New York: Oxford University Press.

——(2005), *Western Muslims and the Future of Islam*, New York: Oxford University Press.

——(2009), *Radical Reform: Islamic Ethics and Liberation*, New York: Oxford University Press.

Remes, P. (2008), *Neoplatonism*, Ancient Philosophies, Durham: Acumen.

Ricoeur, P. (1970), *Freud and Philosophy: An Essay on Interpretation*, New Haven, CT: Yale University Press.

Rousseau, J.-J. (2004), *Discourse on the Origin of Inequality*, New York: Dover Publications.

Rumi (2004), *Selected Poems*, Penguin Classics, trans. by Coleman Barks, London: Penguin.

Ruthven, M. (2000), *Islam in the World*, 2nd edn, London: Penguin Books.

Sachedina, A. (2009), *Islamic Biomedical Ethics: Principles and Application*, Oxford: Oxford University Press.

Sadra, Mulla (1999), *Risala fi huduth al-'alam [On the Incipience of the Cosmos]*, ed. by S.H. Musaviyan, Tehran: The Sadra Islamic Philosophy Research Institute.

Shariati, A. (1980), *Marxism and Other Western Fallacies: An Islamic Critique*, Jakarta: Mizan Press.

Soroush, A. (2002), *Reason, Freedom, and Democracy in Islam: Essential Writings of Abdolkarim Soroush*, New York: Oxford University Press.

Strabo (2002), *Geography* XVII: 1, 8; quoted in D. Heller-Roazen, 'Tradition's Destruction: On the Library of Alexandria', *October*, vol. 100, pp. 133–53.

Talbi, M. (1989), 'Religious Liberty: A Muslim Perspective', *Liberty and Conscience*, vol. 1 no. 1, pp. 12–20.

Tibi, B. (2007), *Political Islam, World Politics and Europe: Democratic Peace and Euro-Islam versus Global Jihad*, Abingdon: Routledge.

Vahid, S.A. (1964), *Thoughts and Reflections of Iqbal*, Lahore: Sh. Muhammad Ashraf.

Vasalou, S. (2008), *Moral Agents and Their Deserts: The Character of Mu'tazilite Ethics*, Princeton, NJ: Princeton University Press.

Vatikiotis, P.J. (1987), *Islam and the State*, London: Croom Helm.

Wadud, A. (1999), *Qur'an and Woman: Re-Reading the Sacred Text from a Woman's Perspective*, 2nd edn, New York: Oxford University Press.

——(2006), *Inside the Gender Jihad: Women's Reform in Islam*, Oxford: Oneworld.

Watt, W.M. (1963), *Muslim Intellectual: A Study of al-Ghazali*, Edinburgh: Edinburgh University Press.

——(2008), *Islamic Philosophy and Theology*, Piscataway, NJ: Aldine Transaction.

Westphal, M. (1977), *Suspicion and Faith: The Religious Issues of Modern Atheism*, 2nd edn, New York: Fordham University Press.

Wright, R. (2008), *Dreams and Shadows: The Future of the Middle East*, London: Penguin

Wuthnow, R. (1989), *Communities of Discourse: Ideology and Social Structure in the Reformation, the Enlightenment, and European Socialism*, Cambridge, MA: Harvard University Press.

Yaqubi, A. (1892), *Kitab al-Buldan (Book of Lands)*, ed. by M.D. Goeje, Leiden: Leiden University Press.

Index